D1223245

The human stage

The human stage

English theatre design, 1567–1640

John Orrell
Professor of English, University of Alberta

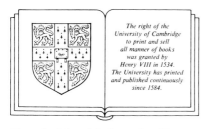

The right of the
University of Cambridge
to print and sell
all manner of books
was granted by
Henry VIII in 1534.
The University has printed
and published continuously
since 1584.

Cambridge University Press

Cambridge
New York   New Rochelle   Melbourne   Sydney

Published by the Press Syndicate of the University of Cambridge
The Pitt Building, Trumpington Street, Cambridge CB2 IRP
32 East 57th Street, New York, NY 10022, USA
10 Stamford Road, Oakleigh, Melbourne 3166, Australia

First published 1988

Printed in Great Britain at
the University Press, Cambridge

British Library cataloguing in publication data
Orrell, John
The human stage: English theatre design,
1567–1640.
1. Theatres – England – Design and
construction – History – 16th
century   2. Theatres – England –
Design and construction – History –
17th century
I. Title
725'.822'0942   NA6840.G7

Library of Congress cataloguing in publication data
Orrell, John
The human stage: English theatre design, 1567–1640 /
John Orrell.
    p.   cm.
Includes index.
1. Theaters – England – Construction.   2. Architecture,
Renaissance – England.   3. Architecture, Modern –
17th–18th centuries – England.
I. Title.
NA6840.G7076   1988
725'.822'0942 Dc 19   87-31158

ISBN 0-521-30859-3

FP

For Emma

Contents

Plates

Figures

Preface

The aim of this book is to present the theatres of the time of Shakespeare and Ben Jonson in the light of contemporary architectural thought and building design. Many notable studies have been published on the Elizabethan and Jacobean theatre seen from the point of view of the audience, the player and the playwright, chief among them the swelling volumes of Glynne Wickham's *Early English Stages*. Since the publication in 1940 of George Reynolds's *The Staging of Elizabethan Plays at the Red Bull Theater, 1605–25*, great advances have been made in the systematic treatment of play-texts as evidence for playhouse practices and performance techniques. We are now beginning to see the huge fund of theatrical information for the period methodically installed in computer databanks, ready for access, and at least one exhaustive study of the dramaturgy of the whole period is under way. The documentation of individual playhouses has also made some advances, more modest but not without significance. C. J. Sisson, Leslie Hotson and Herbert Berry between them have discovered new information about the Boar's Head playhouse and its players, an institution that emerged only as a fleeting shadow among the papers available to Sir Edmund Chambers when he published his standard history, *The Elizabethan Stage*, in 1923. More recently Janet Loengard has turned up a most important document describing the Red Lion theatre in Whitechapel, dating from 1567; and I have myself published a detailed plan of a theatre set up in the hall at Christ Church in 1605.

The steady accumulation of such documentary evidence over the years is bound to modify our view of the development of theatre design, and the present study is intended in part to incorporate the new information into a broad history of the playhouse structure. But I have also aimed to set the buildings and their theatrical fittings in a context of architectural thought that is not always immediately evident in the documents themselves, nor in the work of the theatrical scholars who interpret them today. Here the studies of the architectural historians are of the greatest value, for they have clarified, in Rudolf Wittkower's accurate words, the *Architectural Principles of the Age of Humanism*. Not everyone will agree with all of Wittkower's more recondite arguments, but his book is largely a reminder of what is obvious about Renaissance design: that it takes its departure from theories about the ideal proportionality of the cosmos. Nowhere is this more evident than in the theoretical accounts of the design of that most human of social institutions, the theatre, and it is part of my intention to suggest that in the Italy of the cinquecento, and in London too, the design of the playhouse was often influenced by such ideas.

When the experienced designer Simon Basil prepared a scheme for a theatre at Christ Church in 1605 he specified that the auditorium should contain what he called 'a slight Portico ... of hoopes & firrpoales' at the rear of the seating degrees. 'This portico', he added, 'giues a great grace to all the Theater, & without it, the Architectur is false.' The complete design, that is, constituted a true architecture of the theatre, and it has been my purpose in writing this book to discover what such an architecture might be. For three of the chapters I have risked a sort of literary coyness that I don't much like by venturing titles that use the discontinued word 'goodly': Spenser's 'goodly theaters', Holinshed's 'goodlie devise', and Shakespeare's (or Hamlet's) 'goodly frame'. When it was current the epithet was ordinarily used of someone's personal appearance, or of its representation in a picture, and meant, according to the *OED*, 'good-looking, well favoured or pro-portioned'. The hard-nosed practical information that is contained in most of the legalistic documents by which we know the details of the theatres' construction leaves little room for such language as this, but in their own way the fusty deeds and contracts do sometimes betray the more imaginative motives of the craftsmen and owners who signed them.

The pursuit of this 'goodly' idea of the theatre has led me to Serlio's book of architecture, and beyond that to the more general theories of Alberti and even of Vitruvius. Here I tread a path that has been little explored by students of the English theatre, even though the trail was blazed long ago in Lily B. Campbell's *Scenes and Machines on the English Stage during the Renaissance*, and more recently revisited by Frances Yates in *Theatre of the World*. That I do not agree with everything in these two remarkable books will be obvious to the reader of the ensuing chapters, but so will the debt that every page owes to their vigorous pioneering work.

In completing the study I have had the generous assistance of the Social Sciences and Humanities Research Council of Canada, and of the University of Alberta, whose award of a McCalla Research Professorship made the whole thing possible.

Parts of this book have appeared before in a rather different form, as essays in theatre journals whose editors have kindly given permission for their reappearance here. Something of chapter 6 was published in *Theatre Notebook* 38 (1984), as 'Sunlight at the Globe'; part of chapter 8 was printed in

Shakespeare Survey 35 in a paper called 'The Theatre at Christ Church, Oxford, in 1605'; chapter 12 contains material from 'The Private Theatre Auditorium', *Theatre Research International* 9 (1984); and chapter 13 was largely published as 'Serlio's Practical Theatre Scheme' in *Essays in Theatre* 3 (1984).

Acknowledgments

The University of Alberta Library: plates 31, 33, 34, 43, 45
The Bodleian Library, Oxford: plates 8, 29, 30, 44
The British Library: plates 2, 5, 9, 26, 28, 32, 35, 36, 40, 41, 46, 47
The Syndics of Cambridge University Library: plate 20
The Courtauld Institute of Art: plate 48
The Devonshire Collection, Chatsworth. Reproduced by permission of the
   Chatsworth Settlement Trustees: plates 19, 49–58
The Guildhall Library: plates 3, 4, 11, 14
Ordnance Survey, Crown Copyright: frontispiece
Pentagram Design: plates 23–5
Queen's University, Belfast: plate 7
The Royal Library, Stockholm: plates 12, 13, 15–18, 27
Bibliotheek der Rijksuniversiteit, Utrecht: plates 1, 6, 10
The Provost and Fellows of Worcester College, Oxford: plates 37–9, 42
Yale Center for British Art, Paul Mellon Collection: plates 21, 22

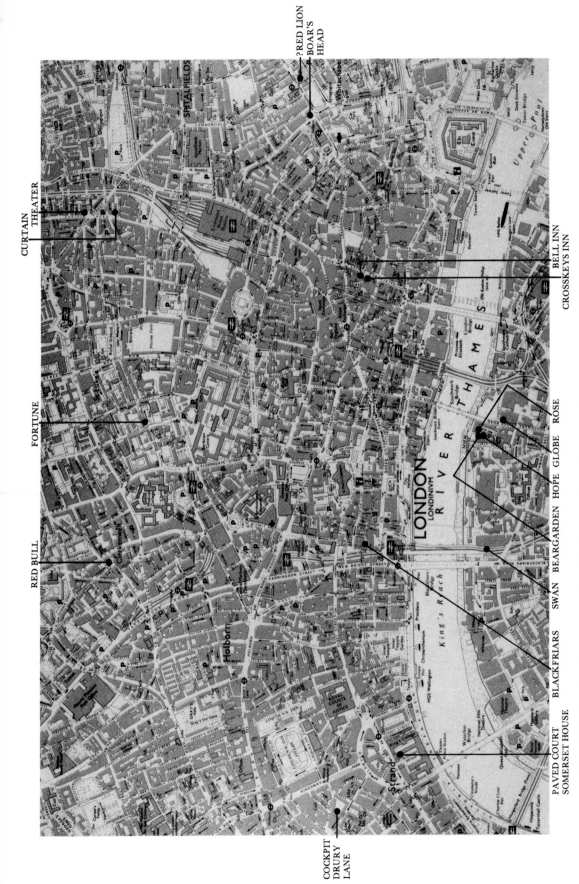

Sites of the London theatres mentioned in the text, located on a modern map.

Prologue

It is one of the tricks of a child's imagination – and of a scholar's too, if he knows what's good for him – to move like some planetary traveller in space and time across the landscapes of the past. An interest in the theatres of Elizabethan London might bring us in the mind's eye to hover high above the Thames on a bright summer's afternoon, to see the river winding in the sunlight (its gloomy flotsam happily invisible from here); the tide is ebbing, and we can see the pattern of its motion unmoving in the moving water, especially where the starlings of the bridge conspire to stem the flow. Below that thin strip of houses laid perilously across the water the large craft go about their business, docking at Billingsgate or Wapping, making sail to catch the tide, some in the shallows on their beam ends, bottoms up for careening. Above the bridge the Thames is alive with watermen's dows crossing and recrossing the stream, for here the river is less vigorous in its movement, a little like a lake above a dam.

There is a pattern in almost everything when seen from such a height as this. Downstream the Tower marks the end of the city, and beyond it are fields and smallholdings. Mile End is open country. At the northern end of the bridge the lines of traffic fan out among the densely clustered streets and alleys, most of them invisible from our vantage point, deeply shaded narrow clefts between the terracotta fields of tiled roofs. Here and there – but rarely – a tree breaks through. At every corner, it seems, a squat church tower rises a little above the height of the tiled peaks, and sometimes sports a lead-covered spire whose imposing height, though hardly to be comprehended from our point of view, nevertheless lends stereoscopic depth to the scene. Not much of the old city wall is to be seen, but its gates block the main traffic routes at the periphery of the most thickly built-up area. Like the bridge, they impose themselves on the composition before us, for to one side they flank almost solid urban construction, wood, brick and tile, while to the other they look out on the green plots, hedgerows and tentergrounds of the more sparsely populated suburbs.

There is a pattern, too, in the separation of this contained city from its neighbour to the west and south. Beyond Ludgate the densely built-up Strand crowds its jettied houses and innyards beside the courts and formal gardens of the great villas by the river. To the north Drury Lane and Lincoln's Inn Fields are what their names imply: a country lane amid rural fields. Yet further west the red brick of St James's can just be made out, but the eye is caught more firmly by the still resplendent ashlar of the aptly named Whitehall to the south, beyond the bend in the river. Here is the biggest of all the villas of the bank, its grounds strung with two-storeyed access galleries, the main courts obvious enough, but between and around them a wondrous huddle of undistinguished rooftops. Further south, there is nothing undistinguished about Westminster, where hall and Abbey ripple their Gothic stonework warmly in the sun.

Almost everything in the scene below us is the work of man. Even the river, to whose soft running the best of Elizabethan poets tuned his song, is channelled a little by human handiwork, in wharf and dock and many-arched bridge. Within its pewter sheen we can now make out, with eyes grown accustomed to the light, the tarnish of outflow from the Fleet as it joins the paler hue of the main stream. Knots of boats tied up beside Whitehall Stairs, Paul's Wharf and a hundred other landing points show how regularly its surface is scored by the activities of the thousands of boatmen who are reputed to make their living from its traffic. The patterns of land traffic too may be seen in the Strand, along Cheapside, the tracks etched deep up Bishopsgate and disappearing into the built-up deck of London Bridge to fan out again on the other side in Southwark, down Borough High Street, along Tooley Street one way and into Bankside the other.

These patterns, like those imposed by agriculture on the surrounding countryside, are assuredly human, but they are no intentional part of a human design. They are the tracks, the spores, of civilization, signs of other designs. The coal landed at St Katherine's dock feeds the furnaces of Gracechurch Street, and lighter, wharf, crane, cart and smoke give evidence of its traffic: the design of the northern miner to produce it and of the London craftsman to consume it in his workshop. The scene below us is crossed and crossed again with the evidence of such collaborative trade. Among the houses near Aldwych a new roof is arising, but like the others it does not address itself towards our point of view. Its shape is an accidental echo of the floors below, and soon it will take its undistinguishable part among the rest, its builders concerned that it should be weathertight and not at all worried about the contribution it makes to our bird's-eye view.

Were we to revisit the scene a mere half-century later we should find rather more evidence of Londoners appearing to address themselves to the skies. The open meadows at Smithfields and Lincoln's Inn would be partly covered, built up in regular terraces and planted in neatly ruled rows of trees, all forming a fine geometric pattern when viewed from above, though perhaps a little monotonous on the ground. The piazza at Covent Garden would be laid out, the model for many a later London square, but there would still be nothing to resemble the astonishing declivities of Nash's time, the emphatic patterns of Regent's Park and Street, though the seminal idea would have been planted: cities should be designed to a plan.

There is not much sign of an intentional plan in Elizabethan London. The ribbons of shadow which mark those of the streets that are visible at all follow something of a Roman grid, perhaps, but it is everywhere modified by an organic growth of lanes and alleys. Here and there a more or less regular courtyard catches the eye, a coaching inn perhaps, or an Inn-of-Court, but these are isolated passages of visual order in the jumbled roofscape. Only the churches seem to be much influenced by deliberate planning, for most of them – by no means all – face one way, like boats anchored in a tidal flow. Among them two stand out: the abbey church at Westminster, and in London the huge pile of St Paul's, dominant at the centre of the scene. Its site is the best in the city, on a rise well above the river. Its tall central tower, spireless since the fire of 1561, rises high towards us, and around it the nave, choir and transepts spread their dark leaded roofs. The whole assembly is cruciform, a plan intended to be read from above, *sub specie aeternitatis*. But churches are not the only buildings in the townscape to give evidence of a notably patterned design. To the north of Bishopsgate, in the fields at Holywell, the Curtain theatre stands, a wooden O, about as large in diameter as St Paul's chancel is wide. It is therefore, from this point of view, an outstanding building, bulky enough to call attention to itself and moreover distinctive in design. To the south of the bridge, not far from the river at Bankside, we can see similar structures: the Globe south of Maid Lane, the Rose nearby and the Beargarden closer to the bank. Further west is the Swan, like most of the others a large building about 100 ft across, polygonal in plan and with a central courtyard largely open to the elements. With the exception of the Beargarden all these wooden rings boast some kind of roof covering part of the yard, always located to the southwest of the frame; and if we peer directly down into the Globe we can see that in the afternoon sun the whole area beneath its roof is in deep shade. The actors are even now at work, but from here they are tiny figures, almost too small for sight. Sunlight penetrates to the framework of some of the galleries opposite them, where part of the audience is visible, attentive to the play and to each other, and not at all to the sky above. They experience, each one for himself, what we can see as a collective fact: the capacity of the building to focus attention inward, from the periphery to the centre. An audience in one of these playhouses is in no need of Jaques' 'inuocation, to call fools into a circle', for they are there already.

At the heart of the city, then, lies the distinctive cruciform outline of the Christian cathedral; at the outskirts, where the congregation of tile and thatch gives way to green fields, stand the equally remarkable theatres, all much the same in plan as if built to a standard design, in their roundness vividly contrasting with everything else in view. From a distance, at least, these are the two most noticeable architectural forms to stand out from the largely mediaeval prospect before us. When Inigo Jones drew a panorama of the town for a scene in Davenant's masque, *Britannia Triumphans*, he centred the view on St Paul's – as who would not? – but in the foreground, neatly aligned with the cathedral, he placed the characteristic outline of the Swan. Everything else in his picture is a rectangular box, with or without a pitched roof. Yet in the town itself, if not quite in Jones's image of it, the form of St Paul's is clearly related to the scores of churches which crowd the streets around it. It is linked to them often by a common orientation, and often too by a similarly cross-shaped plan. The theatres seem to find no such echo in the architecture of the rest of London. If we look closely we shall see other round buildings, to be sure. A small tiled amphitheatre in Shoe Lane houses cockfights, and to the west there is the round stone Temple of the Knights of Jerusalem, but these show no obvious signs of kinship with the great poly-gonal auditoria in the suburbs. The theatres are both distinctive and without obvious parallel. Yet the very particularity of their form, with all the special demands it must have made upon the carpenters who built them, argues that their design was neither an instant whim nor a routine application of commonplace trade practices. Our sight of them from above, like the sight of St Paul's, makes palpable the determined human agency of their design. These are no mere spores of civilization, like the swelling aggregation of sheds and huts beside Tooley Street. Nor are they simply signs of other activity, like the ruts in the lanes or the smoke about Gracechurch Street. They are deliberate human structures, complex in design because they serve a complex human function. Save for the great churches, no other class of building in the prospect announces with such certainty that it is shaped by an idea transcending the utilitarian, or bears so clearly the imprint of the human spirit.

I FESTIVE THEATRES

I
Goodly theatres

So much for mere intuition: we had better come down to earth again, to confront more mundane questions. Granted that the Elizabethan theatres were unusual, outstanding structures, where did the builders find their model? No new type of building is altogether without antecedents, a fact which led the greatest of our theatre historians, Sir Edmund Chambers, to agree with the Victorian idea that the open playhouses had developed from the innyards of such institutions as the Bel Savage, the Bell and the Cross Keys. There – so the argument went – the players had performed their London seasons before the establishment of the Theater in 1576. The innyard formed a ready-made auditorium, enclosed on every side (though open to the sky above) and therefore controllable: no audience could melt away at the sight of a collection box, and the presumed existence of surrounding galleries made for a degree of comfort for those who could pay the extra to command a place in one of them. The stage might be placed against the wall opposite the main entrance to the yard, and rooms contiguous to it made available to the actors for their tiring house. The utilitarian pattern thus established led – it was argued – to the pattern shown in de Witt's famous drawing of the Swan (plate 1), which shows a similar disposition of galleries, stage and yard. Although the Flemish traveller wrote his notes in Latin, and labelled the central floor of the Swan as *planities sive arena*, Sir Edmund was confident enough of the inn theory to suggest the provenance of the English term:

This is the space ordinarily known as the 'yard', a name which it may fairly be taken to have inherited from the inn-yards, surrounded by galleries and open overhead, in which, in the days before the building of the Theatre in 1576, more or less permanent playhouses had grown up.[1]

Such a theory requires for its proof the existence of sound evidence that innyard galleried theatres did indeed exist before 1576, after which year the presence of the Theater among the entertainment houses of the capital would exert an irresistible influence on subsequent playhouse design. For the Theater was a 'vast' polygonal frame of three storeys of galleries,[2] and without doubt it was the source of the design of the Swan and other public playhouses of the age. Once this model had been constructed in the fields of Shoreditch there was little enough need to look beyond it for examples of how to build, and the surviving carpenters' contracts for the Fortune and the Hope contain many clauses referring questions of design to the existing models (to the Globe for the one and to the Swan for the other).[3] Doubtless the Swan contract, had it survived, would have referred the builder directly to the Theater or its neighbour and near contemporary, the Curtain. Moreover innyard theatres dateable only after 1756 are as likely to have been influenced by the public playhouses as vice versa, and may have little to contribute to our present enquiry.

There can be no doubt that innyard playhouses did exist in London before John Brayne and James Burbage put their heads and their money together to build the Theater, but the evidence does not appear to indicate that they were many or of long standing. The clearest account is given by Richard Flecknoe in his 'Short Discourse of the English Stage', published in Restoration times as an appendix to his *Love's Kingdom*:

about the beginning of Queen *Elizabeths* Reign, they began here [in London] to assemble into Companies, and set up Theaters, first in the City, (as in the Inn-yards of the *Cross-Keyes*, and *Bull* in *Grace* and *Bishops-Gate Street* at this day is to be seen) . . .[4]

This account appears to indicate an early date for the theatrical conversions, but in fact the first allusion to a play at the Bull dates only from 1578, while at the Cross Keys the earliest such reference occurs three years later.[5] That the yard of the Bel Savage in St Bride's parish was equipped with galleries and used theatrically is indicated by the first edition of William Lambarde's *Perambulation of Kent* (1576), in which the system used for gathering money from pilgrims at Boxley Abbey is somewhat loosely likened to the customs at the London houses of entertainment:

No more then suche as goe to Parisgardein, the Bell Sauage, or some other suche common place, to beholde Beare Bayting, Enterludes, or Fence playe, can account of any pleasant spectacle unlesse they first paye one penny at the gate, another at the entrie to the Scaffolde, and the thirde for a quiet standing.

In a later edition, of 1596, Lambarde stresses the similarity of inn and permanent playhouse by including the Theater in his list of show places.[6] Certainly the Bel Savage was used for entertainments, whatever its structure, but the earliest of plays there anticipated the date of the Theater by very little: George Gascoigne wrote slightingly of the 'merrye Iest' and 'vayne delight' of 'Bellsauage fayre', but not until 1575.[7] The first record of a fencing prize at the Bel Savage is in an entry for 1568, but prizes in earlier

1   Johannes de Witt, The Swan theatre *c.* 1596 (copy by Aernout van Buchel).

times had generally been fought in such open courtyards as that at
Leadenhall, without benefit of stands for an audience. Lambarde's comment
of 1576 remains the earliest evidence of a built auditorium at any of the
innyard theatres.[8]

Thus far I have introduced only what might be called 'accidental' records
concerning these inns. But there is also a collection of routine bureaucratic
documents referring to them, though in disappointingly ambiguous terms.
Professor Glynne Wickham, in opening the assault on the innyard theory on
which our present discussion is largely based, has reviewed them so thoroughly that here we need only provide a brief summary and echo his
conclusions.[9] Beginning with the Parliamentary Act of 1543, a series of Acts
of Common Council and Lord Mayor's Precepts reiterated a determination
to exercise jurisdiction over stage interludes and other performances, and

listed the sort of places that were subject to control. The earliest of these proclamations limited the permissible locations to the 'houses' of noblemen, the Mayor and aldermen, gentlemen or 'sad [i.e. grave] Comminers or hed parisheners'; to 'the open stretes . . . as in tyme paste it hathe been vsed & accustomed'; and to 'the commen halles of the Companyes fellowshipps or brotherheddes of the same Citie'.[10] No mention here of inns or their yards, but in 1553 the city fathers spelled out more fully that they meant to control playing 'within eny parte of' a person's 'house or houses yarde gardein or baksyde'.[11] Thereafter similar injunctions included the word 'yard' only occasionally, and usually in imitation of the 1553 document.

Thus while the records concerning the attempts to bring play-acting to heel give some countenance to the idea that plays might have been performed in the yards of inns during the 1550s, 1560s and 1570s, they indicate rather more surely that the performances were commonly given within doors. Their witness is sometimes rendered a little obscure by the ambiguity of the terms they employ. In 1574, for example, an Act of the Common Council alluded to the evils of crowds attending plays and getting up to no good 'In greate Innes, havinge chambers and secrete places adioyninge to their open stagies and gallyries'.[12] The phrase 'open stagies' has been taken to signify playing areas open to the sky, but Glynne Wickham cites cognate usages of the word in similar records where it clearly means 'public' as opposed to 'private'. The galleries in question might as well have been indoors as out.[13]

In all the documents only Lambarde's allusion to the system of payment at the Bel Savage gives any certain indication of a genuine innyard auditorium before 1576. If we turn to the provinces we find that the earliest record of a play in an innyard dates from Norwich in 1583, when an affray caused a fatality that was later examined in court. The records reveal that the performance was in the yard: 'this examynate sayeth that on satturnday last in the after noone he was at a play in the yard at the red lyon in St Stephans and hee dyd see three of the players rvnne of the Staige with there Swordes in there handes'.[14] There is no suggestion, beyond the mention of the stage, that the inn was specially equipped as a theatre. Moreover the account is not only the earliest we have of an innyard production in the provinces; it appears also to be unique. Perhaps others will yet come to light, but they are unlikely to change the present state of our knowledge very much: before 1576 innyard theatres were rare.

There is little enough reason, therefore, to encourage the view that Burbage and Brayne took their pattern for the Theater from the inns of Gracechurch Street, though obviously it would be absurd to deny the Bel Savage and its like any influence at all. In later years the story is rather different. Of one innyard converted to theatrical purposes we have certain and complete notice. The Boar's Head in Whitechapel was dedicated to use as a playhouse by a number of alterations made there in 1598, alterations which effectively prevented its continuing in the way of the victualling trade and turned it instead into a theatre. The greater part of the inn consisted of a long courtyard on the northern side of the street, just beyond the city bars. An existing gallery on the northeast side of this irregular space was useful for theatrical purposes, but because there were no others already on the site new ones were built on posts across the larger middle part of the court, and a fourth was added against the range of buildings on the southwest side. A stage was placed out in the yard some ten feet away from the forward edge of the southwestern gallery. In this rather minimal guise the Boar's Head took its place, illegally to be sure, amongst the several playhouses of Elizabethan London. It seems to have thrived, for within a year its proprietors regrouped and rebuilt. The galleries of the previous year were torn down and replaced by others which extended three or four feet further out into the yard, though because they were all on posts the area of the yard itself remained unchanged, save perhaps for the space occupied by a tiring house built beneath the new southwestern gallery, against which the stage was now moved to abut. At the opposite side an upper gallery was also introduced. The consequence of all this activity was that an ordinary innyard – which possessed, we should notice, no more than a single narrow gallery before the conversion – became a regular if rather small Elizabethan playhouse with a tiring house to the southwest, a stage located next to it so that its surface should be shaded in the afternoon, elevated galleries on every side so that its players performed 'in the round', and a yard for groundlings, open to the sky.

Everything that we know about this conversion – and that we know so much is largely due to the insistent researches of Herbert Berry[15] – confirms that the design was approached in an *ad hoc*, pragmatic way. It was intended from the start to make an upper gallery over the extended one on the northeast side, and when one of the owners, Oliver Woodliffe, found the builders measuring up for it in 1599 it occurred to him that the whole gallery structure of the theatre might profitably be expanded, and that there was no time like the present for doing it, before work on the upper gallery proceeded. 'I would pull downe this older gallery to the ground', he said, 'and buylde yt foure foote forwarder toward the stage into ye yarde.' He took a lath in his hand to show what he meant: 'yf yt were buylt so farr forwarder then would there be roome for three or foure seats more in a gallery, and for many mo people, and yet neu*er* the lesse roome in the yarde'.[16] So the yard was converted and adapted for good practical reasons, measured roughly with the sweep of a lath over the ground. Another witness testified – for all this knowledge comes from the litigation so fortunately indulged in by Elizabethan theatre folk – that Woodliffe had advised building the new gallery 'foure foote or thereab*outs*' further forward, and in fact when the job was done 'yt was not set out so farr into yᵉ said yard as [he] did appoint yt by a foote at leaste'.[17]

Such approximations were doubtless typical of the work of entrepreneurs like Woodliffe and his associates. Their motives were mundane and rational enough, and had little to do with any intellectual programme of architectural design. The *idea* of the Boar's Head was profit, whatever the quality of the works actually performed in it. Presumably the earlier innyard theatres, the Bel Savage among them, had similarly come by whatever specific theatrical equipment they possessed. It is hard to see building work of this rough and ready type as much influencing the design of the great polygonal frames that were to arrive in Shoreditch in 1576 and set the pattern for the public stages. James Burbage had been a joiner in his day, but not even he could imagine and plan the vast Theater with only a lath in his hand.

Sometimes, in order to account for this apparently miraculous birth a thousand paces north of Bishopsgate, adventurous commentators have turned to show a parallel theatrical development taking place a thousand miles further south.[18] There, stages destined for the work of Lope de Vega and Calderón de la Barca flourished beneath a more reliable sun, their open yards surrounded by degrees, boxes and galleries, their stages partly covered – like many of those in London – by a tiled roof. The Spanish playhouses were administered in part by charitable brotherhoods – the *cofrades* – and in part by the municipal authorities, with the result that some of them are now far more handsomely documented than any of their English counterparts. We hear of fascinating details, such as the construction of a drainage basin at the centre of the yard, or the provision of counter-weighted pulleys for the flight machinery. But we hear too of more substantial matters, and it is plain that like the Boar's Head these theatres were largely *ad hoc* structures, developed piecemeal over the years to satisfy the demand for revenue and changing audience conditions. The best-documented of them all is the Corral del Príncipe built – or rather begun – in the Calle del Príncipe in Madrid in 1582.[19] The site was an empty court between the blank walls of flanking buildings. For the first production there was simply a stage and some seating platforms beside it, but soon lateral ranges of degrees were built along the flanking walls, together with boxes and a *cazuela* (a 'stew-pot' or enclosed gallery) for women in the two-storey block along the street frontage. By 1602, a row of boxes had been added above the *cazuela*. Some thirty years later the whole auditorium was enlarged when the owners of rooms in the neighbouring buildings cut viewing windows in the party walls at second-floor level, thus introducing rows of boxes above the degrees. At about the same time a new third floor of *desvanes* or attic boxes was constructed along both sides of the building, and across the façade block. Much later still, in 1713, the yard was entirely roofed over.

Clearly the Corral del Príncipe was not a fully worked-out design to begin with. It grew by stages, as if by an organic process. The side boxes cut through from the neighbouring houses were the result of commercial enterprise, not deliberate architectural thought. In applying to the Protector for permission to create three of them, Francisco Garro de Alegría and his partner, who had probably bought into the building next door only months earlier, cited their reasons with transparent disingenuousness:

We state that since there is ordinarily a lack of rooms and boxes in the corrales de comedias, and gentlemen are seeking ways to see the plays, given the few rooms, and we have bought a house on Prado Street which gives onto the Corral del Príncipe, in which three boxes can very easily be opened in order to accommodate gentlemen, since they will be very good ones, we ask Your Grace's permission for them to be made and opened . . .[20]

The petition was granted and the boxes were opened up. Almost immediately Alegría petitioned again, with equal success, to open *desvanes* above his new boxes. So the auditorium grew, its finances as fractured as the ownership of the disparate parts of its auditorium.

There are suggestive parallels between the *corrales* and the London public theatres, to be sure, and not only in the matter of open-air staging. The brotherhoods who initiated the Spanish playhouses intended the revenues to be devoted to the running of their hospitals, a charitable purpose which finds a faint echo in the contributions often made by the English acting companies to the poor of the parishes in which their houses were located. Equally the ownership of galleries in the Swan or the Globe as much as in the Boar's Head was divided among different parties. At the Theater the players received the money paid by people who stood in the yard, but the takings of the galleries were divided between the 'housekeepers', John Brayne and James Burbage.[21] Fortunately for us the arrangement caused many disagreements, especially after Brayne's death when his widow found herself apparently cheated of her inheritance, and so we come to know not only a few of the facts of the theatre's financial affairs but also a little of the often less than cheerful atmosphere in which they were conducted. There was, for example, a 'Commen box' in which the gallery takings were supposed to be placed, well secured with two locks, Brayne holding the key to one and Burbage to the other. After the play the two men would come together like officers in a submarine about to fire a nuclear missile. Both keys would be produced, and the box would yield its riches. But in depositions years later, Brayne's friends remembered him saying that Burbage possessed 'A secret key which he caused one Braye A Smyth in Shordiche to make for him' with which he 'did by the space of about ij° yeres purloyne & filche therof to him self moch of the same money'.[22] For all the opportunist flair with which the auditorium of the Príncipe was developed, nothing in the Spanish records quite equals this for low suspicion.

13

There seems to be no inherent reason why the London entrepreneurs should have been led to construct a playhouse more clearly all of a piece than that initiated in the Calle del Príncipe by the Cofradía de la Pasión y Sangre de Jesucristo, unless they had available to them some idea or model of what they might take a complete theatre to be. And Oliver Woodliffe, lath in hand at the Boar's Head, with the Theater, the Curtain, and the Swan to guide him, could propose only the improvisation of enlarged galleries. Not for him the remarkable integrity of design noticed in the London theatres by de Witt and conveyed in his drawing.

It has sometimes been suggested that the pattern of the Theater was derived from the circular or polygonal animal-baiting arenas which had graced various Bankside sites at least since 1546. If the public playhouses of the nineties struck the observer's eye with their particularity of design, we have a number of early prospect maps to show that the baiting rings were similarly noticeable. All these maps derive from a large, many-sheeted copperplate original, most of which is now quite lost.[23] Mercifully it was copied, at a reduced scale, by Braun and Hogenberg for their atlas *Civitates Orbis Terrarum* (Cologne, 1572), and approximately full-size in a rather crude woodcut version published originally *c.* 1562–3 and wrongly attributed in the nineteenth century to Radolph Agas.[24] Here among the fishponds of the

2   G. Braun and F. Hogenberg, detail from a map of London in *Civitates Orbis Terrarum* (Cologne, 1572), showing Bankside.

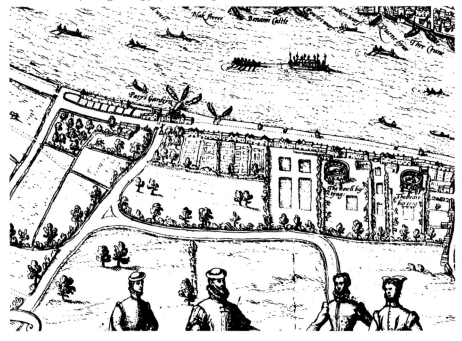

bank, which have been rendered neatly rectangular by the topographer's tidying hand, the two rings stand: to the west 'The Bowll bayting' (I cite Braun and Hogenberg) and to the east 'The Beare bayting' (plate 2). They are both certainly registered as round structures, though because they appear to be made of wood they will just as certainly have been many-sided polygons in fact. In the one a bull is in animated conversation with a dog; in the other a bear (undistinguishable in the woodcut map) is being similarly worried. Outside both establishments a large number of dogs are tethered to their kennels.

Standing before these sheets spread out on the table of a museum print room we may be a little too ready to compare them with the later maps which show round theatres in the Bankside area, and to conclude from our comparison that the one sort of building must have led by some necessary progression to the other. When the famous topographical artist Claes Jan Visscher made his lovely panorama of London *c.* 1616 he took one of these maps – almost certainly, as we shall see later on, the Braun and Hogenberg atlas – and for his view of Bankside translated it quite faithfully into the form of a panorama, putting down, for example, almost every detail of the housetops along the bank (plate 4). But because he knew that theatres had been built in the neighbourhood he placed tall polygonal structures on the old circular sites: the Globe where the Bearbaiting used to be, the Beargarden in the place of the Bullbaiting. Then he added a third in a more or less vacant spot upstream for the Swan. At the Beargarden he transposed one of the original map's ranges of kennels to his panoramic mode, and placed beside it a couple of human figures leading a dog. He carefully omitted these

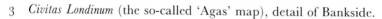

3 *Civitas Londinum* (the so-called 'Agas' map), detail of Bankside.

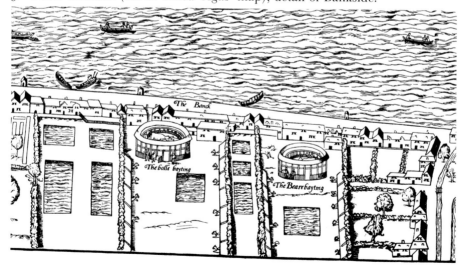

4   Claes Jan Visscher, *Londinum florentiss[i]ma Britanniae Urbs* (Amsterdam, 1616), detail showing Bankside.

appurtenances of baiting from the Globe, though he did retain a group of spectators standing outside its walls, peering in as if to see the play. Such figures also appear in Braun and Hogenberg and the woodcut map outside the baiting rings. But Visscher borrowed his visual idea of the playhouses from the depictions of the Swan and the Beargarden contained in John Norden's panorama of 1600 (plate 12), and in placing them so meticulously on the sites of the old structures he may have implied that the baiting rings had simply evolved into theatres.

Yet there are persuasive reasons for believing nothing of the sort. It is true that in 1613, before Visscher etched his view, the bearbaiting arena had been rebuilt as the Hope, a dual-purpose house intended to serve both for baiting and for plays. Far from reproducing the form of the old baiting rings, however, the new building copied the general shape and dimensions of the Swan playhouse. We shall return to its design later, but it is in any case unlikely to be the structure intended by Visscher, who had never been in England and whose topographical information was derived mainly from the Norden panorama of 1600. The confident air of his image of London has misled many commentators, but in fact his testimony is second and third-hand and of small consequence. Far more important is the account given of the baiting rings by the earlier maps and other contemporary evidence. Both the printed maps and a coloured drawing probably by the topographer William Smith (plate 5)[25] show what appears to be nothing more elaborate than a circular wooden screen. Within it the activity of the baiting takes place, while outside both Braun and Hogenberg and the woodcut show spectators standing on the ground. Some of them lean on a ledge formed by the closed-in lower part of the screen, evidently to get a comfortable and

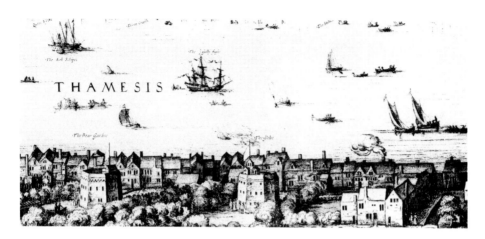

close view. Smith shows no spectators, but does indicate the ledge. Alone among these early maps the woodcut gives details of the access doorways into the rings and of a narrow roof or awning surrounding them.

In his lucid examination of the early history of the baiting arenas, Oscar Brownstein finds that the maps show nothing more than one would have expected of a mid-century bullring. Distinguishing carefully between the kind of structures appropriate for bull and bear baitings, he observes that the former was normally 'a circular barrier from 20 to 30 feet in diameter'; such rings were to be found in almost every town, where they enabled butchers to bait their bulls in order to improve the meat before the slaughter. 'The barrier', he says, 'had to be large enough in circumference to permit the bull to charge, and high and sturdy enough to keep the bull in and any spectators out.'[26] Although bearbaiting had different structural requirements, at the simplest needing only a stake to which the bear was chained, the earliest Beargarden appears to have included a safety screen also, on the pattern of the bullring and presumably to protect onlookers from the excited dogs. The pictures show this minimum arrangement, a mere safety wall of post and beam construction, with an in-filled section below, rising to about waist height. Presumably a grate covered the upper part of the screen, transparent enough for the spectators to look through it.

It would be a mistake, therefore, to conclude with Visscher that these purpose-built rings were early versions of the glorious theatres of Bankside. Yet we must also note that the pictures tell only part of the story. Public baitings had been held in the area, not far from Paris Garden, since at least 1546.[27] The maps, based as they are on an original of *c.* 1560, show two rings, but the Bullring seems to have enjoyed only a brief life, leaving one arena generally called 'The Paris Garden' to house baitings of every sort. In 1562 an Italian visitor found that a fairly complex structure had been developed to house them. There was, noted Alessandro Magno, 'a circular place surrounded by scaffolds, with their awnings against the rain and the sun', but he added that the ring itself was 'closed in all round, and one could not get out unless they opened one of the doors'.[28] This enclosure must have been a screen of the type reported by Braun and Hogenberg, but the accommodation for spectators was evidently more substantial than that shown in the maps. Already there was an auditorium sufficiently developed to permit the sort of entrance system that Lambarde was later to notice, the people 'paying one penny to stand below . . . and two to go up into the scaffolds'.[29] At about this time Paris Garden belonged to William Payne, who in a much later interrogatory was reported to have erected 'low scaffolds or standings' at his arena. Payne died in or before 1574 and was succeeded by a new deputy of her majesty's game of bears, named Wistow, and the same interrogatory asked whether he or one Morgan Pope did 'cause or procure instead of the said scaffoldes or standinges certaine galleries to be built about the said baytyng place'.[30] Unfortunately this question elicited no information, but it implies that such galleries did replace the 'low scaffolds' at some time after

5   William Smith, 'London', detail showing Bankside.

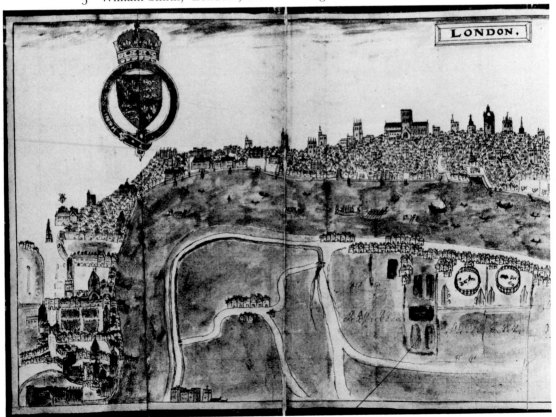

c. 1574. In 1583 the audience accommodation at Paris Garden suffered a spectacular and fatal collapse:

about foure of the clocke in the afternoone, the old and vnderpropped scaffolds, round about the Beare-garden, commonly called Paris Garden . . . ouercharged with people, fel soddainly down, whereby to the number of eight persons, men, and women were slaine and many others sore hurt . . .[31]

The event having occurred on a Sunday afternoon, and on the baleful 13 January at that, it became a matter for instant moral comment. John Field promptly published *A Godly Exhortation*, in which he revealed the divine hand behind the disaster. Presumably he was not an eyewitness, but his visualization of the event is specific enough to command attention:

Beeing thus vngodly assembled, to so vnholy a spectacle and specially considering the time; the yeard, standings, and Galleries being ful fraught, being now amidest their iolity, when the dogs and Bear, were in the chiefest battle, Lo the mighty hand of God vppon them. This gallery that was double, and compassed the yeard round about, was so shaken at the foundation, (y^t it fell as it were in a moment) flat to the ground, without post or peere, that was left standing, so high as the stake whervnto the Beare was tied.[32]

Most of the casualties were numbered amongst those who 'stood vnder the Galleries on the grounde, vpon whom both the waight of Timbre and people fel'.[33] It is possible that Field's moralizing temperament made him describe the Beargarden in terms more appropriate to the Theater and the Curtain, centres of entertainment to which he was at least equally hostile, but on the whole the detail of his account carries conviction. At this date therefore the baiting ring was probably surrounded by a 'double' gallery, underpropped with posts and elevated above an area where people stood. Field estimated the crowd as 'farre aboue a thousande'.[34] Four years later, so even-handed is Providence, his son Nathan was born, the playwright, famous actor and spirited defender of the stage.

The galleries at the Beargarden were promptly rebuilt. When Lupold von Wedel visited a baiting in August 1584 he found a theatre-like structure in which baitings were held in sequence with a type of spectacular show that brought the crowd teeming into the arena itself:

There is a round building three stories high, in which are kept about a hundred large English dogs, with separate wooden kennels for each of them. These dogs are made to fight singly with three bears, the second bear being larger than the first and the third larger than the second. After this a horse was brought in and chased by the dogs, and at last a bull, who defended himself bravely. The next was that a number of men and women came forward from a separate compartment, dancing, conversing and fighting with each other: also a man who threw some white bread among the crowd, that scrambled for it. Right over the middle of the place a rose was fixed, this rose being set on fire by a rocket: suddenly lots of apples and pears fell out of it down upon the people standing below. Whilst the people were scrambling for the apples, some rockets were made to fall down upon them out of the rose, which caused a great fright but amused the spectators. After this, rockets and other fireworks came flying out of all corners, and that was the end of the play.[35]

The Beargarden had become a kind of theatre in its own right, a process carried still further in 1613 when Philip Henslowe replaced it altogether with a larger structure called the Hope. This was built on or close to the site of its predecessor, but it was deliberately designed as a dual-purpose house, 'fitt & convenient', as the builder's contract put it, 'in all thinges, bothe for players to playe Jn, And for the game of Beares and Bulls to be bayted in the same'.[36] There was a tiring house to accommodate the actors, and the stage was set on trestles so that it might be carried away to clear the yard for baiting. For this reason the stage cover or 'Heavens all over the saide stage' was 'to be borne or carryed without any postes or supporters to be fixed or sett vppon the saide stage'. There were special provisions for the bulls and horses, but the fundamental design of the house was that of a theatre, the carpenter being bound by his contract 'to builde the same of suche large compasse, fforme, widenes, and height as the Plaie house Called the Swan'.[37]

The rebuilt Beargarden, and even more the Hope, certainly resembled the playhouses, but that is not to say that the playhouses grew out of the baiting rings. Once again, as with the case of the innyards, the theatres seem to have been the more potent influence. The early baiting rings were too slight, too undeveloped and too specialized to have shaped the great auditoria of the Theater and the Curtain. One would not seek to deny their influence altogether, for doubtless the round stands, with their awnings, as well as the system of audience admission at the Beargarden formed part of James Burbage's awareness of the possibilities of playhouse design as he deliberated with John Brayne over the layout of the Theater. But it seems unlikely, to say the least, that the baiting rings were the sole or even significant progenitors of the playhouses on the other side of town.

There was, in fact, something of far greater urgency in John Brayne's mind. The Theater was not the first playhouse venture he had launched upon. Nine years earlier he had engaged with a carpenter, William Sylvester, to make certain theatrical provisions for him at a 'house' called the Red Lion in Stepney. The contract led to complaints about performance, and an appeal was made to the Carpenters' Company, whose court book registered the following reaction:

Memorandum that at courte holden the daie & yeare abovesayd that, whear certaine varyaunce, discord & debate was betwene Wyllyam Sylvester carpenter on thone partie & John Brayne grocer on thother partie, yt is agreed, concluded & fullie determyned by the saide parties, by the assent & consent of them bothe, with the advise of the Master & wardeins abovesayd that Willyam Buttermore, John Lyffe,

Willyam Snellinge & Richard Kyrbye, Carpenters, shall with expedicon goe & peruse suche defaultes as are & by them shalbe found of in & aboute suche skaffoldes, as he the said Willyam hathe mad at the house called the Red Lyon in the parishe of Stebinyhuthe, & the said Willyam Sillvester shall repaire & amend the same with their advize substancyallie, as they shall thinke good. And that the said John Brayne, on Satterdaie next ensuenge the date above written, shall paye to the sayd Willyam Sylvester the some of eight poundes, tenne shillinges, lawfull money of England, & that after the playe, which is called the storye of Sampson, be once plaied at the place aforesaid the said John shall deliver to the said Willyam such bondes as are now in his custodie for the performaunce of the bargaine.[38]

Persuaded perhaps by the colourful name, commentators have nearly always seen this as what Sir Edmund Chambers called 'the Red Lion playing-inn',[39] the earliest of the courtyard theatres of which certain notice survives. Although the Carpenters' memorandum makes no mention of a yard, nor even of an inn in explicit terms, the general analogy with what little we know of the Bel Savage or even the great deal we know of the Boar's Head is so persuasive that these omissions have seemed scarcely worth the notice. No one had remarked on them, not even C. J. Sisson in his astute discussion of the memorandum in his book on *The Boar's Head Theatre*.[40] No one, that is, until an alert American legal historian, Janet Loengard, running her eye down the rolls of King's Bench pleas for the eleventh year of Elizabeth's reign, came across an entry concerning John Brayne and his Red Lion enterprise, and recognized its significance.[41]

Even as he had contemplated pursuing the negligent Sylvester through the agency of the Carpenters' Company, Brayne – we now discover – entered into a performance bond with a second workman, John Reynolds 'citizen and carpenter of London'. The bond was for the performance of a building contract, and when the time came Brayne refused to deliver it, an action which brought both men to the court of King's Bench in 1569. Here Reynolds' attorney entered a plea that part of the work had been performed 'well and in workmanlike manner' and completed before the agreed deadline, on 8 July 1567, but that Brayne himself had impeded the completion of the rest. As a normal part of the proceedings the original bond and its endorsed condition were read into the records, and it is the condition – the description, that is, of what Reynolds had undertaken to perform – that contains a mine of new information about the Red Lion. It must be quoted in full:

The condicion of thys obligation is suche that if the withinbounden John Raynolds hys executors or assignes or any of them att hys or theyre proper costes and charges do frame make or buylde and sett upp for the wythyn named John Braynes wythyn the Courte or yarde lying on the south syde of the Garden belonginge to the messuage or farme house called and knowen by the name of the Sygne of the Redd Lyon about the whiche courte there are galloryes nowe buyldinge, scituate and beinge at Myle End in the Paryshe of Seynt Mary Matfellon otherwyse called Whyte Chappell without Algate of London, sometyme called Starke House, one Skaffolde or stage for enterludes or playes of good newe and well seasoned Tymber and boords whyche shall conteyne in height from the ground fyve foote of assyse and shalbe in lengthe Northe and Southe fortye [word deliberately blanked out] foote of assyse and in bredthe East and West thyrty foot of assyse Well and sufficientlye stayed bounden and nayled wyth a certayne space or voyde parte of the same stage left unborded in such convenyent place of the same stage as the said John Braynes shall thynk convenyent. And yf the sayde John Raynolds hys executors or assignes do make frame sett up uppon the sayde skaffolde one convenyent turrett of Tymber and boords which shall conteyne and be in heyghte from the grounde sett upon plates thirtie foot of assyse with a convenyent flower [floor] of Tymber and boords within the same turrett seaven foote under the toppe of the same turrett and that the same turrett be in all places sufficiently brased pynned and fastened for the byndynge together of the same turrett and do also make and frame and sett up uppon the toppe of the same turrett some suffycyent compasse brases of good and well-seasoned tymber, and yf ye same turret so to be made framed and sett up bee fullye fynyshed ended and workmanly done in alle thynges accordyngly before the Feaste daye of the Natyvyte of Seynt John Baptest next comyng after the date hereof and also that the sayde skaffolde or stage so to be made bee fullye fynyshed wrought and workmanlye ended and done before the eyght daye of Julye then next ymedyattlye ensuynge withoute fraude or further delaye That then thys oblygacion to be voyde and of none effecte or ells to stande and abyde in full strengthe and vertue.[42]

To this Reynolds' attorney entered a plea alleging that Brayne himself had impeded part of the work, and Brayne asked that the matter should be sent for a jury trial. Unfortunately no further record of the subsequent proceedings has been found.

   This richly informative document, so happily discovered, tells us something about Brayne as a theatrical designer, for according to Reynolds it was his busy interference that held up the work. But it tells us far more about the theatre itself. To begin with this was no mere conversion of an inn, nor indeed was the Red Lion an inn at all. The Carpenters' Company alluded to it as a 'house', and Brayne's condition calls it 'the messuage or farme house called and knowen by the name of the Sygne of the Redd Lyon'. The term 'farm' here might conceivably mean that the building was leased out 'in farm', but nothing else in the document suggests that this was so and we should probably conclude that it was a farm in the agricultural sense. The location of the house is not certain, for the plea roll gives it as 'Myle End in the Paryshe of Seynt Mary Matfellon otherwyse called Whyte Chappell without Algate'. Until comparatively recent times there was a Red Lion Street to the south of Whitechapel High Street, but it was too close to Aldgate to be associated with Mile End, which as its name implies is a mile away to the east. Wherever it was, the Red Lion possessed a name sufficiently inn-like to have caused much confusion among modern historians, though it was of course customary for all manner of ordinary houses to bear such names and signs. It possessed also a garden to the south side of which there was by the time of Reynolds' agreement a 'Courte or yarde' within which he undertook to set up 'one Skaffolde or stage for enterludes or playes'. The exact nature of the court is unclear. It does not appear to have been a part of the main house, or we should not have been told that it stood to the south of the garden. It seems more likely, therefore, that it was a farmyard,[43] rather than a domestic quadrangle enclosed on all sides by buildings. At the time of the original agreement with Reynolds galleries were in the course of construction 'aboute' the court. These will have been the 'skaffoldes' that Sylvester was contracted to build 'at the house called the Red Lyon', and their inner faces will have defined the yard of the theatre proper. It is possible that they were erected against the walls of existing buildings, but overall the documents suggest rather a new and independent structure. The stage, its turret and the surrounding galleries were all substantial items and together constituted an entire theatre which Brayne was causing to be built under separate but coordinated contracts. His capital investment must have been substantial and so must his active interest as a designer. Reynolds' contract is specific and detailed, giving every sign that Brayne knew exactly what he wanted, including a void space in the stage apparently intended for a trapdoor whose location Brayne himself was to direct during the course of the construction. And then there was the extraordinary turret, which seems to have been the bone of contention between the two men. In his plea Reynolds makes a series of allegations which give a notable insight into the process of construction. He claims to have 'constructed, made and fabricated the structure called the Scaffold specified in the aforesaid endorsement' by the first of July, 'and was prepared to erect and set up the same structure at the aforesaid house . . . but . . . the aforesaid John Braynes then and there impeded, disturbed and prohibited him'. Moreover he also claims that by 20 June, that is eleven days earlier, he had 'constructed, made, joined and built the aforesaid turret specified in the aforesaid endorsement . . . and set up the same turret upon the structure called the Scaffold according to the form and effect of the aforesaid endorsement'.[44]

On the face of it this plea seems to be a piece of arrant nonsense. The stage was 'fabricated' by 1 July, but not yet erected. Yet already by 20 June a turret had been set up on it. What can this lawyer mean? One would have expected such an argument to be laughed out of court, but it was not. Brayne's attorney did not object to the logic of Reynolds' narrative, but claimed simply that his client 'did not impede, disturb or prohibit the aforesaid John Raynolds from erecting and setting up the said structure . . . in the mode and form as the aforesaid John Raynolds alleged above in his pleading'. Both were agreed, therefore, that the work was not completed in time; the point on which they joined issue was whether Brayne was himself responsible for the delay. It appears that neither he nor his lawyer saw anything odd in the logical progression of Reynolds' account.

The litigants agreed that a scaffold was fabricated but not yet set up at the Red Lion by 1 July, though some days before that a large turret had been built and set up 'upon' it. Because a court full of legal minds saw nothing to object to in this story we have no alternative but to attempt to make sense of it ourselves. In fact a solution is not far to seek. Elizabethan timber building practice involved a good deal of what we should today call prefabrication: timbers might be dressed, cut, jointed and numbered at some distance from the actual building site, at what was commonly known as the 'framing place'. Here the joints would be tested for a good fit, and whole sections of the building might be framed up before being carted away for their final assembly.[45] It appears from Reynolds' account that both scaffold and turret were prefabricated at such a framing place; that the main structural parts of both were assembled before the feast of St John the Baptist (24 June) in order to try them out; that it was intended that Brayne should check the work and probably point out where the trap was to be located; and that subsequently the whole affair was to be demounted, conveyed within the space enclosed by Sylvester's new galleries, and there erected and set up for good. But Brayne apparently interfered – or so at least Reynolds claimed – presumably after 24 June and before 8 July, the date when the contract was meant to be completed. On 1 July Reynolds 'was prepared to erect and set up' the structure at the Red Lion, but was unable to proceed as had been intended.

Reynolds' testimony also leaves us with a strong sense of Brayne's urge to control the design of the structure even as the carpenter laboured over it. The turret and the scaffold must work together, the 'space or voyde parte' of the stage must be placed just so, the compass braces must be 'suffycyent'. At about the same time Brayne was also finding fault with Sylvester's work on the galleries, but the court of the Carpenters' Company met on 15 July and sought to have the matter resolved by the following Saturday, the 19th. Clearly Brayne had created something of a dust up at the Red Lion late in June or early in July, and was refusing to deliver performance bonds to both of his carpenters until he got exactly what he wanted, if then. He emerges from this affair as a demanding man and a knowledgeable one.

And what did he want? Sylvester's galleries were built 'about' the court; within them a stage was to be set up, 30 ft by 40 ft in area and 5 ft tall, all made of the best new material. On the stage there was to be a turret rising 30 ft above the ground. It was to be 'sett upon plates', but we also hear that it was to be set up upon the stage. Perhaps it was part on and part off, enclosing a tiring house in its lowest level through which the actors might ascend to the platform. If this reading is correct the turret will have risen 25 ft above the stage; 7 ft below its top – or 18 ft above the stage – there was a floor, presumably for theatrical use as an 'above'. Higher still, at the very top of the

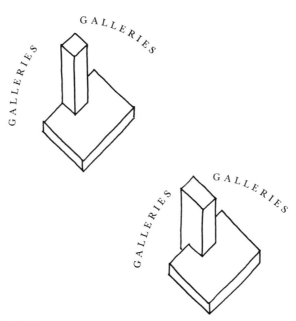

Figure 1   The Red Lion, Whitechapel. Axonometric diagrams showing alternative
arrangements of the stage turret.

turret itself, 'compass brases of good and well-seasoned tymber' were
installed, four of them if these are the 'four [leus?] brases' acknowledged by
Reynolds in his plea. The reading *leus* is Dr Loengard's, and I cannot
improve upon it. A 'lewis' (spelled variously 'lowys', 'louis' and 'luis' in
contemporary documents) is an χ-shaped cramp used for hoisting masonry,
consisting of two iron crescents back to back, united where they touch by a
ring. Compass braces are curved ones, and it seems likely that they were
assembled in the χ-pattern of a lewis for structural rigidity as well as good
looks. The stage was set with its wider sides facing east and west, and while
these cardinal terms are doubtless only approximate they are consistent with
the orientation of the Boar's Head stage as well as with what we know of the
Globe. And finally we have to note that what Brayne wanted was very large.
The area of his stage was slightly greater than that of the Fortune, the only
other Elizabethan public stage whose dimensions are known: 1200 ft^2 as
against 1182.5 ft^2. Some of it may have been occupied by part or all of the
base of the turret, but it is important to notice that this earliest of the
purpose-built theatres possessed a stage whose size and proportions closely
resembled those of a playhouse built 33 years later. Assuming that there was
some yard space left between the elevated stage and the surrounding galleries we may reasonably conclude that the external dimensions of the entire
structure can hardly have been much smaller than those of the Fortune (80 ft

6   *The View of the Cittye of London from the North towards the Sowth* (>1599).

square) and may even have approached those of the Globe (100 ft in diameter). Here was a large, complex, galleried theatre, completed if not finally assembled in June 1567, fully nine years before the construction of the Theater in Shoreditch. John Brayne had established the pattern of the Elizabethan theatre long before the earliest records of the use of innyards for the staging of plays in London, and his enterprise at the Red Lion was a far more substantial affair than anything that would be built at the baiting rings for another twenty years. And while it owed little or nothing to the gaming houses and inns it came into being under his insistent personal control, reflecting in its design a well developed idea of what a theatre should be.

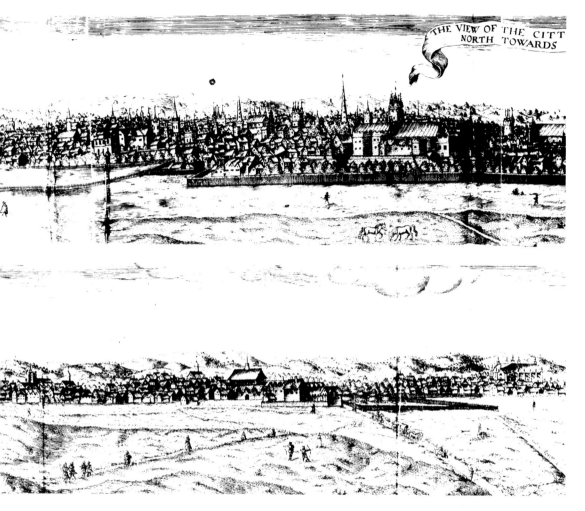

One recent theorist of the stage has summed up the evolution of the early London playhouses with blunt but mistaken simplicity:

James Burbage was no architect but a carpenter-turned-actor who merely copied existing structures – an animal-baiting arena and a Tudor hall stage – that he jammed together without regard for architectural coherence.[46]

The baiting arenas did not provide an adequate model for Burbage, who benefited as much from Brayne's experience at the Red Lion as from any lessons that the game of bears and bulls might have taught. The Red Lion's stage, 40 ft wide and surmounted by its lofty turret, little resembled anything that might have been set up in a Tudor hall. To be sure, the Whitechapel playhouse had been constructed by two carpenters under separate contracts, one for the frame and another for the major fittings, but Brayne had insisted

27

on overseeing their careful integration. The idea of the theatre that he carried to the enterprise must surely have influenced the planning of his next playhouse venture nine years later in Shoreditch. Unfortunately the shape of the Red Lion remains unknown, but the Theater had one of the polygonal frames that were to become characteristic of the Elizabethan public playhouse. De Witt, writing in about 1596, included it in a class of four 'amphiteatra Londinij',[47] and it appears as a tall, angled structure in an anonymous 'View of the Cittye of London from the North towards the Sowth', also probably dating from the late sixteenth century (plate 6). The documents at the Public Record Office concerning its construction and subsequent management were ferreted out and transcribed by C. W. Wallace, and have been expertly summarized by Herbert Berry.[48] From them we know that it was sited among other buildings, most of them 'very symple buyldinges but of twoe storyes hye of the ould fashion and rotten'[49] and therefore not actually incorporated into the new structure. It was so solidly built that once it was up a 'ruynous and decayed' barn nearby 'was shored vppe with twoe or three Shores from the Playhouse Called the Theater'.[50] Other materials used in the construction included wainscoting, tile, brick, sand, lime, lead and iron.[51] Neither stonemasons nor thatchers were involved either in its construction or in its maintenance, and it seems likely that the foundations were of brick and the roof of tile. There is no mention in these records of a polygonal plan, but we hear that there was a 'Theater yard' as well as 'the Attyring housse or place where the players make them readye'.[52] There were galleries for spectators, and although their number is not mentioned we do hear of a 'door going vppe to the said Gallaries'[53] at which money was taken. In them presumably were the 'vpper romes' where one could 'have such convenient place to sett or stande to se such playes as shalbe ther played'.[54] A German traveller who was in London in 1585, before the building of the Bankside theatres, wrote that 'Comedies are given daily . . . There are some peculiar houses, which are so made as to have about three galleries over one another, inasmuch as a great number of people always enters to see such an entertainment.'[55] He must have had the Theater and the Curtain in mind, and the picture of the former in the long view of London from the north shows it with three storeys of windows in the outer wall. It also shows the upper part of some kind of roofed turret rising above the top of the main frame, an echo perhaps of the 30 ft high turret at the Red Lion. There are two stair turrets, one at each side, which doubtless provided the way of 'going vppe to the . . . Gallaries'.

In the broadest terms, then, we know something of the design of the Theater. Its polygonal timber frame stood on a foundation of brick; it was enclosed on the outside presumably with lath and plaster; its roof was tiled. There was a yard surrounded by three levels of galleries which were reached by attached external staircases, though it is not clear whether the doors leading into them were external or opened from the arena. We have no word of the stage but there was a tiring house and at least by the 1590s a roofed turret erected within the yard, tall enough to be seen above the polygonal frame. The Theater was a freestanding structure, not incorporated into other buildings on the site, though one of them was eventually shored against it. Once built, in fact, its main frame could hardly be adapted, so all of a piece was its conception and design. At the Boar's Head old galleries could be taken down and other ones built; when necessary a new one could be added to enlarge the auditorium. In Madrid the auditorium of the Corral del Príncipe might grow step by step like a crystal. But we hear of no such developments at the Theater, nor at any of the subsequent purpose-built open playhouses. Their fittings might be changed from time to time, as when Henslowe added a flight machine at the Rose,[56] and they could of course be redecorated. But no one ever added a new storey of boxes, or expanded the ground plan, or radically changed the relation of stage to auditorium. Such alterations, however desirable for commercial or even theatrical reasons, were entirely precluded by the highly integrated design of the original structure.

2
The festive tradition

An anonymous topographical artist took himself some four hundred years ago to a spot in the fields near Islington from which he could get a clear view of St Paul's. In the background of his prospect ranged the Surrey hills, where today we should see the great television masts of Crystal Palace and Norwood. Immediately to the left of St Paul's he could make out the tower of St Saviour's, Southwark, now Southwark Cathedral. As his eye scanned the wide vista before him it soon came to the distinctive 'crown spire' of St Mary-le-Bow rising a little to the left of St Bartholomew-the-Great. In the foreground here were the castellated ranges of St John's Priory, beyond which soared the spire of St Lawrence Poultney, the tallest object in the view. From there the topographer could count off a succession of church towers and other distinctive landmarks: the Guildhall, St Dunstan-in-the-East, the flamboyant tower of the Exchange, the Tower of London. To the right of St Paul's he could remark St Sepulchre, St Martin's Ludgate, the Middle Temple and, much closer to, the hall at Gray's Inn. As he contemplated the expanse of the view, the artist found that the whole fell conveniently into a symmetrical composition if he made his central axis the tower of St Paul's and followed the spread of the city equally to east and west. This enabled him to close the design to the right with the distinctive, immediately recognizable form of Westminster Abbey. To the left a nondescript barn offered itself in the foreground, but above it he could make out the remarkable form of the Theater, with its polygonal wooden frame and flag-topped turret.[1] London was still a mediaeval city of churches, but here was a secular building notable enough to balance an abbey in his composition. The result of his endeavour was the broad panorama to which we have already referred, 'The View of the Cittye of London from the North towards the Sowth' (plate 6).

The artist's station point may be deduced from the alignments of the landmarks in the engraving: it was on what is now the Pentonville Road, close to the reservoir in Claremont Square.[2] His line of sight towards Westminster crossed the palace of Whitehall, but unfortunately in his print he omitted this cluster of Tudor buildings, the better perhaps to display the Abbey.[3] Had he shown Whitehall he would have included the great Banqueting House which Elizabeth had caused to be erected there to entertain Alençon's embassy in 1582, and which stood to the west of the great hall until it was pulled down by James I. For years the capital was flanked by these remarkable houses of drama and entertainment, to the south west the fantastic Banqueting House originally built as a glorified tent of timber and canvas, to the north east Brayne and Burbage's Theater and its neighbouring Curtain. It is our business in the present chapter to trace something of the common ancestry of these structures in the festive architecture of Henry VIII.

That the Theater had an ancestry there can be no doubt. The Red Lion will have been close among its kin, and Paris Garden and the Bel Savage may also have been part of the family. Yet none of these provided a wholly satisfactory model, because before 1576 none was sufficiently developed in design to convey to Elizabethan builders the perfectly integrated idea of the great three-storeyed polygonal frames which they were to establish in Shoreditch and later along Bankside. The erection of so large, complex and unadaptable a structure as the characteristic public playhouse of the sixteenth century required a great measure of entrepreneurial confidence, and it is unlikely to have been undertaken at all without some assurance, no matter how remote in time or place, that such a building could indeed be realized and serve its purpose.

And in fact, as Richard Hosley has observed, the Theater was not a new thing on the face of the earth in 1576.[4] There had been something of a fashion for such structures among the grand monarchs of Europe a little over half a century before, and the finest of them had been built by Henry VIII's English craftsmen at Calais in 1520. The auspices were of course very different from those of the London playhouses: Henry's banqueting theatre was erected for a large but exclusive diplomatic audience, not the general public, and its programme of design reflected its aristocratic origins. Indeed the political importance attaching to the occasion for which the house was built – Henry's meeting with the Emperor Charles V immediately after the conclusion of the Field of the Cloth of Gold – ensured that nothing in the way of decorative and emblematic splendour should be left to chance.

The theatre at Calais was set up in an area in front of the Exchequer from which several modest buildings had been cleared. It was polygonal in plan, described in Turpyn's *Chronicle of Calais* as having 'xvj. principals made of great mastes, betwixt every maste xxiiij. fote'.[5] A Venetian observer called it variously 'an amphitheatre' and 'a theatre' [*theatro*], estimating its diameter at 'more than fifty paces' [*più di cinquanta passa*].[6] Turpyn's figures imply an external diameter of just over 120 ft; the Italian's more than 125 ft, assuming a pace to be $2\frac{1}{2}$ ft. The outer walls were closed with wooden boards and covered with canvas. Attached to them, doubtless forming part of their structure, were three storeys of galleries:

with in rownde abowt by the syds were made thre loftes one above anothar for men and women for to stond upon, and they that stode behynd myght see over the hedes that stode before, it was made so highe behynd and low before.[7]

The Venetian confirms that the galleries were one above another:

All round inside the walls run three orders of galleries or balconies [pogioli], 8 ft deep and 9 ft high. The parapet in front is as high as a man's waist. From one to the next it is 10 ft, and they have sloping floors so that the lastcomers see over the top of the first to arrive, and are able conveniently to look and see what goes on on the ground floor. These tiers, as I have said, are in three orders and are spacious, one above another; they are made for the service and convenience of the spectators, musicians, trumpets, etc.[8]

A French account reported 'trois galeries les unes sur les aultrez' (three galleries, built one above another).[9] As Sydney Anglo remarked, when he first brought this house to the public's attention, 'The basic similarity here, though in a very simplified form, to the later public theatres is remarkable.'[10] The polygonal frame of superimposed galleries, three storeys of them, is just what we find later on at Shoreditch, but at Calais it formed part of an ensemble that included a great canvas ceiling painted with an elaborate cosmic decoration. The timber frame struck contemporaries as being theatrical in shape and construction, by which evidently we are to understand that it reminded them of the wooden theatres which Servius had observed were common in the territories of ancient Rome. The canvas roof, however, with its *mappa mundi*, evoked more modern associations, for it resembled many another that had been installed on festive occasions over the political and social ceremony of the banqueting chamber. At the centre of the arena stood a huge timber column made of eight masts lashed together. To the Venetian indeed it looked like the mast of a ship, for it was fitted with iron hoops and rings from which ropes were rigged to the walls behind the galleries. At the top was a canvas roof, intended for service. Below it, resting on ropes radiating from a hoop lower on the mast, a second canvas ceiling covered the entire building within, and on it was painted the main programmatic decoration. It was a vast representation of the four elements, its intellectual content derived in part from Aristotle's *Meterologica*. First, running like a border round the outer parts of the house, there was a landscape of the earth, with mountains, woods, forests and meadows, filled with windmills, towns, houses, trees and churches. Beyond it, closer towards the central mast, was an artificial sea – Turpyn records 'many shipps under sayles' – and in the midst of all 'was payntyd the element *with* [MS.; transcript reads 'of'] starres, sonne, and mone, and clowdes, with divars othar things made above men's heds'. Beneath this striking cosmological

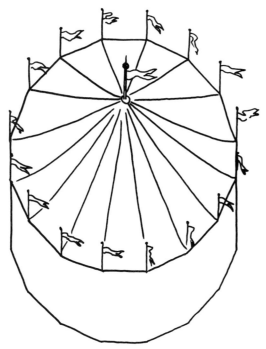

Figure 2   The Calais banqueting house. Axonometric diagram.

display there stood, in Turpyn's words, 'greate images of white wykers, like grete men, and they were set hyghe above on the highest lofts and stages'.[11] They represented men and women alternately, as the Venetian reported, clad in silk and each with a torch in its hand. Between these figures were marvellous chandeliers, suspended from the ropework of the ceiling, while still more light was given by candlesticks shaped as cornucopias fixed to the masts. Evidently there were 16 chandeliers, for the Italian reported that they hung 'at each angle of the theatre'; there must therefore have been an equal number of statues, one at the centre of each of the 16 bays, and as many cornucopias.

The building was ostensibly intended to celebrate and encourage the alliance between king and emperor, but its form and lavish provision in fact glanced sideways at the recently concluded negotiation with France. The Field of the Cloth of Gold had also been lavish, and had openly declared the ideal of a Universal Peace in which the centrifugal forces of national pride might be tamed by a united Christendom. But just as openly it practised the competitive rivalry it professed to supersede, finding its most characteristic expression in the ritualistic combats of chivalric sport, where symbols of reconciliation coexisted with a real and often bitter national jealousy. After the sentimental clichés of its public declarations the very fact of Henry's

33

meeting with the emperor must be read as an equally ambiguous sign of his intentions: the affair at Calais was as much a rebuff to France as a genuine attempt to achieve a widening unity. Nevertheless the programme of the banqueting theatre straightforwardly asserted a Tudor/Imperial equality, contained in a vessel of cosmic order. The house was approached through a vestibule, planned on a double square 30 ft by 15 ft, at either end of which stood a gateway adorned with statuary maintaining what Anglo calls 'the careful equipoise demanded by protocol'.[12] There was Arthur as a representative of chivalry, flanked by a crowned king to one side and Hercules to the other, symbols of the Tudors and the emperor, whose respective arms also appeared. At the inner gate blind Cupid stood between an English archer and an Imperial knight, and this balanced symbolism was carried into the theatre proper, where shields of arms on every pillar were alternately English and Imperial.

The overall supervision of the design and construction of the preparations for the Field of the Cloth of Gold had been entrusted to Sir Edward Belknap, who had at his command a host of artisans from the Royal Works. Three of them are mentioned in a letter of the commissioners, who note their concern about the delay in preparations for the palace at Guisnes, where Henry was to entertain the French king:

And Richarde Gybson who shuld cover the rofes with seared canvas ys not yet commen, and yt is highe tyme hys warkes were in hande, for yt muste be paynted on the owte syde, and aftir curiouslye be garnisshed under with knottis and batons guyltt and other devises, whiche busynes is committed to John Rastell, Clement Urmeston and other. Thies warkes be of greate and importunate charges, and we be in doubte how they shall overcumme the same by the daye appointed.[13]

Belknap and his team were also responsible for the construction of the Calais theatre, whose ceiling was to be more elaborately decorated than those of the temporary buildings at Guisnes.[14] Both John Rastell and Clement Urmeston were interested in the 'devises' in more than a passing fashion. Two years later, when Charles made his complementary entry into London, Rastell designed one of the pageants, a mechanism which, as Anglo observes, echoed the themes of the Calais theatre.[15] In it England appeared surrounded by sea and populated with mechanical animals. Images of the king and emperor, each bearing a sword, emerged by means of a device, and having beheld each other threw down their arms and embraced in a machine driven clinch. Whereupon the Father of Heaven moved into sight at the top of the pageant, bearing the scripture 'Beati pacifici qui filij dei vocabuntur' (Blessed are the peacemakers: for they shall be called the children of God; Matthew 5.9). The cosmic preoccupation was also evident in Rastell's printer's device, in which the Father of Heaven appeared along with the planets and the four elements. Some years before the Calais visit, indeed, he had revealed his cosmic propensities in an interlude, *The Nature of the iiij Elementes*, and presumably did so again in his lost work, *Canones astrologicos*. He may have passed such preoccupations on to his friend and colleague Clement Urmeston, for the latter developed a theory of kingship – which he proposed to Cromwell – along lines so fraught with cosmic thinking that he confessed that his musings on 'goddes lawes namyd to be in ligt of sone and moone and sters perchaunce are straunge and mysticall to erthly mens understanding'.[16]

The Calais theatre's cosmological decoration was no mere reflex of a courtly routine; it was initiated for good political reasons and carried through by court artists at least two of whom believed so far in its themes as to explore them in their own writing. The programme was developed by men whose modes of thought were of the Renaissance and would be of the Reformation, by turns humanist and cabbalistic, modern and mediaeval. They must on this occasion have found much food for thought, for in the event, as Turpyn reports,

on the same morninge the wynd began to ryse, and at nyght blewe of all the canvas, and all the elements with the sterrs, sonn, and mone, and clowds, and the same reyne blewe out above a thowsand torches and tapers that wer ordayned for the same; and all the kyngs seets that was made with great ryches that cowlde be ordaynyd, besyds all othar things, was all dashed and lost.[17]

The Venetian observer put the matter more charmingly:

The western wind, hearing the report and doubtful lest they might find it too hot in so enclosed a place, blew off both the roof and the sky-cloth, upset the fire, the sea and the earth and left the building to the spectators. I suppose that in such a ruin there was no room left but for such as had stood there.[18]

The timber frame, as might have been expected, had stood firm.

'All dashed and lost': one may prefer the Englishman's dour fatalism to the Italian's *sprezzatura*, for the collapse of so elaborate a building must have taken many hearts with it. At the centre of the floor there had been stages ready for music and players:

abowght the highe pece of tymbar that stode up right in the mydste was made stages of tymbar for organs, and othar instruments for to stand in, and men for to play upon them, and for clarks syngenge, and othar pagents for to be playde when the kyngs of England and of Romayns shuld be at theyre banqwete . . .[19]

Yet the English men of learning and of craft who had devised the building might have been forewarned. Only a few weeks before, as part of the preparations at Ardres for the Field of the Cloth of Gold, the French had built a group of festive pavilions in which to feast their visitor. One had been especially elaborate:

And the said king had another [pavilion] built, outside the town. It was covered with canvas, as had been done at the entertainment at the Bastille, and it was made in a form like that which the Romans, in past ages, used for their theatre: all in a round, constructed of wood, with loges, rooms and galleries. [It had] three storeys, one above another, and all the foundations were of stone. For all that it came to nothing.[20]

A storm had blown away its canvas roof. Our commentator, the seigneur de Fleurange, notes that the structure resembled a Roman theatre, checking off a series of points which emphasize the similarity: the round shape, the wooden construction, the storeys of galleries and the stone foundations. These are also characteristics of the Calais banqueting theatre. Fleurange found evidence of the ancient building form in the great wooden frame, but not in the gorgeous decoration of the canvas ceiling, which brought to mind rather the blue cloth, painted with stars and planets, with which the court-yard at the Bastille had been covered some two years earlier when the English ambassadors were received by Francis I. The banqueting house at Ardres, like its simular at Calais, enshrined the Roman idea in its substantial timber frame, but its canvas roof derived from more contemporary sources.

At Calais Belknap's artisans seem to have produced a structure remark-ably like that which had already succumbed to the summer winds at Ardres, but it is unlikely that they were merely copying the French design. The proposals for Henry's temporary palace at Guisnes, in which he planned to entertain the French king, had been set in train well before the beginning of the year, and the king's painters put to work on its programmatic ceilings. It seems likely that they began their labours on the Calais structure at much the same time, a task they cannot have undertaken without a clear know-ledge of the shape and size of the building. Sir Nicholas Vaux, trying desperately to move the construction forward on the site, wrote to Wolsey on 10 April that although the lack of materials was holding up the work at Guisnes, at least 'The Frenche kyng maketh but lityll prep[aration] at Arde'. But by 18 May, when Vaux's anxiety was even more acute, he wrote – the letter is now partly burnt away – that

the Frenche kinge . . . at Arde . . . hathe taken . . . iiij howses of the towne and a greate peace of the abbaye there called Anderne. And entendeth to make greate [build-ings,] wherin moche of his pastymes shalbe showed, as the maistre [of the] workes there didd report. And that there ys provided and redy at Rouen certein tymbre redye framed for the same buyldinges . . . the same tylt, counterlistes, stages, and bariers that were set upp in Parys. And so by soche meanes they be in a greate forwardnes of thier provisions.[21]

In the event Francis changed his plans, abandoning the project to convert buildings in Ardres itself, and instead erected his pavilions outside the town. The fact that the tilt and barriers were brought from Paris as ready-made structures suggests that the last-minute pavilions may have had a similar source, and especially the round theatre mentioned by Fleurange as being reminiscent of the entertainment at the Bastille. The origin of its three-storeyed galleried auditorium may well have been that diplomatic occasion of eighteen months before.[22]

Such buildings could be disassembled and moved about the country because of the nature of their construction. As Vaux reports, it was possible to frame a timber building at Rouen, then move it as a kit of parts to the site 100 miles away, there to assemble it as a piece of prefabrication. At Guisnes, where Henry was intent on outscaling the French if nothing else, it was intended to erect three huge chambers so large that 'there ys not such iij. in noo one howse in England'. The great chamber was to be 124 ft by 42 ft, and 30 ft high; the dining chamber 80 ft by 34 ft and 27 ft high; and the privy chamber 60 ft by 34 ft, also 27 ft high. There were plans for galleries and chapels, and for a banqueting house 220 ft long, 70 ft wide 'and to be so highe as tymbre woll serve us'.[23] Not all of these great structures were begun, but by 18 May a brick foundation and basement had been laid for the greater part of them, raised to a level eight feet above the ground. Then followed the timber framing, some of which was prepared in London and shipped across ready cut. The construction was so rapid that it became a marvel, and afterwards, when Henry and his retinue had returned home, Martin du Bellay told the story:

the king of England feasted the [French] king near Guisnes in a wooden building which had four main blocks, and which he had had constructed in England, and brought over by sea ready made. It was covered in canvas painted to resemble ashlar, and adorned within with the richest tapestries that could be found, in such sort that one could only conclude it to be one of the loveliest buildings in the world. Its design was based on that of the Merchants' Exchange in Calais. Afterwards it was disassembled and returned to England . . .[24]

In fact most of the dressing and framing of the timbers had been done on the site,[25] but the dismantled parts will certainly have been transported back to England. Like the French king's pavilions, the palace of Guisnes was a demountable structure. Its roofs, which Sir Nicholas Vaux described as works 'of greate and importunate charges', will have been rolled up and returned whence they came. And what was true of Guisnes may surely be applied also to the round theatre at Calais. Its roof too will have been prepared in London and sent out ready-made; its frame, whether constructed in London or on the site from raw timber, will have been taken apart and sent back home along with the canvas and the great masts. For all this festive architecture of 1520 was as transportable as a geodesic dome in a modern international exhibition.

The polygonal banqueting houses at Ardres and Calais were both three-storeyed frames of wooden galleries, and both emerged from a tradition of festive building that seems to have been common to the French and English Courts. Both could rapidly be dismantled and carted away, but were none the less splendid for that. The accounts of the emblematic decoration show their kinship with many other places of courtly entertainment of the time, but in their shape they do seem to have been unusual for such large projects. The structure at Ardres looked to one observer like a theatre of ancient Rome, and it seems likely that the similar work at Calais made much the same appeal to the learned of the day. The most obvious characteristics of the buildings were their programmatic coherence of design, their temporary, demountable methods of construction, and their generic allusion to the splendours of the antique world. All of these qualities interpenetrated one another: the method of construction relied on the coherence of the programme, and the programme expressed the idea of antiquity, especially in its evocation of the Roman theatre. These are elements of design that we find again, generations later, as the Elizabethan public playhouse springs to vigorous and astonishing life in the suburbs of Whitechapel and Shoreditch.

Occasional building in the festive mode continued in England throughout the period of Wolsey's ascendancy, a fine example being the banqueting hall and disguising theatre erected for the French embassy at Greenwich in 1527. But with the events of the Reformation there came a decline in the Court festivals and in the elaborate temporary buildings designed to house them. The young Edward VI, anxious to emulate the deeds of his father, made some attempt to revive the traditions of courtly entertainment, and banqueting houses were set up in Marylebone and Hyde Park to welcome a French commission in 1551, but his reign saw no major essays in the genre. Neither Mary nor the younger Elizabeth was to countenance much in the way of festive building, and it was not until another French embassy – that of the Duc d'Alençon in 1581–2 – that the Works was required to undertake the construction of a large banqueting house in Whitehall. The Surveyor approached this task using some of the techniques that had been employed at Calais: a framework of masts was covered externally with canvas, but far from being blown away by the first storm the structure stood – periodically strengthened to be sure – for twenty-five years before it was demolished to make way for a successor made of brick and stone.

Holinshed left what appears to be an accurate account of it:

there was a banquetinghowse made in manner & fourme of a long square 332 foot in measure about, 30 principalls made of great mast*es* being xl foot in length apeece, standing vpright between eu*ery* one of these mast*es* x foot a sunder & more The walls of this howse was closed with canvas and painted all ye out sides of ye same howse most arteficially with a worke called rustick much like vnto stone This howse hath 292 light*es* of Glas The sides within ye same howse was made with x height*es* of degrees, for men & weomen to stand vpon and in ye top of this howse was wrought most cunninglie vpon canvas, worke of Iuie & holy with pendant*es* made of wicker rod*es*, & garnished with baies Rue & all maner of strang flowers, and garnished with spang*es* of gould, as also garnished with hanging Toseans, made of holly & Iuie, with all man*n*er of strang fruit*es*, as pomegarnett*es* orreng*es* pompions Cowcombers grapes carrett*es* Reav*es* [i.e. strings of onions] with such other like, spanged with gould & most ritchlie hanged betwene these work*es* of baies & Iuie were great spaces of canvas which was most cunninglie painted y^e cloudes with y^e starres y^e sunne and sunne beames with diu*er*se other coates of sundry sortes belonging to Queen*s* ma*jestie*, most ritchlie garnished with gould . . . This howse was made in 3 week*es* & 3 Dai*es* / and ended on the 28 [April 1581] \ it cost 1744 19 ij^{d}ob, as I was credebly enformed by Tho*mas* Crane, Surveyor vnto her ma*jestie*s work*es*.[26]

Although more than sixty years had passed since the constructions at the Field of the Cloth of Gold and at Calais the old methods of fabricating this specialized type of building had not been forgotten. A few minor examples had perhaps helped to keep the tradition alive: after the great banqueting hall at Greenwich in 1527 there had been a temporary one made of masts at the same palace in 1559, and another at Whitehall for a French embassy in 1572. Now, on the site that was later to be occupied by Inigo Jones's famous building, the Works renewed the old techniques. The total cost according to the Declared Accounts was £1887.2s.8½d., a little higher than the figure reported by Holinshed, and among the emptions the largest individual sums expended were for the masts and deal boards (£131.1s.0d. and £127.10s.0d. respectively). It seems likely that the 30 principals mentioned by Holinshed were supplemented by other masts, perhaps to form an aisled structure. At the upper end stood 'a sort of stage [*theatre*], where the queen was seated on a dais',[27] and this will have been lit by 'two great Baywindowes' mentioned in the taskwork accounts.[28] To the east and west there were wooden 'Clerestorie light*es*' framed by the carpenters, and on the walls were stretched 2000 ells of canvas and 1000 ells of 'vandelle' or sail canvas at a cost for the material of £125. All this was painted, for a similar price, in the fashion described by Holinshed.

The entry in the Declared Account for 1581–2 records payment for

makinge of sundrie Ronninge Scaffoldes, hewinge of mast*es* Joistinge of the Banquet-tinge fflour, Reringe of a platt with Shoores under the same enclosing upp thendes, frayminge of hallpaces and two stage Cuburdes with railes, sawinge of Timber, Cuttinge of Crownes p*or*tcullic*es* Luces [fleurs de lis] Pendaunt*es*, Comp*ar*timent*es* and makinge uppon boorde in paste A Lyon and A draggon Dealetables Joyned ffourmes and doores with the drawinge and planinge of the flowers [floors], sowinge the walles roofes Selinges windowes and ou*er*heddes with Canves, makinge of Armes Scutchins uppon Pendaunt*es* aswell with wier as with Twigges and roddes . . .[29]

In 1606 this late Tudor structure – which Sir John Summerson has called 'the most interesting Elizabethan feature of [Whitehall] palace'[30] – was finally demolished to make way for a replacement suitable for the masques of the Jacobean Court. It stood, therefore, throughout the greater part of Shakespeare's activity as a playwright, until the year of *King Lear*. *Othello* was performed in it in November 1604.[31] But its treatment as a theatre rather than a banqueting house reared for a special occasion belongs in a later chapter; what concerns us for the present is the evidence it gives that the Tudor traditions of festive design were still active in London in the 1580s. The mast-and-canvas method of construction recalls the round house at Calais, as does the scheme of decoration, with the canvas ceiling painted with an elaborate sky effect of 'cloud*es* with ye starres', enlived with 'gold-foile', 'Grenefoile and Tinfoile' and 'Two pound of Archdin' cut into shapes, along with gold and silver paper. As at Calais, there was 'worke of Iuie and holy', or what the Declared Account records, in its more material way, as

Trees and hearbes viz hollie Ivie and mestletowe Rosmarie and Baies Birch and diverse fflowers used about the said Banquitting house.[32]

The use of wickerwork recalls the great human figures that surrounded the Calais house, though here the craft is employed in the framing of decorative escutcheons mounted on the pendants in the ceiling.

Although a temporary structure, the Banqueting House was not an altogether slight one. The walls were of canvas, but they were penetrated by hundreds of wooden windows with lights of glass. So much money was spent on wooden boards that it seems likely that they formed a more substantial backing to the canvas in many parts of the house, as they had done at Calais. Lead was used somewhere about the structure, presumably on the roof, and the walls had decorative battlements. Expenditures in the following years record the existence of more than 70 pendants of various sizes in the roof, together with a similar number of 'towsions' – possibly 'Tuscans', or plaited decorations.[33] Since these coexisted with the painted canvas they were presumably attached to a timber structure which supported it, in place of the ropes that had served so inadequately at Calais. There was very little brickwork, most of the labour payments being due to the carpenters and joiners, together with the sawyers who prepared their materials. Tailors were paid £43.5s.0d. for their work on the canvas, and the basketmakers earned £10.7s.0d. for preparing the wicker scutcheons in the ceiling.

The ranks of degrees fitted at either side of the house will each have required a space some 15 ft deep. leaving room for a central wooden dancing floor, raised up on shores and planed smooth. The elevated halpace at the upper end, to the south if later custom already prevailed, would have had the appearance of a raised theatrical stage, though the 'two stage Cuburdes with railes' may not have been located on it. A stage cupboard was often a very large, almost architectural, piece of joinery designed to display expensive plate in the manner of an *étagère*. One provided in 1549 for an entertainment at Binche rose over 20 ft in three storeys, was lit by candelabra and possessed an elaborately decorated canopy supported by two large Doric columns.[34] In view of the prominence of joiners among the craftsmen working on the Whitehall Banqueting House it is likely that the cupboards there were similarly lavish, and made a strong visual contribution to the effect of the whole chamber.

The room therefore bore a general resemblance to a Tudor great hall, with its bay windows, its porch and its allusions – in pendants and towsions – to a hammerbeam roof. But its stage, degrees and dancing floor also made it substantially a Court theatre, suitable for masques and interludes. In a later chapter we shall trace the alterations which were gradually to confirm it in this role, and to strengthen its fabric sufficiently to make it last until it was replaced in 1606.

For all its longevity, the Banqueting House was essentially a temporary building, constructed like the festive theatres at Calais, Ardres and the Bastille to be taken away as readily as it was put up. Yet in their portability all these structures were closely related to the normal characteristic of Tudor timber-framed building. We have seen how the stage and turret for the Red Lion were measured, cut and jointed at John Reynolds' 'framing place', assembled there for testing, then demounted and transported to the Whitechapel site, where Sylvester's galleries had been erected under a separate contract. The result was doubtless intended to be a permanent structure, the prefabrication being no more than usual building practice. But there is some evidence that John Brayne's other playhouse, the Theater in Shoreditch, was actually constructed with the possibility of its future dismantling in mind, so that when required the whole timber frame could be taken down and carried away, massive and complex though it was.

The Tudor builder prepared his timbers at the 'framing place', rather than on the construction site itself, for obvious reasons: there was better security, both for the materials and for the tools, and more room for the trial framing of parts of the structure. The process was fitted to the nature of the work, for the timbers, which were dressed trunks and major branches of trees rather than milled lumber, were far from standard in their dimensions and had to be matched individually to the developing structure of the frame. Much depended on the strength and efficacy of the mortise and tenon joints, and these too had to be cut individually to match. An ordinary three-bay country house might consist of upwards of 50 principal timbers – sills, posts, bressummers, plates, principal rafters and purlins – each to be measured, cut and jointed to fit into its exact place in the scheme. Each was marked so that it could be recognized when transported to the site, and remarried to the mortises or tenons that had been prepared to fit it. A single-bay townhouse of three storeys would require fewer timbers, but their precise jointing and marking would still be essential. When the timbers had been delivered to the site it was necessary to sort and identify them, and then proceed to erect them according to an exact sequence enjoined by the need to have room at every point for the tenons to be slotted into their mortises. Some easement might be gained by pegging the joints only loosely at first, so that timbers might be prised apart to admit a tenoned member between them, but there were narrow limits to such margins. In smaller structures parts of the frame could be assembled flat on the ground and then 'reared' into position on the brick or stone foundation walls with the help of a shear truss and pulleys. Larger buildings had to be assembled timber by timber, and called for very thorough planning if the sequence were not to go wrong. First the sills had to be bedded onto the foundation walls; then principal posts were slotted into the mortises prepared for them. These heavy members were held in place by temporary supporting rods until they could be made firm with the lateral bressummers and tie-beams. Next came the wall plates, followed by the principal rafters together with their collars and any crown posts and purlins. As every angle of the frame was constructed the necessary braces had also to be incorporated, each in its allotted place in the whole constructional sequence. Every stage in the process had to be foreseen and allowed for.

All this was complicated enough in the matter of a small house, but at one of the great public playhouses the difficulties were much greater. In *The Quest for Shakespeare's Globe* I have given reasons for believing that the Theater, like the first and second Globes, was a timber-framed structure of three storeys, 100 ft across, polygonal in plan and with a large number of sides, perhaps 16 but more probably 24. There must have been well over 500 principal timbers, excluding joists and rafters, and probably as many braces, all to be cut, jointed and marked at the builder's framing place, then assembled in exact sequence in Shoreditch.[35] Moreover the unusual angles of the joints all had to be allowed for, and procedures normally governed by the rectangular planning of most structures adapted to the demanding polygonal forms. The shoulders of many tenons, for example, would need to be precisely sloped, and sway braces in the roof accurately cut to intervals greater or less than the customary 90°. Plainly the business of building such a frame was not to be undertaken lightly: it must have strained the builder's skills as well as his resources to the very limit. And perhaps most of all, it must have challenged his imagination.

Nevertheless by 1581 when the Works were busy setting up their masts and canvas for the Banqueting House at Whitehall, the public playhouses of Shoreditch were in constant use, routinely denounced from the pulpit and regularly patronized by a growing and sometimes disorderly public. The lease of the site for the Theater contained a clause which had committed the tenants to spend at least £200 within the first ten years from Lady Day 1576 on improving the buildings then existing on the premises. This Burbage and Brayne eventually accomplished, but first they had laid out some £700 on their new playhouse. A further clause in the lease permitted them also to 'take downe and Carrie awaie . . . all such buildinges and other thinges as should be builded erected or sett vpp . . . either for a Theatr or playing place'.[36] Timber-framed structures could generally be dismantled if required, for once the superficial plaster and tile were removed the frame itself could be taken apart in the reverse sequence of its original assembly. It was not uncommon for houses to be moved in this way, and re-erected elsewhere;[37] in our own time many framed houses threatened with destruction have taken down and rebuilt in the relative safety of a theme park such as the Weald and Downland Museum at Singleton, West Sussex. Yet although most timber buildings were capable of being taken to pieces and carted away, few were built with such an eventuality in mind from the start. In this respect, as in so many others, the Theater was unusual: a great polygonal timber frame of three storeys, evidently made to be demountable, and in fact dismantled in 1599, carted to Southwark and re-erected as the Globe.

A demountable building is likely to be a temporary one. It is constructed from the beginning with a definite term in mind, even if that term be long and its conclusion not altogether certain. Any timber-frame structure requires careful planning, especially if its design is complex, and all the more so if in addition it is intended to be demountable. It must be developed, that is to say, all of a piece, as a fully integrated scheme, for an accretion of additions and extensions over the years will certainly not be as retainable as the original structure. The Calais banqueting house was such a building, its polygonal plan carefully established in association with the details of the canvas ceiling. It was essential to ensure that the roof and frame would match when they were brought together on the distant site. The foresight required to guarantee the smooth progress of its erection would serve also to enable its efficient dismantling, though this was doubtless of smaller consequence. At the Theater it appears that the processes of assembly and dismantling had both to be borne in mind by the builders as they set about the planning of their house. Quite as much as the designers of the analogous theatre at Calais they were governed in their work by a coherent idea of what they were about; they built, that is to say, to a realizable programme.

Part – perhaps even the principal part – of the Calais programme was given by the cosmic organization of the canvas roof, with its methodical exposition of the four elements. From this idea stemmed, we may be reasonably certain, the doubly fourfold layout of the sixteen-sided auditorium, with its decorative provision of sixteen wickermen and as many candelabra. The similar house at Ardres had reminded Fleurange of a Roman theatre, and Calais itself was adorned with emblems of Imperial power. In Shoreditch Burbage and Brayne were governed by no such obvious motive as the cosmic ceilings, but the end of their enterprise was much the same, a polygonal auditorium, galleried in three storeys, all assembled out of predetermined and identifiable parts. They too must have conceived the idea of their structure with absolute clarity before they began to formulate its construction with their builder, and our only clue to what went on in their minds at that moment of high endeavour lies in the name they chose to conjure with: the Theater.

For it was a moment of wonderful like-mindedness, a harmony whose sweetness may be judged from the shrillness of the bickering it was soon to descend to. Before long there would be the tiresome accusations about the 'commen box' in which the money gathered at the plays was kept; one day a witness would record that 'Burbage did there strike [Brayne] with his fist and so they went together by the eares Jn somuch that this deponent could herdly part them'.[38] Years later, when Brayne was dead and the quarrel was being pursued by his widow Margaret, the Burbages were capable of thrusting her away violently from the theatre door. James told her partner Robert Myles that the Chancery brief he held in his hand was nothing 'but A paper which he might wype his tale with', and his youngest son, Richard, confronted another of Margaret's associates in characteristically dramatic fashion, the victim later testifying how the actor had threatened him, 'scornfully & disdainfullye playing with this deponentes Nose'.[39] All this is the sad counterpart of what had once been a powerfully creative partnership. Burbage the player had entered into the ground lease on his own account, but Brayne the man of business had soon brought capital to the enterprise as well as his experience as the builder of the Red Lion. Between them the two men settled on a design, later to be described by de Witt as an *amphiteatrum*, with a tiring house, yard, galleries, and stair to go up to them, all items mentioned in the copious records of the subsequent litigation. The litigation also shows that they were brought together by the hope of profit, but of its nature it cannot tell of other, less tangible motives. Both men had previously been drawn to the stage, one as an actor and the other as a promoter. Both are recorded to have had a practical interest in the craft of building, for Burbage had been 'by occupacion A Joyner and reaping but A small lyving by the same gave it over and became A commen Player in playes'.[40] Brayne, besides his close control over the detailed construction of the Red Lion, joined Burbage on the actual building work at the site, though even this sign of commitment later became a cause of wrangling. Brayne worked unpaid, while Burbage was alleged to have taken a workman's wages from the business.[41] Whatever its practical limits, their commitment was to an enterprise that had the momentary distinction of being unique. There was no need to give it a particular name; the generic one would do very well. 'The Theater' was a confident, definitive title, an obvious choice when no other purpose-built playhouse besides the apparently ill-fated Red Lion had yet arisen to make its contribution to the daily life of Londoners. In part the confidence was economic: when Brayne became alarmed at the escalating costs of the enterprise, Burbage is reported to have said to him that 'it was no matter praying him to be contented it wold shortlie quyte the cost vnto them bothe'.[42] It would, for the moment at least, be the only game in town. But the confidence resides also in the bold use of the classical term, with its claim to continuity with an ancient tradition. It was bold enough to offend the learning as well as the sensibility of a schoolmaster such as John Stockwood, who preached against it from the pulpit at Paul's Cross:

I know not how I might with the godly learned especially more discommende the gorgeous Playing place erected in the fieldes, than to terme it, as they please to haue it called, a Theatre, that is, euen after the maner of the olde heathnish Theatre at Rome, a shew place of all beastly & filthie matters.[43]

Nevertheless, if a learned divine had reservations about the parallel between the architectural form of the new and the ancient playhouses, travellers better versed in contemporary European culture did observe the similarity. Repeatedly they used the terms *theatrum* and *amphitheatrum* to describe the playhouses of Shoreditch and Bankside, and occasionally made their point more explicitly. In 1600 a tourist visited Bankside:

1600 die Lunae 3 Julij. We heard an English play; the theatre was constructed in the style of the ancient Romans, out of wood. It was so built that spectators could very easily see from every part.[44]

Johannes de Witt, struck by the similarity of the Swan to the theatres of the ancients, drew his picture of it to illustrate the parallel.

It has been argued that de Witt's perception of the Swan may have been coloured by his interest in the scholarly archaeology of Justus Lipsius, whose illustrations of a Roman amphitheatre established the graphic mode of presentation adopted for the sketch.[45] But this observation, while it helps to account for de Witt's special interest in the playhouses, does not negate the truth of what he reported, especially since so much of what he noted down differed from the conceptual model. He saw three storeys of galleries surrounding a circular yard, into which the stage thrust in a fashion not illustrated in any of the treatises on Roman architecture. Though the yard was mostly open to the sky, the surrounding galleries were sensibly roofed, but in a quite un-Roman style. Standing forward of these roofed galleries, and possibly constructed on the stage itself, a great turret rose to a lofty height, in the manner of the one constructed by John Reynolds at the Red Lion.[46] This too was roofed, and against it a lean-to stage cover was placed, its front supported by columns of a giant order. On the face of it, there was not much here to call forth de Witt's comment that 'its form seems to approach that of a Roman structure'.[47] Yet two aspects of the building had struck him with particular force. The first was the sheer impressiveness of all four of the amphitheatres – the Rose, the Theater and the Curtain as well as

45

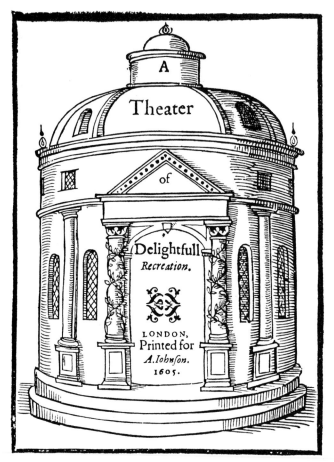

7   Samuel Rowlands, *A Theater of Delightfull Recreation* (1605), title page.

the Swan – and the fact that the largest of them would contain as many as 3000 people. While this is hardly a capacity to compare with the Circus Maximus it was enough to move de Witt to admiration when he came across it in suburban London. And the second point was what he called the 'noteworthy beauty' of them all, and of the Swan in particular, with its 'wooden columns painted in such excellent imitation of marble that they might deceive even the most prying [*nasutissimos*]'. In detail the Swan differed from any Roman theatre de Witt had seen illustrated in the text-books, or indeed encountered on his travels, but in its size and its painted magnificence it laid claim to a monumentality worthy of comparison with antiquity.

De Witt, we may be sure, knew his Vitruvius and perhaps his Alberti. He was an enthusiast for Lipsius. When he contemplated the structure of the

8   *Cornu-copiae, Pasquils Night-cap* (1612), title page.

Swan he looked at it through eyes long accustomed to the charming engravings with which their ideas of the ancient theatre and amphitheatre had been publicized throughout Europe. But neither Francis Langley, who built the Swan, nor James Burbage, who built its predecessor and model, had enjoyed the Dutchman's humanist education and background. If their playhouses really did imitate those of the Romans they will have done so in broad strokes, not erudite details. The possibility that they might have designed the Theater along the lines described by Vitruvius has been advanced by the late Frances Yates,[48] but although it is an idea of enormous imaginative appeal it can hardly be documented with any conviction. Neither of the entrepreneurs was an especially literary man. Even their insults, if we are to credit the court records, lacked intellectual bite. The Vitruvian text, though it was represented in many English libraries,[49] was usually sparsely illustrated, and sometimes not at all. No English translation had appeared, and although John Dee had summarized part of its content in his Preface to Euclid he did not include an account of the theatre in the subjects he covered. Dee owned no fewer than five editions of Vitruvius, and two of Alberti's book on architecture.[50] The image that most of these books gave of the ancient theatre was by no means uniform. A learned commentator such as Daniele Barbaro – a scholar and diplomat who spent a tour of duty in London during the reign of Edward VI – might offer a carefully researched plan and

47

elevation, the result of long archaeological investigation of the remains as well as an attentive reading of the Latin text, and all mediated through the learned pen of his illustrator, the architect Andrea Palladio.[51] Other editions were more perfunctory, and it was their picture of the ancient theatre that was more likely to be propagated in English woodcuts and book illustrations. In these the building is sometimes a full round, not D-shaped, and it is often presented as a tall domed tower. For an example of this curious imaginative idea of what a theatre might look like one might turn to the title page from Samuel Rowlands' *A Theater of Delightfull Recreation* (1605) (plate 7). A cross-section much in the manner of the de Witt sketch, with the top arc sloping downwards and the floor plan extended in a full circle towards the observer, adorns the title page of *Cornu-copiae, Pasquils Night-cap* (1612), a work sometimes attributed to Nicholas Breton and published by Thomas Thorpe, the printer of Shakespeare's sonnets (plate 8). These blocks give some idea of what popular, unlearned notions of the ancient theatre were like even as late as the early seventeenth century. There seems to be little enough cognizance here of Vitruvian *symmetria* and the refined system of setting out the building along the lines of an astrological diagram. Yet surely if James Burbage and John Brayne thought about the Roman theatre in 1576 when they conceived and named their own new playhouse they will have imagined something more like these curious images than Palladio's careful reconstruction.

It is necessary, therefore, to think our own way back past our holiday experiences at Verona, past the beautiful engravings through which our forebears knew the ancient world, past even Barbaro's brilliant Latin edition of Vitruvius, published in 1567, the year of the Red Lion, to a less fully developed notion of the Roman theatre, if we are to investigate its possible influence on the earliest London playhouses. It is as well to remember the round banqueting house at Ardres, with its three levels of wooden galleries, and the observation of the urbane Fleurange that it was built 'de la façon comme du temps passé les Romains faisoient leur théâtre'. Yet we must remember also Fleurange's distinction between the 'Roman' style of the timber frame and the more contemporary themes of the painted decorations in the ceiling. The first London theatres had no roofs adorned with stars and planets, only a round or polygonal frame of timber galleries, together with the players' special equipment of stage, turret and tiring house. In their structure the theatres repeated what was most noticeably 'Roman' about the festive banqueting houses, but appear to have derived little or nothing from the cosmic allusions of their elaborate décor. If the coherent, integral design of the theatres can be traced to a controlling idea, it is to that of the ancient building type as understood by Belknap and his French counterparts, and not to the rich plenitude of emblems contained in the festive banqueting houses of the Tudor monarchs.

3
Goodly devices: emblematic design

The distinctive shape and the daring size of the earliest of the Elizabethan public theatres reflected the integrity of the idea that lay behind them. Without a firm notion of what they were about, John Brayne and James Burbage could hardly have established their great wooden ring in Shoreditch, with its vast auditorium and broad open stage. The idea was one of function: it responded to the need to provide a satisfactory viewing place for large audiences, as well as a raised platform on which the players might perform. But mere functionalism is unlikely to have been a sufficient cause of the Theater and the Curtain, nor even of the Red Lion. Beyond the practical needs of the actors and their audience lay a common sense of what they were about when they entered into that that conspiracy of playing that creates the drama. To some contemporaries the very name of the Theater seemed to indicate a culture at once hedonistic and un-Christian that was alien to the stricter Elizabethan proprieties. The term evoked images of the pagan entertainments of ancient Rome, of wickedly excessive expenditure on matters of pleasure, next only to the follies of the stews. Such at least was the case amongst people like the schoolmaster John Stockwood, whose sermon we quoted on p. 45. A more sympathetic view is that of Edmund Spenser, whose description of the ruins of the city he calls *Verlame*, on the banks of the Thames, contains that curiously double vision in which the facts of the present world coexist with the memories of the past:

> High towers, faire temples, goodly theaters,
> Strong walls, rich porches, princelie pallaces,
> Large streetes, braue houses, sacred sepulchers,
> Sure gates, sweete gardens, stately galleries,
> Wrought with faire pillours, and fine imageries,
> All those (O pitie) now are turned to dust,
> And ouergrowen with blacke obliuions rust.   (*Ruins of Time* 92–8)

The brave houses and sweet gardens belong as much to Elizabethan England as to the Roman culture of Verlame, and so do the 'goodly theaters'.

49

The theatre was, in Spenser's day, a characteristic of the London scene; but it retained also its ability to evoke the splendours of ancient Rome. The language of the stanza illustrates our theme when it describes the wonders of the antique world in terms that are equally suitable to the Elizabethan, quietly insinuating the judgment that the modern world has at last achieved a civilization worthy to be compared with that of antiquity.

Beside the function, therefore, of the Elizabethan playhouse, there existed a controlling idea of its place among the artifacts of culture: it was a necessary part of a complete city, and its model was to be found among the great amphitheatres of Rome. But our quotation is a witness also to the prevailing style of Elizabethan architecture. At Verlame the public works were high, strong, large and sure; the living quarters were fair, rich, brave and sweet; and there was a further category of structures whose qualities were more social than these: goodly, princely, sacred and stately. This group, isolated at the ends of the lines in Spenser's stanza, consisted of theatres, palaces, sepulchres and galleries, the last an especially Elizabethan touch. The palaces and galleries of Spenser's London too were built in a tradition of courtly festive design, as were the 'sacred sepulchres' that we know in the vigorous crestings, strapwork and other enrichments of Elizabethan funerary work.[1] With these belonged the 'goodly theatres' of Shoreditch, like their antique forerunners exemplars of a public and celebratory art. Sydney Anglo has put this matter so well that we can hardly do better than quote his words at length:

It will be remembered that the French pavilion at Ardres, like the English round-house at Calais, had been adorned with a cosmological design – a suggestive feature in view of the numerous similar examples one can adduce. The temporary palace, erected in Paris for the reception of English ambassadors in 1518, had been set with gilt stars and the zodiacal signs. The English masterpiece in this genre, built at Greenwich in 1527, boasted a decorative scheme showing the land, sea, and heavens in scholarly detail. And, much later, the theatre erected for Queen Elizabeth's reception of the French embassy in 1581 had a similar cosmological roof decoration. All these buildings were employed for the production of masks and plays; and the representation of the heavens, together with the terraced auditorium, the seats placed in horseshoe fashion around the stage, and, more especially, the tiers of galleries in the Calais round-house, afford interesting parallels with the public theatre, as it developed later in the century.[2]

As we have seen, the roofs of these buildings gave them one sort of programme, cosmological in its imagery but often political in its immediate purpose. The Calais structure, like the others, was intended to make a bold public announcement of peace and unification, and it did so in terms borrowed from the histories of England and the Empire: Arthur for the one and Hercules for the other, the red dragon and the black eagle, the English archer and the Imperial *lanzknecht*. Holinshed, printing Turpyn's account in his *Chronicles*, added the observation that the round house was 'like a theatre'.[3] The 'goodlie deuise' of its design alluded to the prime antiquity within which the other more detailed images were set: the great tent was a theatre of history, and its messages were contained in an envelope sealed in the ancient world.

One feature that the buildings mentioned by Anglo have in common is that their decorative programmes have meaning. At Calais the shields of arms and the wicker men and women were interspersed with Latin mottoes, or what a contemporary English account described as 'The posies and writinges that were in the rownd howse made at Callais for the feasting and banqueting of the Emperoʳ Charles'.[4] The Venetian observer spent much of his time in the building noting down the images and words with which the place was filled, and a French account recorded the 'bones allegations et propositions philosophales'. 'Amicitiam omnibus rebus preponamus', 'Nox illuminabitur in deliciis', ran two of them, but there were more than fifty others. The cosmic organization of the ceiling, with its depiction of the four elements, caused one observer to think of the 'auctorite philosophale de sa generation qui estoit chose belle avoir a gens amateurs de science' (philosophical authority for the development of its design, which was a lovely thing for the learned to contemplate).[5] Clearly the decorative scheme had its lessons to teach or learning to celebrate, but the fact that the ceiling had been prepared in London and shaped to the theatrical plan of the banqueting house argues that the latter was not without its semantic contribution to make to the whole effect. Here was a modern theatre of the Roman type, suitable for the entertainment of a Roman Emperor of the modern kind, and suitable too as a worthy container for the propagandistic flourishes of the Tudor Court. At Verlame Spenser's nymph remembered the goodly theatres: at Calais 'there was builded a banketting house . . . like a theatre, after a goodlie deuise'. It is the goodly device of its design that sets the building apart from a purely functional structure.

The theatre at Calais is only one of many instances of the literary character so often found in the more elaborate Tudor buildings. The other examples quoted by Anglo – the festive halls at Greenwich and Whitehall – shared something of its capacity to enshrine a verbal programme, and much the same is true of many an Elizabethan mansion in the shires. Sometimes literature itself provided the cues, although the relation between some carved motto or painted rebus and the actual design of a structure was often a complicated one, hardly ever as rigid or complete as later traditions imply. John Aubrey, always alive to a good story, observed that the Countess of Pembroke, Sidney's sister, laid out the grounds of her house near Ampthill 'according to the Description of Basilius's house in the firste booke of *Arcadia*'.[6]

The Lodge is of a yellow stone, built in the forme of a starre; having round about a garden framed into like points: and beyond the gardein, ridings cut out, each aunswering the Angles of the Lodge: at the end of one of them is the other smaller Lodge, but of like fashion; where the gratious *Pamela* liveth: so that the Lodge seemeth not unlike a faire *Comete*, whose taile stretcheth it selfe to a starre of lesse greatnes.[7]

The ruins of Houghton House still stand on the open hillside beyond Ampthill, a haunting and lovely place of warm Bedford brick. But nothing about them or the surviving ground gives the least material hint of the pattern that Aubrey reported. His 'reading' of the estate may well have been no more than a literary fantasy.

Nevertheless there can be no doubt that gardens especially were often laid out to a semantic design. Sir Roy Strong even identifies the 'emblematic garden' as the type characteristic of the middle and late sixteenth century,[8] a type that often took as its point of reference the figure of the queen herself. In an anonymous royal entertainment at Theobalds someone impersonating a gardener came forward to expound on the design of a garden actually set out nearby at Pymms by Sir Robert Cecil, Burghley's son. It was, he said, 'the younger sonne of ye owner of this house' who 'devised a plot for a garden, as me thought in a place unfytt for pleasure . . . and besides so farre from ye house y^t in my Cuntry capacitie a pounde had bene meeter y^{en} a paradize'. The ground was readied, the moles destroyed, and the whole site was divided into four quarters, of which the gardener then provides a description of only the first:

in ye first I framed a Maze, not of hissope and tyme but y^t w*h*ich makethe tyme itselfe to wither w*i*th wondringe. All ye vertues, all ye greaces all ye muses wynding, and wreathinge about y*o*ur may*e*stie eache contending to be chiefe, all contented to be cherished. And this not of pothearbes but of flowers & of flowers fairest and sweetest for in so heavenly a maze, w*h*ich astonished all earthly though*tes* what did not bewtye bringe, what dyd not fortune promyse.

The Vertues were done in roses, flowers fitt for ye xii vertues having in y^{em}selfes, (as wee Gardyners have observed) above an hundred. The Graces of pawnces partie collored in one stalke, sisters never asunder but dyverselye beautified. The Muses of ix^{en} severall cullors being of sundrye natures yet all sweete all soveraigne.[9]

Here the motive is less literary than in Basilius's five-pointed garden, but the organization is according to the associations of the flowers rather than their specific appearance. The author imagines Cecil devising a semantic plot for the whole, and its effect must be 'read' before it can be fully felt.

We do not possess the programme for all of the garden planned at Pymms, but there is no need to suppose that it would have been any less emblematic in the other quarters. Somewhere close to the flowery maze of the virtues, graces and muses stood an arbour of eglantine, the five-pointed rose of

Elizabeth herself, a plant deep rooted in the soil of England, 'making it so grene y^t ye sonne of Spaine at ye hotest cannot parch it'. The relation of the queen to the virtues is perhaps clear enough, but their association with the graces and the muses seems merely an Elizabethan excess, not a wholly integral system of compliment. A similar but Jacobean plenitude is to be found in a ceiling at Boston Manor, in Middlesex, painted in 1623. Here Faith, Hope and Charity consort with the five senses, the four elements, Plenty, Peace (twice) and War. A leading motive in the design seems to have been a simple desire to pile emblem upon emblem. Yet the whole set of sixteen panels oversails a chimneypiece of Abraham and Isaac, the clue perhaps to its interpretation as illustrating the heated struggle between devotion and the claims of the world.[10]

The garden at Pymms, almost as much as the plasterwork at Boston Manor, was essentially a decorative scheme. The quartering of the plot was simply a geometrical division of the land, no part in itself of the semantic programme. Similarly the pattern of intersecting ribs in the Boston Manor ceiling, though conveying its own sense of order, merely provided a field for the display of the emblematic panels. In both cases the system of reference in the emblems was independent of the measured setting-out. Yet the geometrical development of structural designs sometimes lent a kind of symbolism to Elizabethan buildings, even though the concentration of purpose required to carry through such schemes was inevitably rare. At Lyveden New Build Sir Thomas Tresham, a Catholic convert, began a garden lodge which, had it ever been completed, would have contained an architectural expression of the fivefold symbolism of the Passion. The plan is an equal-armed cross, each arm 23 ft wide and 23 ft deep. At each of the four ends there is a five-panelled window bay. Over the centre Tresham intended to erect a twelve-sided lantern whose upper stage was resolved into an octagon, the whole topped by a large egg-finial (plate 9). The building was set in gardens that carried the design across the surrounding land, somewhat in the manner of the lodge at Houghton as described by Aubrey. The meaning of all this complex numerical symbolism is to be found in a series of Tresham's papers now at the British Library, in which number symbolism merges with quotations from Augustine and Chrysostom;[11] it is also indicated by a series of roundels in the lower frieze of the building, containing the instruments of the Passion. Rather less complex, but even more thoroughgoing, is the symbolism of the Triangular Lodge at Rushton. This is planned as an equilateral triangle, and alludes to the Trinity. Each side of the triangle is about two rods long, or 33 ft; each has three triangular gables. The entablature bears three legends, one to each side, each containing 33 letters.[12] Trefoil patterns are everywhere, in the windows and at the doorhead. Even the date wrought into the heads of the tie-bars on the first floor of the three-storey structure is fudged a little as 1593, a good trinitarian number

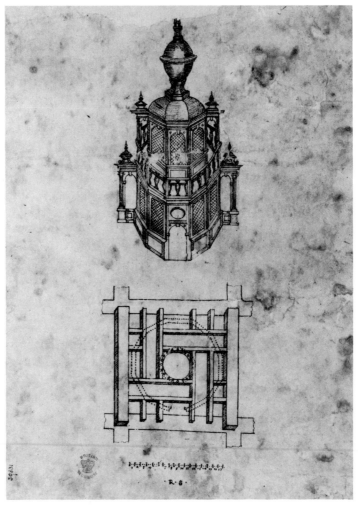

9   Robert Stickells, project for a roof and lantern for Sir Thomas Tresham.

but a little earlier than the actual building year of 1594. A further inscription points to the numerical programme behind the whole design: *Tres testimonium dant* (There are three that bear record), a play also on Tresham's name. Only the date on the triangular chimney resists the imperious idea, and records the topping-out season of 1595.[13]

Tresham's lodges, eccentric as they are, belong in a domestic tradition of Elizabethan banqueting house design. It was not unusual for great mansions to possess these small buildings for pastime in the grounds, often located, like the arbour of eglantine described by Robert Cecil's gardener, in a fancifully emblematic relation to the surrounding gardens. Even suburban London

54

could offer such pretty little structures. Contemporary maps of the area around Moorfields show several of them set in small plots to the west of Bishopsgate outside the city walls, one shaped like a domed temple, another curiously fashioned like a beehive. The spirit of Wemmick has a long history among the Londoners. Habits of unrestrained symmetry of design could here find their fullest expression, there being few functional offices for the building to perform. All that was required was a pleasant unheated space, quite small, where friends might gather for a collation and perhaps to admire the view. A banqueting house at Wimbledon, for example, is recorded in a survey plan by Robert Smythson, which shows it to have been developed from a square, with a small projecting bay on each of the four sides. The whole was set on a square plot surrounded by hedges directly to the garden side of the house.[14] Whether this building had any programmatic kinship with the rest of the grounds at Wimbledon we do not know, but at Nonsuch we have the careful account of a traveller from Basle, Thomas Platter, to convey a fuller idea of the emblematic principles of its design.[15] Here, in a grove named after Diana, the goddess of chastity, and beyond a fountain celebrating her, there stood a little temple, vaulted and adorned with Latin mottoes praising the virtues of the chaste life, the pleasures of rest and contemplation and the purity of the fountain itself. Nearby was a pavilion in which the queen sat to observe the hunt, living out her role as the chaste huntress. The buildings and their surroundings supported one another's theme, the whole group making an effect quite as emphatic as those of the pageants and entertainments with which the queen was so often received on her progresses.

The triangular theme of Tresham's Lyveden Lodge had found an earlier and larger expression at Longford Castle, built by Sir Thomas Gorges not far from Wilton, beginning *c.* 1580. An early gloss to the structure is given in a schematic plan by John Thorpe, where the three corner towers are labelled, in an explanatory diagram, *Pater*, *Filius* and *Spiritus Sanctus*.[16] The three main blocks joining these towers are marked by the phrase *non est*; there are connections marked *est* to a central circle in the midst of the triangular plan, but this feature, marked *Deus*, appears to have been notional rather than an achieved part of the building. Although the trinitarian theme seems so powerful there is no further indication of it in the house, and Gorges seems to have had other motifs in mind. An engraving of the house made about 1670 shows a device of Neptune sailing a boat in a niche at the top of the entrance bay, an allusion to Sir Thomas's wife, Helena Snakenborg, *alias* Bat (or, in English, Boat). The late-seventeenth-century versified *Longford Inventory* describes something of the decorative scheme within, a scheme that seems to have little enough to do with the apparently theological bias of the plan. The main hall, in the northwestern block, was painted with a medley of mythological subjects and the twelve Caesars. Standing here one could look into the southwest tower:

> Through a fair entry doth ye Parlour shine
> Gilt round (as Ovid did Sol's house designe)
> With pleasant closetts & a safe retreat
> For Clymene's (but nott for Mars') his heat,
> Since we behold Mars caught by Vulcan's art –[17]

The overmantel still exists, with its relief of Mars and Venus, similar to work at Hardwick Hall with which it is contemporary. Upstairs, above this place of pagan solace, the chapel made a more Gothic effect with its fan vault of stone and great central pendant, but even this was qualified by the Corinthian columns that surrounded the room.

Whatever the force of Longford's classical decoration, its plan could seem piously trinitarian to an observer such as John Thorpe. A motive of a similar type caused Sir John Strode to devise the E-plan of his reconstruction of Chantmarle in Dorset. The surveyor for this work, undertaken in 1612, was Gabriel Moore, but Strode himself must have been responsible for the overall programme, noting down its theme in a few Latin words: 'Constructa est in forma, de Littera (E) sc. Emmanuel. id est, Deus nobiscum in Eternum' (It was made in the form of a letter E, for Emmanuel; that is to say, our Lord everlasting.)[18] In the account book of the project he records payments to Moore 'for his paines only, to survey and direct the building to the forme I conceived and plotted it'.[19] Here the relation between the original conceit and the achieved building is quite clear. It is less so at Chilham Castle, built by Sir Dudley Digges beginning in 1616. The plan consists of three main blocks whose central axes form the sides of an equilateral triangle. Two smaller blocks act as corridors between them, leaving the third angle of the triangle open, and forming altogether what might be described as an incomplete hexagon. Evidently the motive behind the plan was strongly felt, for there was a good deal of juggling of chimneys caused by the need to fulfil the pattern, and much ingenuity was expended on the arrangement of the rooms within. But the name of the architect, if any there was, is unknown. The main influence on the design may have been what Christopher Hussey called 'the Digges' trait of mathematics',[20] but the architrave above the front entrance, which is loosely Doric in articulation, contains an inscription between the triglyphs of the frieze which may indicate a prime motive as theological as that at Longford: 'THE LORD : IS MY : HOUSE OF : DEFENCE : AND MY : CASTLE'. Perhaps the house was a kind of amulet. Beneath these words were more routine ones: 'DUDLEY : DIGGES : A.D. : 1616 : MARY : KEMPE.'

Sometimes a building might contain a deliberate sequence of experiences to be encountered by the visitor in a determined order. At Gonville Hall, Cambridge, Dr John Caius built a New Court, beginning in 1565, with an entrance from Trinity Street called the 'Gate of Humility'. It was a simple gateway in the wall, with classical mouldings and the word HUMILITATIS

56

carved on the frieze. An avenue led to the 'Gate of Virtue', which was raised high and ascended by steps. This was in four superimposed orders, the arch decorated with female figures in the spandrels, and bearing on one side the inscription VIRTUTIS. Finally came the 'Gate of Honour', which led from the college to the Schools and was an altogether more elaborate structure. Its design derived from Serlio's *Architettura*, and recalled the triumphal arches of antiquity. At the top was a hexagonal superstructure resting on a square base, and on each of its six faces a dial was placed. The gates constituted a progressive sequence, but Caius evidently intended them to embody something of the diurnal routine as well as the purposive direction of collegiate life. He left explicit instructions about the hours of their opening and closing, and the dials set on the Gate of Honour shadowed the passing of the days through which the achievements of the intellect were to be won.[21]

In most of these emblematic projects the design expressed in diagrammatic form an idea which was conveyed by the owner to the mason, carpenter or gardener, and which in turn stood for some great human or religious experience, whether of the five senses or the Trinity or the name of the Saviour. We are fortunate to possess the owners' instructions in many instances, and it is therefore possible to distinguish between their recorded motives and the interpretations – often mistaken – which later generations have put upon their works. At the London playhouses, which in scale and distinctive appearance were a match for some of the greatest of the Tudor country mansions, we find no similar expressions of the builders' imaginative motives, but a great quantity of interpretive comment in the playtexts, which often – especially in the seventeenth century – allude to the round theatre as if it were a model of the cosmos.[22] In later chapters we shall have to approach this testimony with some caution, for there is a risk of confusing the poets' metaphors with the builders' conceptions, thus creating an unsatisfactory circular argument.

In ordinary circumstances few buildings or gardens could fully express the formative ideas of any single person, whether owner or surveyor. The process of construction was too long drawn out, too chancy and flexible, for any definitive programme to retain its integrity in the finished work. The well-documented case of Kyre Park, in Worcestershire, illustrates the various stages and accidents through which a building came into being. The records are extant in a set of accounts kept by Sir Edward Pytts, starting in 1588 with a summary history of the descent of the house to its present owner,

Who beginneth to provide Stone Bricke Tymber and other necessaries for the re-edifyeng thereof this yeare of our Lorde God: one thousande five hundred eightye eight. beinge the thirtith yere of the Raigne of our most famous quene Elizabeth, viz: When God wonderfully vanquyshed the invincyble ffleet (as they cristened it) of the Spanyardes.

> Soli deo omnis gloria.
> Nisi dominus aedificaverit domum, frustra
>   laborant qui aedificat eam.
> Began to provide Stone Brick Timber Wainscott, and
> other necessaries for the buildinge of Kyer House
> by Edward Pytts anno Domini 1586 anno q^e Regine
> Elizabeth 28 mense Augusti
>   Dat veniam deus.[23]

There follow accounts of the preparation of ashlar and the firing of bricks. Only later is there an entry for 'Symons To John Symons of London for drawing my first platt for my house . . . 40s.' Then comes a similar entry: 'To the same John Symons for drawing my latter platt according to my newe purpose . . . £3.' All this is amongst the documentation of the gathering of materials. Evidently the work began without a specific design, and even when this was acquired from the London craftsman – John Symonds had become the Master-Plasterer at the Works in 1585 – still the proposals could change, Pytts himself exercising a controlling 'purpose'. The work at the site was not undertaken by Symonds, but by John Chaunce, a mason. As it proceeded the need to supply important parts of its interior decorative scheme prompted some negotiations with one of the Flemish Holleman family for a pair of chimneypieces:

Garrett Hollyman Bargayned with Garrett Hollyman a dutch carver the Ist of Marche 1592 to make 2 Chymney peaces, the carving thereof being the storeyes of Susanna and Mars and Venus . . .

The work seems to have been done by Gerard ('Garrett') and his son Jasper, both of London, and cost something close to £30. The theme of Susannah as the chaste soul made a delicate match with that of Venus in her benign aspect as the controller of Mars, and together these images may well have expressed something of the generous piety with which Sir Edward opened his account book. But it was only later, in 1595, that he set out a scheme of what he called 'Titles for my House'. These consisted of verses and mottoes, some in English and some in Latin, evidently intended to be inscribed about the building. One was to be set 'Over the Dore', another was 'For Mars & Venus Story'. The English verse gives little sense of an architectonic programme:

> Feare God: lyve well:
>   regarde his lawes,
> Be firme: please not
>   popular Dawes.

Later, in 1611, Sir Edward caught the building virus again, and agreed with his old mason, John Chaunce of Bromsgrove, to supervise the work. At about this time too he was engaged on building a new house in London, and paid one Carter of St Giles' Lane 40s. 'For drawing the upright of the fore part' of it. When, therefore, we find that two years later he had engaged Robert Stickells, the Surveyor of the Royal Works at Richmond, to provide him with further drawings, it is not clear whether the work was intended for the London house or for yet another revision at Kyre Park:

Paid to Stickles of London for drawing the platt of my house anewe December 1613 . . . £3.

When Sir Edward died in 1618 he left £2000 to his son James to finish the country house 'according to the platte remaynning in Chaunce's handes drawne by my dictation'. No matter how experienced the local craftsmen and their London advisers, the owner retained a firm intellectual control over the 'purpose' of the building. Yet there is little sense, in all the scores of manuscript pages by which the project is documented, of a coherent emblematic scheme, beyond the general and rather vacuous pieties of the inscriptions. Kyre Park is a warning to anyone who would seek to reduce Elizabethan architecture to a verbal conceit.

But at Shoreditch the Theater, unlike Kyre Park, was built as it were in a day. We know very little about its decorative scheme, and not much more about those of the other Elizabethan playhouses. That they were richly painted there can be no doubt: de Witt tells us of the convincing marbling at the Swan, the Fortune contract alludes to the painting 'in or aboute the saide fframe house or Stadge',[24] Henslowe paid ''ffor payntinge' his Rose playhouse in 1596[25] and we even have Gabriel Harvey's terse note about 'the Theater, or sum other paintid stage'.[26] Some were equipped with a Heavens, a feature that may have made its contribution to a larger emblematic scheme. But the essential 'device' of the public playhouse lay in the geometric development of its plan. The design of the Theater was all of a piece not merely because its structural form could admit no wilful variation, but because the building process had to be carried through as a single concentrated job. Sir Edward Pytts's house might grow by degrees, and its plan might change from one year to another. No such developments could occur at the Theater, whose polygonal frame exercised an imperious self-limiting control, and where the initial idea, whether functional or emblematic or some combination of the two, governed the builders' every move. When Burbage and Brayne addressed themselves to the difficult matter of the design of their new playhouse they will certainly have been concerned with such things as the audience capacity, acoustics, sightlines and provision for the needs of the players. They will have devoted much thought to its structural viability, and to the provision of suitable materials. But because it was a timber-frame structure every major part of its design had to be firmly established before the carpenter set to work at his framing place. The process of its construction, quite as much as the economic conditions of the time, required them to approach their project with a clear and perfected image of what they wanted. Their choice of a name for the new building suggests that their thinking was coloured by an idea of the Roman theatre, which in turn led them to model their scheme on the round houses of the festive tradition, the fullest modern expressions to date of the ancient theatrical form. Elizabethan and Jacobean architecture provides many examples of buildings whose design is influenced by a respect for some such driving intellectual motive, whether literary, religious or political. The playhouses of Shoreditch and Bankside, described from time to time by their builders, their audiences and their critics as modern restatements of the Roman theme,[27] lack no company among the lodges, banqueting houses and country mansions in the Tudor line of emblematic building.

4
The stage cover

The programme of the round houses of Ardres and Calais was largely contained in the emblematic imagery of their roofs, which had necessarily to be prepared in conjunction with the development of the design of the main polygonal frame. The frame itself, with its galleries and central arena filled with stages, musicians and more emblematic imagery, embodied the dignity of the ancient theatre transformed to modern political uses. We know that some Elizabethan public theatres were equipped with a roof, often called a Heavens, which extended over part of the yard, and, armed with this fact as a prime piece of evidence, it is tempting to press the analogy with the festive banqueting houses. If the cosmic decoration of the Calais building could lend programmatic meaning to its actual structure, might not the Heavens at the Swan or the Globe serve a similar purpose? The theory is elegant enough, but a few brute facts conspire to destroy it. For it appears that at the time when John Brayne developed his design for the Red Lion, and when he and Burbage chose to construct a vast polygonal frame for the Theater, the decorative 'Heavens' roof was not in use, and cannot have shaped their architectural thought. Nevertheless an enquiry into the structure and purpose of the Heavens reveals some of the very practical ways in which the design of the public playhouses developed, following imperatives quite different from the 'goodly device' of a neo-Roman programme.

The earliest public theatres consisted of an open galleried yard containing a stage and probably a tiring house. At both the Theater and the Curtain the galleries were so formed as to be characterized as an *amphitheatrum* by de Witt, and the Curtain was repeatedly described as 'round' by other witnesses.[1] In addition the Theater had an 'Attyring housse or place where the players make them readye',[2] and the Red Lion was fitted with its lofty turret, but at none of these houses do we hear of a 'Heavens' or other roof over the stage. Nevertheless some kind of cosmically decorated covering was found in the antique theatre as well as in the Tudor banqueting houses. Though Vitruvius makes no mention of the *vela*, Alberti is careful to discuss it, adding a few observations about the technique for fitting it up:

And over all this [i.e. the auditorium including the portico], as a Cieling to the Theatre, both to keep off the Weather, and to retain the Voice, they spread a Sail all strewed over with Stars, which they could remove at Pleasure, and which shaded the middle Area, the Seats, and all the Spectators . . . Upon the upper Cornice on the Outside of the Theatre, Mutules and Stays must be contrived to support Poles, like the Masts of Ships to which to fasten the Ropes for spreading the Vela or Covering of the Theatre . . .[3]

A canvas covering, strewn with stars and suspended on ropes from masts: it might have been a specification for the lovely but frail roofs at Ardres and Calais. The Greenwich disguising theatre of 1527 had a double fabric roof like these; an outer one against the weather, and an inner ceiling painted by 'Master Hans', almost certainly Hans Holbein:

the rofe of this chambre was conninglie made by the kynges Astronimer, for on the grounde of the rofe, was made the hole earth enuironed with the Sea, like a very Mappe or Carte, and by a connyng makyng of another cloth, the zodiacke with the xii. Signes, and the fiue circles or girdelles and the two poles apered on the earth and water compassing the same, and in the zodiak were the twelue signes, curiously made, and aboue this were made the seuen planettes, as Mars, Jupiter, Sol, Mercurius, Venus, Saturnus, and Luna, euery one in their proper houses, made accordyng to their properties, that it was a connyng thing and a plesant syght to beholde.[4]

All this painterly learning was displayed above an auditorium which, though made out of wood and canvas, resembled stone and marble as surely as the Swan ever did. The rows of degrees that flanked the room to either side

were all of Marble coler, and the railes like white marble; in the middest of this Chamber, was a gate, the Arches whereof stretched from side to side, this Arche was figured masonrie on water tables with haunses receiuyng pillers wrapped, beyng Dormants Antike . . .[5]

Like the Greenwich theatre, the Banqueting House at Whitehall had a roof of painted canvas, but its design was less elaborate and it was enhanced with evergreens. In later years architects were to install *velaria* of canvas and calico in many Whitehall Court theatres: at the Cockpit-in-Court in 1629, at the Masquing House in 1638 and at the Hall Theatre in 1665. Others were fitted at the Paved Court theatre at Somerset House (1633) and at Windsor (1674).[6] The Roman *velarium* had been spread across the theatre, stage and *cavea* alike, on a network of supporting ropes, and at their most archaeological the English designers sought to imitate this effect, as Wren did at the Sheldonian, fashioning the great net in gilt moulded relief work of wood and plaster. His painter there, Robert Streeter, was also responsible for staining the cords which supported the ceiling cloth at the Hall Theatre.[7] Canvas *velaria* do not seem to have been employed in the public theatres of London, no doubt because most of the audience was sheltered by the roofed-in structure of the galleries and the yard had to remain open to admit enough daylight for the performance to be seen. Of course the utility of a canvas cover was not forgotten. In 1614, when King Christian of Denmark descended unannounced on the Court of James I, he was entertained in part by a display of fencing performed on a hastily erected outdoor stage at Whitehall. It was 40 ft square, and stood on trestles 3 ft 6 ins above the ground. The date was July, and the fencers needed to be able to see what they were doing without being dazzled by the sun, so Thomas Green was paid

for lv ells of canvas to hang before the ffencers to keep the Sun from their eies . . . for cords packthreed and small threed for the same Canvas . . . and for v daies worck of one man to sowe and bind the same . . . [and George Weale] for iiij large bedcords for the drawing vp of Canvas to keep the sun from the fencers eyes . . .[8]

When a Heavens was introduced in the public theatres of London it was related to the stage, partly to shelter it from the elements, partly to shade it from the sun, partly perhaps to act as a sounding board, and partly for the emblematic effect of its astrological decoration. The tendency to identify it with a built roof over the stage in the classical theatres was widespread. Thomas Heywood, describing Julius Caesar's gorgeous amphitheatre in *An Apology for Actors*, alluded to

the couerings of the stage, which wee call the heauens (where vpon any occasion their Gods descended) . . .[9]

The *Apology* was written *c.* 1608, but before it was published in 1612 Randle Cotgrave, in his *Dictionarie* of 1611, had already defined the French word *volerie* as '*a place ouer a stage which we call the Heauen*'.[10] The link between the Heavens and the stage is nowhere more explicitly stated than in the building contract for the Hope theatre, a dual-purpose house intended for bearbaiting as well as plays, where the stage was to be removable. In order to accommodate this flexibility, the builder was required to

builde the Heavens all over the saide stage to be borne or carryed without any postes or supporters to be fixed or sett vppon the saide stage, And all gutters of leade needfull for the carryage of all suche Raine water as shall fall vppon the same . . .[11]

Evidently the Heavens was to be at least as large as the stage beneath it, and one of its acknowledged functions was to provide shelter from the rain. When Peter Street contracted to build the Fortune in 1600 he was required to provide 'a shadowe or cover over the . . . Stadge', though whether over part of it or the whole is not specified. The latter seems more likely, for there was also to be 'a sufficient gutter of lead to Carrie & convey the water frome the Coveringe of the saide Stadge to fall backwardes'.[12] The language of the contract is not quite definite, but it seems unlikely that so much trouble would have been taken over the guttered cover if it were to shelter only part of the platform beneath. The formula for the Hope ('all over the saide stage') is probably to be understood in the terms of the Fortune contract too. Here we know that the stage was to be 43 ft wide and to extend forwards to the middle of the yard, a total of 27 ft 6 ins from the inner surface of the frame. A 'shadowe' large enough to cover the area must have been a substantial structure, especially since the contract required its roof to be constructed with tile, a heavier material than thatch or – for every foot covered – even lead.

Neither of the contracts alludes to another known function of the Heavens, its role as the point of departure and return for descent machines. Yet in 1595 the owner of the Rose theatre on Bankside, Philip Henslowe, undertook extensive renovations at his playhouse, costing £108.19s. and accomplished during the long Lenten closure. Some six weeks later, on 4 June, he paid out £7.2s. 'for carpenters worke & mackinge the throne In the heuens'.[13] There can be little doubt that this throne was the kind of thing mocked years later by Ben Jonson in the prologue to his revised *Every Man in his Humour*, a play as sound, he avers, 'as other plays should be',

> Where neither *Chorus* wafts you ore the seas;
> Nor creaking throne comes downe, the boyes to please . . .

Once having raised his eyes to this upper part of the house, the Prologue continues the list of cheap effects that might, on a less auspicious occasion, be expected to originate there:

> Nor nimble squibbe is seene, to make afear'd
> The gentlewomen; nor roul'd bullet heard
> To say, it thunders; nor tempestuous drumme
> Rumbles, to tell you when the storme doth come . . .[14]

To these we might add at least a bell, together with the 'chambers' or cannon whose firing is called for in several plays and which proved disastrous at the first Globe when a piece of batting from them sparked the thatch. If the 'shadowe' was as large as the stage there could have been no shortage of floor space for all these devices, even though the headroom would have diminished to an unusable proportion towards the eaves.

No such stage roof or Heavens is recorded in the documents relating to the Red Lion, the Theater, or the Curtain. De Witt shows a partial cover at the Swan, together with a taller roofed structure above it. Henslowe tells us that the Rose possessed a Heavens, at least by 1595. The Boar's Head in Whitechapel was equipped with a 'coueringe ouer the stage' when its yard was fitted up as a theatre in 1599, but there is no detailed evidence of its design.[15] The Fortune and Hope contracts specify Heavens, the former in terms that imply a similar structure at the Globe. The second Globe, rebuilt after the first burned in 1613, had an enormous stage roof recorded by

Wenceslaus Hollar, and in later years – in 1653 – Sir Aston Cockayne looked forward to the day when he might see again

> The Bull take Courage from Applauses given,
> To Eccho to the *Taurus* in the Heaven.[16]

In any case it is plain from the stage requirements of plays performed at the Red Bull that it possessed a cover capable of providing flight effects.[17] For the second Fortune, built after the first was burnt in 1621, no such assumption can be made, though in general the new building represented an enlargement and improvement upon the old.

From this brief review it is evident that the earliest external reference to a Heavens at any of the theatres is Henslowe's in 1595. The structure may have been added to the Rose in that year, or perhaps in 1592, when extensive carpenter's and thatcher's work was paid for, or it may have been incorporated from the beginning in *c.* 1587. No playhouse before that date is recorded to have been provided with this expensive facility, nor is there any evidence in the play texts of its presence. The few descents, or possible descents, in early plays could well have been managed with a simple hoist from the highest part of the tiring house: none makes mention of a Heavens trap, a feature that Shakespeare could take for granted when he wrote *Cymbeline*.[18]

10 *The View of the Cittye of London . . .*, detail showing the Theater.

The Heavens, with its painted representations of the stars and planets, was not an original part of the Elizabethan playhouse as conceived by Brayne and Burbage. They provided an open yard surrounded by galleries. At the Red Lion, as we saw in chapter 1, the large stage was surmounted by a tall timber turret, substantial enough to be capable of supporting a simple descent machine if required, but apparently innocent of any structural cover over the platform. Of the Theater we have the picture that appears in *The View of the Cittye of London from the North towards the Sowth* (plate 10). This shows a gabled roof emerging from within the main polygonal frame of the theatre and rising somewhat above it. The structure must be supported from below, and because it appears to be independent of the frame it is probably merely the topmost part of a turret like that at the Red Lion. It is possible that a similar design was followed at the Curtain. De Witt's drawing of the Swan is often ambiguous, but in one thing it seems clear enough: the *mimorum aedes* is built forward of the galleries of the main frame and rises – with some diminishment in width – to the so-called 'hut' with its flag and trumpeter. The sketch shows that the back wall of this topmost element touches the front of the galleries, so that the whole affair stands out in the yard, just as the turret did at the Red Lion. Against the tall turret, with its hipped roof apparently of thatch, the builders have erected a lean-to and rather inadequate cover over the stage, supported by two substantial Corinthian columns. De Witt found this arrangement more impressive than those he had witnessed at the Theater and the Curtain, which presumably lacked the lower roof and its marble-painted supports. But it was little more than an *ad hoc* development from the turret of the Red Lion, combining the lofty rise of the

Figure 3   The Theater, Shoreditch. Axonometric diagram.

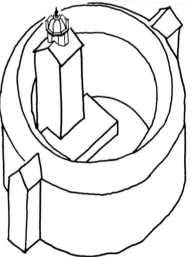

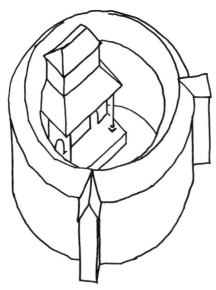

Figure 4   The Swan. Axonometric diagram.

old form with the newer Heavens which Henslowe had pioneered at the Rose.

Scholarly reconstructions of theatres later than the Swan have generally proposed that they too shared most of the characteristics of its backstage design, though few have followed the drawing in placing the entire *mimorum aedes* structure forward of the gallery fronts. Common sense suggests that the tiring chamber ought to be located within the bays of the timber frame behind the stage, so that the actors might easily make their entrances from it through the sort of stage doors that are depicted at the Swan by de Witt, or at the Cockpit by Inigo Jones (plate 38). These prime pieces of evidence show its contiguity with the stage very clearly, but its location in the frame of the public playhouses is much less certain. In contracts and legal records it was the custom to describe the tiring house as one of the separate component parts of the building, to be listed independent from the galleries and stage. At the Fortune, for example, Peter Street was to build the frame of galleries with its seats and staircases, and in addition provide it 'With a Stadge and Tyreinge howse to be made erected & settupp within the saide fframe . . .'[19] Two years later the Court of Chancery described part of the Boar's Head theatre in Whitechapel as 'the stage Tyring Howse and galleryes scytuat on the West syde of the great yard of the said Inne',[20] language that was later echoed by the actor, Robert Browne: 'Richard Langley . . . aboutes two yeares past or thereabouts vnlawfully entered into the said Stage Tyringe howse and galleryes and offered to disturbe the said Playes and Comodyes to be acted on the said Stage . . .'[21] At the Hope in 1613 the carpenter Gilbert

Katherens was commissioned to build a 'Plaiehouse fitt & convenient in all thinges, bothe for players to play Jn, And for the game of Beares and Bulls to be bayted in the same, And also A fitt and convenient Tyre house and a stage to be carryed or taken awaie . . .'[22] Insistently the records repeat that the tire house was an element of the playhouse structure to be mentioned like the stage as an entity separate from the frame or galleries.

De Witt's sketch, our one detailed picture of the interior of an Elizabethan playhouse, explicitly confirms the idea that the *mimorum aedes*, as it is labelled there, is an independent structure, built forward of the frame of galleries but pressing up against it. There is no mention of a tiring house in the Red Lion documents, but the great turret that was to stand either partly or wholly upon the stage resembles the structure shown by de Witt, and may well have been used as a tiring house. Certainly it was to stand independent of the surrounding galleries, which had been built separately by another carpenter. We know that the Theater had an 'Attyring housse',[23] but the records give no idea of its location. At the Rose there was a 'Rome ouer the tyerhowsse' in 1592, and a later inventory listed things 'Leaft above in the tier-house in the cheast'.[24] Apparently the tiring house was, as its name suggests, not merely a room or rooms contained within the framework of the galleries: it was sometimes capable of being at least a two-storeyed structure, taller still at the Swan and – if we accept the idea that it was located in the turret – at the Red Lion.

Such evidence as we have suggests that the tiring house was commonly a separate structure set up within the public playhouse yard, contiguous with the main frame and standing between it and the stage. No other interpretation of the Fortune contract seems possible, for if both stage and tiring house were to be set up 'within the saide fframe' the phrase must surely mean 'within the yard' and not 'within the bays of galleries', the latter sense being ruled out by the impossibility of putting the stage there. One must resist, therefore, a simple evolutionary theory that would have the tiring house originate in the lower floor or floors of the type of turret that had been found at the Red Lion and the Swan, standing out within the yard either upon or next to the stage, then withdrawing into the timberwork of the main frame at the same time as the great Heavens roof was introduced, namely at the Rose and the first Globe. For the Fortune, which evidently set its tiring house in front of the galleries of the frame, was generally modelled on the Globe, and there is at least a strong possibility that the Globe too possessed a tiring house similarly situated.[25] The introduction of a Heavens, especially if it took the form of a substantial roof, tiled and guttered to keep rain off the entire stage below, called for a more radical development of design than that indicated by the Swan's rather makeshift lean-to, but it did not drive the tiring house backwards into the frame. The roof shown by de Witt covers barely more than half the stage, but those required or implied by the Hope and Fortune contracts needed to come much further forward. The compromise recorded in the sketch would not do for Henslowe; indeed in a contemporary engraving there is good evidence that he had already taken the next step in the design of the tiring house and stage cover in his work at the Rose, perhaps even as early as 1587.

5
John Norden's pictures of the theatres

Any study of the architecture of the Elizabethan theatres has to turn sooner or later to the vexed question of the various maps, panoramas and drawings which purport to record their appearance. It is well known that their evidence is contradictory, at first blush so confusing as to seem worthless. But in fact it is possible, with a little patience and fortitude, to steer one's way past most of these Sirens of the Thames. Only a few sing the truth; the rest must be identified and ignored. The most alluring of them all is the fine etching made in Amsterdam by Claes Jan Visscher, and published there in 1616. It shows three arenas along Bankside (plate 4) – the Swan, the Beargarden and the Globe – and to each it gives a tall 'hut' roof something like that recorded by de Witt, though at the Swan and Beargarden it engages so firmly with the roof of the surrounding frame as to meet its ridge. The 'huts' vary in design. The simplest is at the Swan, much as recorded by de Witt, but gabled rather than hipped. At the Beargarden the taller roof is turned around so that its narrow gabled end is tied in with the frame. The most complex of the three is at the Globe, a remarkable T-planned affair, topped by a small turret or louvre with a pyramidal roof (plate 11). This last has found favour with reconstructors of the Globe for a number of reasons. Its broader part, the bar of the T, runs as a chord across the frame, re-assuringly in the manner of the Swan's upper roof as recorded by de Witt, though deeply engaged with the timber structure of the galleries. The central forward extension, unlike anything in de Witt, nevertheless allows the introduction of a Heavens trap further forward over the stage. Descents and ascents might therefore be made in two planes, or the stem of the T might house a minor trap to permit the use of fireworks well away from the flammable surface of the tiring house front below. Furthermore the complex of gables and louvre is rather attractive, and would make a fine sight from across the river, especially on those glad days when the players were in residence and their flag signalled their readiness to act.

It is to be regretted, then, that Visscher's lovely view has no independent authority whatever, and must be resolutely steered past if we are to reach

11   Claes Jan Visscher, *Londinum . . .*, detail showing the Globe.

port in one piece. In 1948 I. A. Shapiro published, apparently for the first time since the seventeenth century, a bird's-eye view of London by John Norden, the *Civitas Londini* (1600).[1] He showed that Visscher had used it as the source of all his information for his depiction of the north bank of the river, which consequently possesses no independent value as a record of the scene as it actually was. If it appears to possess such authority, that is because the etcher's masterly hand has given it the stamp of topographical art. For the south bank, however, Visscher turned away from the *Civitas Londini*, doubtless judging this part of it to be unsatisfactory, and relied instead on an earlier map. As long ago as 1917 John Quincy Adams reckoned to have identified the source: 'in drawing the Bankside, Visscher rather slavishly copied the Agas map of 1560'.[2] Five years later W. W. Braines

71

renewed and extended this observation, though he assumed – without citing any evidence – that Visscher had made independent on-site sketches of the theatres as a preparation for his work.[3]

As we saw in chapter 1, the 'Agas' map shows rows of houses along Bankside, with ditches, lanes and straight hedges making something of a formalized pattern away from the river. 'The bolle bayting' and 'The Beare bayting' rings are located amongst groups of rectangular fishponds, and flanking each of the arenas are rows of kennels with dogs tied to them (plate 3). Braines observed that this regularized layout is exactly what Visscher shows in his panorama, though there the elements are transposed, with no little artistic authority, into a convincingly 'real' perspective form. The schematic tufted trees of the map flourish here as nicely varied specimens. The hedgerows bush out like the real thing, but they are still quite straight even though they are realized as perspective orthogonals. Some of the rectangular fishponds also reappear, similarly foreshortened. And among them, as Braines observed, Visscher places 'The Bear Gardne' and 'The Globe' on sites that had been occupied in the map by the bullbaiting and the bearbaiting respectively.

Visscher's debt, however, is not to 'Agas' but to the smaller map published by Braun and Hogenberg in their atlas, *Civitates Orbis Terrarum*. Its

12   John Norden, *Civitas Londini* (1600), detail showing the Bankside area with the Swan, Beargarden, Rose and Globe.

Southwark section (plate 2) shows the same regularized pattern, though it extends the area covered further south. Both it and 'Agas' were based on a common source, a copperplate map/view of London long thought to have been lost. In the 1950s two of its sections turned up, in the form of the original copper plates whose backs had been used by Flemish artists as panels for their paintings. One covers the area around Moorfields and the other a central part of the city to the north of the bridge.[4] A close comparison shows that both Braun and Hogenberg and 'Agas' derive from the copperplate, both agreeing with it in many fine details. But in one respect they differ from each other. Braun and Hogenberg, working to the small scale called for by their atlas format, reduce the number of houses shown in the densely populated parts by about a third. The 'Agas' map, a rather crude though large-scale woodcut, simplifies their outlines but generally retains their number, and it is this variation between the maps that makes it possible to tell which of them Visscher used.

For the panorama reproduces not only the hedges, ponds and other large features of the landscape from Braun and Hogenberg, but every one of the houses registered by their map along Bankside. Like the ponds and hedges they are all rendered in an apparently authoritative perspective, giving the misleading illusion of an eyewitness record. We can check the matter by adopting Braun and Hogenberg's own topographical code: in their map the schematic rooftops present either a gable or a ridge to the observer (plate 2), and we may therefore follow the rows along Bankside using the simple notation of G for the one and R for the other. Some buildings are registered a little further south of the river, and we may include them in the array, which begins with the row of cottages to the left of 'Parys Gardeyn', thus:

```
GRRRRR         [R]   GR
        [RR]RG RGRGR
     RR                    RGGRRRRRGGRGGRGRRGGRGGRRRRGGRRRRGRRGGRRRRRGGRR
   (G R)G                                        (R)      R       R            G
                                          Bowll baytyng  Beare               R
                                                         bayting             RRG
```

It might have been useful to present a comparably growly 'code' for Visscher, reading similarly along Bankside from the row of houses to the left of the Swan to the little bridge in Deadman's Place, and so to prove – from the close correspondence between them – his dependence on the Braun and Hogenberg map rather than the variant scheme in 'Agas'. But there is no need to print the code again: with the exception of the first item (G in Braun and Hogenberg, R in Visscher), the two series are not merely close but identical, as the reader will see if he or she follows the panorama along house

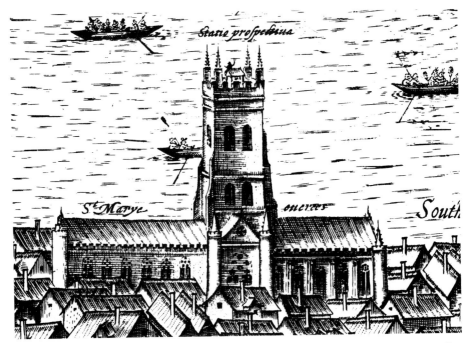

13   John Norden, *Civitas Londini*, detail showing St Saviour's ('St Marye ouerees').

by house from left to right (plate 4). True, the (GR) contained in round brackets are obscured in Visscher by a tree, one (R) is hidden by his tall 'Bear Gardne', and the [R]s in their square brackets are replaced by the Swan, but otherwise the sequence is exactly repeated. Further east Visscher followed the map implicitly until he came to St Saviour's (i.e. 'S. Mary Ouerys'). Here it offered nothing more than a schematic church, and he turned instead to the fuller picture in Norden's panorama for all the details he required, including the six-bay nave and five-bay choir, the corner turrets with their tipes, the grand south transept window and the mistaken parity of ridge height in chancel and nave (in fact the former was higher) (compare plates 13 and 14). Beyond the church – indeed throughout this neighbourhood – Norden had seriously distorted his view by removing the nearer end of the bridge eastwards, presumably in order to present a fuller view of its flank (he published elsewhere an engraved study of its other side). In his panorama the distance between St Saviour's and the bridge is too great, and the angle of the approach road – Borough High Street – is accordingly thrown off to the right. Visscher wisely returned to the map, following it faithfully almost all the way to the edge of his view.

In general, then, the Bankside according to Visscher is a true rendering of what he found in Braun and Hogenberg, but supplemented from Norden

74

with respect to an important individual building. At every point he converted his information into something much more detailed and realistic. Take, for example, the row of buildings shown in the map parallel to the low fence that runs along part of the northern boundary of the quartet of fishponds. The houses are simple boxes with doors and windows marked by perfunctory strokes. In Visscher the palings of the fence are imaginatively reconstructed, convincing chimneys rise from walls and rooftops, and porches and out-buildings are added to the houses, some of one storey and some of two, so that what began in the source as a mere cartographical device has now assumed the air of an authoritative rendering of a real scene. But it is all an invention.

The panorama's depiction of Southwark is entirely faithful to Braun and Hogenberg, and owes nothing to the simplified picture in 'Agas' (nor probably to the lost copperplate map, which is likely to have included more houses). But Visscher has updated his source even so, locating the Globe on the site of the map's bearbaiting arena and the Beargarden where it offered the bullring, all with an exactness that we may judge by reading orthogonally against the code of rooftops along Bankside. The Swan is tucked into a pleasant site by the bank, at the expense of three of the original's roof ridges.

Although the panorama of Bankside is so evidently a rendering of the

14   Claes Jan Visscher, *Londinum . . .*, detail showing St Saviour's ('St. Mary Oueris').

information given in the earlier map, Visscher might nevertheless have based his pictures of the two theatres and the Beargarden on independent and authoritative sketches. But in fact the fanciful buildings he offers are as derivative as the rest of the etching. The spectators gathering outside the Beargarden and the Globe, peering in through the latter's walls, are clearly left over from the figures who cluster about the baiting arenas in Braun and Hogenberg. They are standing, as it were, on the same spot: only the buildings have changed. As for the architecture of the three arenas, one need look no further than Norden's panorama, Visscher's source for the more northerly part of his view and the details of St Saviour's to the south. Here (plate 12) he found the Rose and the Globe lost among trees, as if seen from a high spot nearby, only their polygonal roofs showing. Norden renders the Swan in perspective, but as if seen from a lower angle. Its height is exaggerated for an imposing effect, like that of many of the more notable landmarks in the view, including the Beargarden, which is presented in a straight elevation. All the theatres appear to be hexagonal or possibly octagonal structures, and all fly square flags. Seeking a clearer idea of the Globe than is given by the simple outline of its roof, Visscher seized on the tall profile of the Swan and Beargarden and used it for all of his arenas. He followed Norden in implying three storeys of windows at the Swan, and provided them also at the Globe; at the Beargarden he retained his source's two levels. Beneath the eaves of Norden's Swan a row of tiny windows appears; in Visscher these are carried across to the Beargarden and the Globe, where they reappear irrationally as a form of corbel table or even machicolation. None of Norden's structures has the external staircases we know to have existed at the Theater, the Fortune, the second Globe and the Hope. Neither do Visscher's.

In three matters, however, Visscher goes beyond the information offered in Norden's panorama. He rightly omits the Rose; he gives the Swan twelve sides where his source gave six or eight; and he provides huts for each of the arenas. The omission of the Rose, which had indeed passed out of existence by the time the panorama was prepared, may have been the result of up to date information, but in view of the literalness of the rest of Visscher's adherence to Braun and Hogenberg it is more likely that he simply failed to find a handy arena site in the source. Merian, preparing a revised version of the Visscher view for the *Neuwe Archontologia Cosmica*, printed in Frankfurt in 1638, shuffled the sites of the Beargarden and the Globe about rather in order to reintroduce a third theatre between them, evidently making good what he took to be Visscher's inaccuracy, though by then the Rose had long since faded.

Although Norden shows the theatres as polygonal in his panorama he also provides a small-scale map, revised from an earlier version he had printed in 1593, in which he represents them all as circular (plate 15). This presumably is the source of Visscher's twelve-sided frame at the Swan, the larger number of faces more closely approximating to the round. The little map also gives huts at the Beargarden, 'The stare' (or Rose) and the Globe, each surmounted by a square flag. Here evidently is the origin of Visscher's more elaborate hutwork, in which he composes variations on Norden's artless theme, just as he supplemented the schematic houses of Braun and Hogenberg with delightful porches, windows and chimneys. The little map employs the same formula each time, offering a gable-ended roof rising above the main frame opposite to the observer, and apparently filling a large part of the otherwise open yard. At the Swan, the only exception to the rule, there is no hut at all. Visscher takes the pattern, reshapes it in his perspective mode, and applies it first to the Swan, where it appears integrated with the frame and reduced in proportion, but otherwise unchanged. At the Beargarden he turns the hut round so that its narrow gable end makes contact with the ridge of the frame, and at the Globe he presents what we may take as his crowning achievement in this architectural *capriccio*, a T-planned arrangement of gables, ridges and turret.

But in these matters one eyewitness is worth a dozen foreign artists imaginatively working over their documentary sources. While there is no evidence that Visscher ever set foot in London, John Norden was certainly a personal observer of what he recorded in the *Civitas Londini*. He marks his station point atop the tower of St Saviour's with the tag, *Statio prospectiua*, and

15   John Norden, *Civitas Londini*, detail of inset map of London, showing Bankside.

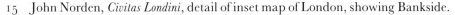
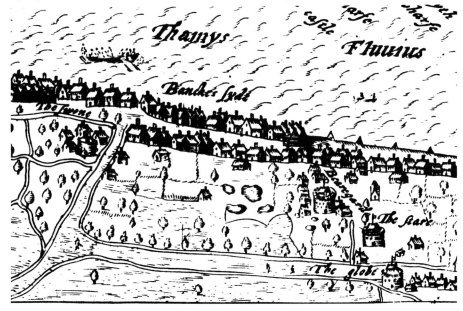

16   John Norden, *Civitas Londini*, detail showing the Globe, whose polygonal roofline may just be seen among the treetops at the centre of the plate.

I have shown elsewhere[5] how accurately the far bank in his view represents
the placing of landmarks as seen from this vantage point. But his presentation of Southwark is altogether different in form and style, nothing like the
townscape as seen from the church tower.[6] The Bankside section appears to
be laid out roughly as an enlargement of the accompanying map. The lines
formed by the river and the more visible lanes make a similar pattern in both
cases, and the theatres are arranged – as presented directly on the sheet – in a
similar relation to each other, though in the panorama the Globe is a little
further north. Yet the buildings are seen not in the conventional elevations of
the map but foreshortened as if actually observed from a real station point.
Common sense tells us that this perspective is imaginary, and in any case the
Beargarden, shown in elevation like most of the houses in the little map,
violates the scheme. Norden's panorama of Southwark is therefore a curious
mixture of plan-map, elevation and foreshortened perspective. Taken separately in isolation, each of the three theatres seems to be presented as it would
appear to a real observer placed not somewhere high to the south but on
Norden's *Statio prospectiua* at St Saviour's. We look down onto the closest (the
Globe and the Rose) (plates 16 and 17) and across almost horizontally
towards the more distant Swan (plate 18). They are located according to the
dictates of a map, but each individually is depicted as it might have been

78

17   John Norden, *Civitas Londini*, detail showing the Rose. As at the Globe, the stage
      roof presents a gable end towards the yard.

seen by the surveyor when he made his original sketches from the top of the
church. It is instructive to compare them with Hollar's later study of the
second Globe and the Hope, as seen from the same spot (plate 22). Here the
spatial relation between the buildings is quite different, because Hollar's
study is a completely integral view made from the single station point, but
the downward line of sight towards the Globe is similar to that found in
Norden. Norden was not only a citizen of London but a professional surveyor, accustomed to making accurate topographical notes. In the small-
scale map he clearly shows that the Globe was thatched, though he depicts
no roof at all at the Swan, and gives too scanty a view of the Beargarden and
'stare' (or Rose) for one to be sure about the roofing material. In the
panorama, however, he carefully distinguishes between the hard-edged line
of the eaves at the Beargarden (a line shared by most of the houses in view)
(plate 12) and the hatched ragged line at the Swan and the Rose (plates 18
and 17). The eaves of the Globe (plate 16) are too hidden by trees for the
distinction to be made. We know from independent sources that the Globe
and the Rose were thatched, and de Witt's drawing of the Swan has seemed
to some to indicate thatch there also.[7] The Beargarden appears always to
have been tiled.

In both the panorama and the inset map the Swan appears without a
turret roof. We know from de Witt that one certainly existed there *c.* 1596

79

18 John Norden, *Civitas Londini*, detail showing the Swan.

when he made his sketch (plate 1). Yet no sign of one appears in an estate map of Paris Garden manor (1627), which gives the playhouse a circular feature of some sort – either a pit or a platform – at the centre of the yard, and offers no hint of a stage.[8] This drawing is probably no more than a map-maker's symbol and of little value to the present discussion, but the picture of the Swan drawn by Inigo Jones in a scene design for *Britannia Triumphans* (1638) plainly show it without an upper roof (plate 19). It may be that the turret had been lost as early as 1597, when the Pembroke's Men, having performed an objectionable play called *The Isle of Dogs* at the Swan, were ordered to be arrested. The authors of the offending work, Thomas Nashe among them, scattered and laid low; Ben Jonson was taken to prison. The theatre's owner, Francis Langley, had connections at Court and in the following months fought hard to protect himself and his investment, but he had to reckon with a Privy Council which had written to the magistrates of Surrey requiring them to

send for the owners [of the playhouses in the Banckside, in Southwarke] and injoyne them . . . forthwith to plucke downe quite the stages, galleries and roomes that are made for people to stand in, and so to deface the same as they maie not be ymploied agayne to suche use [as playing].[9]

80

In fact the Council's bark was much worse than its bite, and no theatre was plucked down, though all were closed for a time.[10] But Langley was in the direct line of fire, the Swan having been the site of a major scandal, and his playhouse never fully recovered from the setback. In the following year he built new facilities of some sort 'near to the Paris Garden play-house'[11] perhaps in an attempt to revive it, but the house did not regain its former reputation and Langley himself transferred some of his interest to the new Boar's Head in Whitechapel.[12] It may be therefore that the Swan actually was defaced in 1597 as a result of the Privy Council's injunction, but that the demolition was limited to the part of the building most obviously dedicated to the players, the tiring house turret which de Witt had recorded for posterity at some time during the brief two years of its existence.[13]

Norden, in short, offers information about the theatres which squares remarkably well with what we know about them from other sources. Within

19   Inigo Jones, 'a prospect of the Citie of London' for *Britannia Triumphans* (1638), showing the Swan.

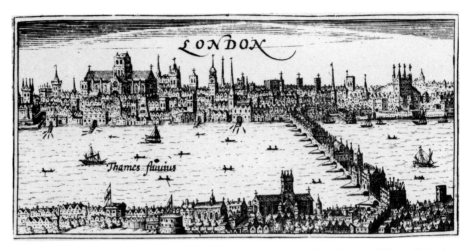

20   Jodocus Hondius, 'London', from the map of 'The Kingdome of Great Britaine and Ireland' in John Speed, *The Theatre of the Empire of Great Britaine* (1611 [−12]).

his limits he is a sound witness, a primary source where Visscher is only secondary. He is not of course infallible. He represents the Globe and the Rose as scarcely taller than the buildings that surround them, and in that may well err in making them too low. But his Swan and Beargarden are far too tall for their width. All of the playhouses, including the Beargarden, probably had more sides than the six or eight he accords them in the panorama. And we know that they had attached stair turrets, which he does not show.

Between them the panorama and the inset map gave other topographers a set of information which they could juggle and reformulate at will. Jodocus Hondius, working far away in Amsterdam, used Norden as his source for a miniature view of London included in John Speed's *The Theatre of the Empire of Great Britaine* (1611). He followed the *Civitas Londini* in general and in particular, repeating for example the displaced angle of Borough High Street and the faulty profile of St Saviour's (plate 20). So literal was Hondius' reading of Norden that he even mistook the southeastern corner turret of St Saviour's for an independent tower, and represented it as such, standing well clear of the main body of the church. (In this delightfully inventive error he was exactly followed by Francis Delaram, in a view of London included in an equestrian portrait of James I.) Using the information contained in the *Civitas Londini*, the map as well as the panorama, Hondius reinvented the Globe, providing it with a round ambulatory at ground-floor level, where in his original the view had been obscured by trees. None of these copies of Norden has any independent authority, and in attempting to reconstruct the design

82

of the first Globe it is necessary to set them resolutely aside. Visscher's picture especially is attractively etched, but whatever is accurate in it is derived from other sources.

Of these Norden's sheets constitute the only authority on the Globe. But Norden, though reliable as an experienced professional, confuses us with his two representations of the playhouse. In the one it has a tall flagged turret rising well above the round thatched frame; in the other it is polygonal, its roofing material uncertain, and its square flag flies above a much lower roof of a quite different character. Indeed both the Rose and the Globe are shown in the panorama with a simple gabled roof presumably over the stage. Its gable end stands parallel to the diameter of the house and its ridge, aligned radially, meets that of the surrounding frame, so that both roofs apparently rise to the same level. No such roof appears at the Swan, nor is there a 'hut' or turret top; the Beargarden, presented in elevation, has no turret rising above its ridge but might possibly contain a covering roof of the lower sort. At the Rose the forward gable of the cover has a window, but none is visible at the Globe. In both cases only the upper part of the roof can be seen, leaving us to guess at its full extent and design below. From each a ridge-mounted mast rises, flying the square flag. And if the angle of our line of sight down into the first Globe here resembles that recorded in Hollar's study of the second, as if Norden's view of the theatre were based on an isolated study, so does the orientation he registers for its ridge. Hollar's roof is larger, raising twin gables well above the frame, but its two ridges run across the sheet in much

Figure 5   The first Globe, with integral stage roof. Axonometric diagram.

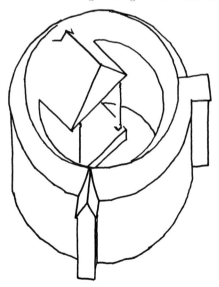

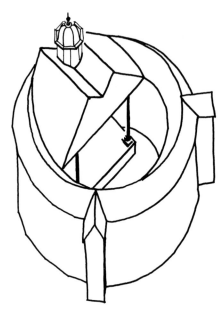

Figure 6   The second Globe, with enlarged integral roof. Axonometric diagram.

the same direction as Norden's single one (compare plates 16 and 21). It appears that the first Globe was aligned on a similar bearing to the second, and that Norden's study of it, made from the tower of St Saviour's, has been set down unchanged within the mixed plan-perspective of Bankside. The comparison with Hollar also suggests that the large roof of the second Globe evolved by a straightforward process from the smaller and simpler one of the first. By contrast with de Witt's drawing of the Swan – and also it seems with Norden's own miniature map versions – the ridges at the Rose and the Globe run radially from the centre of the theatre towards the circumference, not crosswise as a chord. Because their ridges engage those of the frame roof these covers are conceived of as integral parts of the whole building, not the topmost element of a freestanding structure set up within the yard. The contrast is very clear in Hollar's study and it is hardly likely that Norden would casually have invented so firm an anticipation of the actual construction of his Globe's successor. In attempting therefore to decide which of his two depictions of the Globe's roofline is the more accurate we should be guided not merely by the greater general impressiveness of the panorama, nor even by the indications that the theatres are shown in it as seen individually from the *Statio prospectiua* at St Saviour's, but by the consistency of the design of the first Globe with what we know to have come later at the second.

Nevertheless the small map does show tall roofs projecting above the frames at the Beargarden, 'The stare' and the Globe, and it is necessary to consider why Norden chose to represent them in this way. There is, of course, the question of scale: in such a map most buildings are recorded by means of conventional symbols, though some of the more notable ones are also given individualizing touches. Church towers, for example, are generally put down in a simple rectangular form, but Bow Church has its crown spire and St Saviour's is distinguished by its four large pinnacles. In much the same way the playhouses are all reduced to the simple notation of a cylinder about 3.5 mm across. Three of them have roofs, at least one of which (the Globe's) is individualized as thatch. These three also have identical smaller roofs rising above their yards. When compared with the more realistic presentaion in the panorama the minute depictions emerge quite clearly as symbolic notations, and it appears that Norden could assume that such a diagram would strike his public's eye as recognizably standing for a polygonal public playhouse of a familiar kind. In 1600, that is, Londoners expected in a general way to see a tall structure emerging from the top of a typical suburban theatre, and this is just the pattern we have noticed at the earlier playhouses.

It appears, then, that there were at least two forms of tiring house and

21 Wenceslaus Hollar, 'West part o[f] Southwarke toward Westminster,' detail showing the Globe.

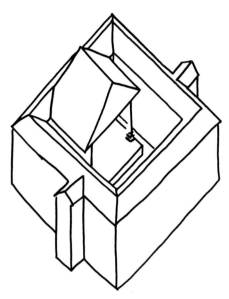

Figure 7   The Fortune, with an integral stage roof, which hides the tiring house. The location of the attached stair turrets is conjectural.

stage cover in the public theatres. An 'integral' structure, neatly tied to the timber work of the main frame, is clearly shown in Hollar's drawings of the second Globe. A free-standing turret is recorded by de Witt at the Swan, its lower storey and perhaps other parts used as a tiring house. The turret is similar to that now documented at the Red Lion, but includes a stage cover or Heavens, a feature not found at the Whitechapel house. The engraving of the Theater shows a tall ridged roof, almost certainly the topmost part of a turret, and it is this feature, with its vivid flag and high visibility, that came in John Norden's imagination to stand for the idea of a public playhouse. Yet already by 1600, as he showed in his panorama, the Rose and the Globe had replaced the turret with an integral stage roof projecting directly from the main frame. At the Globe, indeed, the actors had taken the opportunity of modifying the turret arrangement of the Theater when they moved the components of its frame to Bankside, updating the design in the manner already established at the Rose. At the Fortune in the same year the tiring house was built as a separate structure set up like the stage within the yard, but now presumably under the cover of the great 'shadowe' or roof. It does not appear, therefore, in the list of separate parts of the building that are to be fitted with tiled roofs: 'And the saide fframe Stadge and Stearcases to be covered with Tyle...'[14] By this time the tall roofed turret had become a thing of the past. As a mapmaker John Norden understandably used an old-fashioned image of a public theatre for his tiny conventional symbols,

86

varying it only slightly to indicate special features at individual houses. In the panorama he gave a more realistic if still incomplete reading, and in the process made our only record of the construction of the Heavens at the Rose and the Globe.

6
This majestical roof

The introduction of a Heavens at the Rose, and its subsequent reappearance at the first Globe, the Fortune and the Hope, marks a new stage in the development of the public playhouse. The Swan, with its bastard mixture of turret and penthouse cover, represents a compromise between the two forms, something of a throwback when it was built in *c.* 1595, after the Rose had established the integrated stage roof, and in all likelihood destined for a short life. The turret of the earlier theatres had mediaeval associations, recalling what Glynne Wickham has called the 'timberhouse' of the tiltyard, where the judges sat elevated above the contest:

> This very simple structure . . . was ideally suited to a variety of needs – the scaffold or gallery as a judges' platform for fencing-matches and other athletic games, as private 'boxes' for the owners of the gamehouse, or as a music room; and the area beneath the scaffold or gallery as a tiring-house and property room for actors.[1]

At the Fortune, and probably at the Globe and Rose, the tiring house was still located within the yard formed by the amphitheatre galleries, but now both it and the stage were covered with a substantial common roof. The frame and tiring house structure might support this great covering to the rear, but its forward thrust appears to have been borne on timber posts of the kind illustrated by de Witt at the Swan. In order to span the whole width of the stage it required large trusses, built with tie-beams of exceptional length, and it therefore needed the lightest possible covering. There is direct evidence that the Globe's roof was of thatch, and at the Rose Henslowe employed a thatcher about the building.[2] Thatch is much lighter than tile – as light indeed as lead, and much less expensive[3] – and requires a less weighty structure of purlins and rafters to support it. The development of the large stage roof at these two theatres was therefore quite naturally accompanied by the resort to the lightweight roofing material, though at the Fortune Peter Street was able to contrive the 'shadowe' with tile. A roof of good reed thatch requires a pitch of some 45° at the minimum, and this would have raised the ridge higher than Norden shows it in the *Civitas Londini* if its eaves were not to be inconveniently low over the stage. Evidently the panorama simplifies the rooflines a little, but something of the appearance of the junction of the raised ridge with the frame may be recorded in Hollar's sketches of the Hope (plate 22), where the Heavens originally covered the entire stage, but without benefit of supporting posts. It may be, as C. Walter Hodges has argued,[4] that this roof was subsequently removed, leaving the raised peak so clearly drawn by Hollar.

Soon after the Heavens first appeared at the Rose and the Globe we find Heywood and Cotgrave identifying its starry decorations with features of the Roman stage, but the playwrights soon charged it with unclassical, Christian meaning. In *Dr Faustus* a refulgent throne descends while music plays to conceal the sound of the ropes, and the Good Angel speaks of sad ironies from the tiring house door:

> Faustus behold,
> In what resplendant glory thou hadst set
> In yonder throne, like those bright shining Saints,
> And triumph ouer hell, that hast thou lost . . .[5]

But it would be unwise to conclude from such uses as this that the Heavens was a further Gothic addition to the theatre. It was never a place from which God speaks, as He does in the mediaeval pageants. Its decorative analogies lay in the Banqueting House at Whitehall and the double canvas roofs at Greenwich, Calais and Ardres; in structure it seems to have been a simple innovation, resulting from the need to shelter the stage from sun and rain, but as Henslowe's note makes clear, its value as the housing for a descent machine was very soon exploited. Such machinery had classical antecedents in the *deus ex machina*, but it remains unlikely that the Heavens was constructed simply in order to facilitate descents. No playwright of the period seems to have been as interested in flying effects as was to become common in the masques and the French-inspired 'Machine' drama of the Restoration. Of the plays that may confidently be assigned to the first Globe before 1609 only one positively requires any sort of suspension gear,[6] and even that was almost certainly rigged up independent of the Heavens.

Both of the extant theatre contracts make it obvious, with their talk of rainwater and gutters, that the stage roof was intended to shelter the actors during their performance. There is some evidence – not very strong – that the shelter was welcomed also by a section of the audience. The matter is uncertain because it is not clear whether the custom of sitting on the stage was much followed at the public playhouses before the 1620s. Certainly it was considered usual at the enclosed Blackfriars playhouse by 1604, when Marston's *Malcontent*, after an unsuccessful production there, was offered with a new adult cast at the Globe. This performance included John Webster's specially written Induction in which some of the actors pretended to be

Blackfriars dandies insisting on following their usual practice of sitting on the stage, though now in full view of the Globe audience:

> *Enter W. Sly, a Tyre-man following him with a stoole.*
> Tyre-man.
> Sir, the Gentlemen will be angry if you sit heare.
> *Sly*. Why? we may sit upon the stage at the private house . . .[7]

At the end of the Induction Sly and the friend by whom he has been joined leave the stage for a private room, there to take tobacco. This exchange appears to show that stage-sitting was not tolerated at the public theatres, but in 1596 Sir John Davies had published epigrams that suggest the contrary. 'He that dares take Tabaco on the stage' is the subject of *In Sillam* (no. 28), and *In Rufum* (no. 3) concerns the courtier who, seeking the most 'conspicuous' place to sit at the theatre,

> Doth either to the stage himselfe transfer,
> Or through a grate doth shew his doubtfull face.[8]

These lines appeared in the year after Henslowe first recorded a Heavens at the Rose, and just about the time when de Witt was sketching a part of one at the Swan. The private, enclosed theatres were not active then, and Davies, ever up to date, must have referred to the public playhouse. After the opening of the Blackfriars the habit of sitting on the stage became fashionable among the dandies, but Dekker, in his *Gull's Hornbook* (1609), has the public theatres in mind when he devotes paragraph after satirical paragraph to counselling his foppish client how to advertise himself 'By sitting on the stage'.[9] Sometimes, it seems, the custom was followed at the public as well as the private theatres. Now if one were a late-Elizabethan grandee, clad in slops and dashingly plumed, one would not want to pay good money for a stool in the rain. We first hear of sitting on the stage in the public theatres at precisely the moment when they first offered a cover that would afford reasonably dry conditions below. The Heavens, far from being a direct continuation from a mediaeval tradition of theatrical 'paradises', was an innovation designed primarily to protect the expensive costumes of the players from the elements; thereafter it may have come to protect the expensive plumage of part of the audience too.

The Fortune contract's word for the cover is 'shadowe', a reminder perhaps that shielding from sunlight was almost as important as protection from rain. Cotgrave's *Dictionarie* defines *Ombraire* as 'an Vmbrello, or shadow',[10] and Fletcher in *Rule a Wife* (1624) wrote in metaphor:

> Now you have got a shadow, an *umbrella*
> To keep the scorching worlds opinion
> From your faire credit.[11]

90

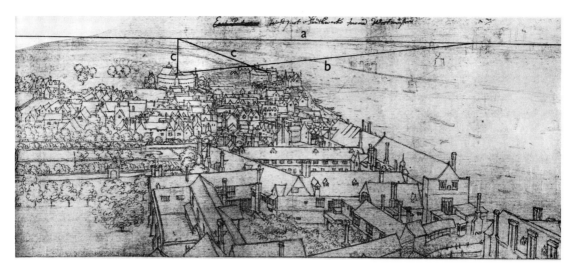

22   Wenceslaus Hollar, 'West part o[f] Southwarke . . .', showing the alignments of
the Globe's stage roof and the stair turrets of both the Globe and the Hope.
   a   horizon line
   b   projection from Globe's stage roof gable
   c   projections from the stair turrets of the Globe and the Hope.

To the modern eye, accustomed to seeing a brightly lit stage from a darkened
auditorium, it may seem strange that the Elizabethans should have placed
their actors in the most shaded quadrant of the theatre, yet the Globe at least
was orientated to achieve precisely such an effect. Our best evidence, which I
have discussed in *The Quest for Shakespeare's Globe*,[12] is Wenceslaus Hollar's
meticulous sketch of west Southwark, made *c.* 1640 from the tower of St
Saviour's with the aid of a drawing frame or topographical glass. Because of
its drafting techniques, the drawing is a precise exercise in linear perspective. A line projected from the stage roof gable to the horizon line, which
Hollar himself ruled across the sheet, strikes it somewhat to the left of St
Paul's (plate 22). It is a characteristic of linear perspective that parallel
horizontals converge on one another at the horizon, and it follows that a line
drawn from St Saviour's tower to the left of the site of Old St Paul's will be
parallel to the Globe's great gable. On a modern map such a line turns out to
lie on a bearing 42° west of north; the Globe's axis, at right angles to the
gable, is therefore 48° east of north. The drawing depicts the second Globe,
built in 1614 on the site of the first, but it is likely that the earlier structure
faced the same way as the later one, the same foundations having served for
both; and we have observed that Norden's engraving of the first Globe,
considered as an isolated study, shows it pointing in much the same direction
as the second as seen from the church.
   Precise information about the orientation of the other theatres is scarce. A

line drawn from the ridge of the visible stair turret roof in Hollar's sketch of the Hope, and passing across the centre of its yard, converges at the horizon with a line of sight drawn straight across the nearer staircase of the Globe (plate 22), indicating that these turrets lay parallel to one another (on a bearing of 100.25° east of north). Assuming that the stairs and frame were similarly located at both theatres, we may deduce that the Hope also shared the Globe's orientation. Norden registers the Rose as pointing the same way as the first Globe, but the engraving of the Theater appears to show its turret to the southeast. The evidence of none of the other printed maps and panoramas is to be trusted. The stage at the Red Lion was longer north and south than east and west; if its placing in relation to the frame was anything like that at the later Fortune it will have been set either to the west or to the east side of the yard. This evidence from Whitechapel is very vague, but in another case from the same area we know the matter quite exactly. Legal documents describing the development of the Boar's Head playhouse repeatedly refer to its stage being situated on the west side of the courtyard. 'West' is, however, not quite what it seems. The lot-lines recorded in Ogilby and Morgan's post-Fire map (1676) indicate that a stage placed against the 'west' side would in fact have faced northeast, at about 46° east of true north, very close to the orientation of the Globe.[13] There is therefore some indication that the two Globes, the Rose, the Hope and the Boar's Head all faced northeast, away from the afternoon sun.

Conditioned as we are by modern habits of stage lighting we are likely to be puzzled by this arrangement, but it was evidently the one favoured by the builders of the playhouses, whatever their reasons. Of course it is true that direct sunlight is hardly the problem in London that it is in the bullrings of Seville, and on all but the brightest days of the year a hazy, diffused light would have been usual. Yet even on the murkiest afternoons the south-west quarter was – and is – the brightest part of the sky, and in relative terms the lighting retains its directionality. It is possible to draw diagrams indicating the angle of the sun's penetration of a public theatre auditorium – admirable examples have been published by R. B. Graves[14] – but the matter seems worth putting to a more practical test. An experiment with a three-dimensional model might reveal more of the truth than a theoretical study. Under the auspices of the Shakespeare Globe Theatre Trust, and with the generous assistance of their architect, Theo Crosby, I joined forces with two enthusiastic engineers,[15] and together we set about the task. We took the large model of the Globe designed by Richard Hosley for the Bear Gardens Museum and shone light into it from a powerful and distant source, representing, as closely as we could practically manage, the parallel beams of the sun. Because we were interested in discovering the 'insolation' at the theatre for various times of the day and year it was necessary to shine our light into it from a variety of angles. The model was too large to be mounted on a

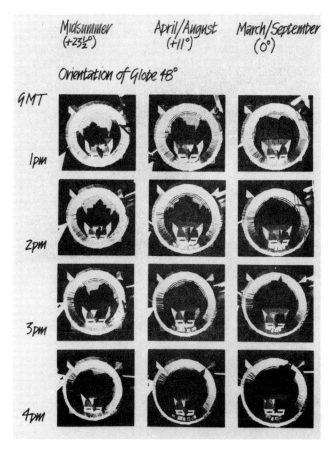

23　The insolation of the Globe.

conventional heliodon, and because it was easier to move the theatre rather than the great lamp we set it on a draftsman's table which was capable both of tilting (to represent the latitude of London relative to the equatorial plane) and revolving (to represent the earth's rotation). In addition we tilted the table itself, along with the model, to represent twelve stages in the varying declination of the earth relative to the sun: $0°$ for the equinoxes of March and September, $+23\frac{1}{2}°$ for the midsummer solstice, and $-23\frac{1}{2}°$ for midwinter; together with $+20°$ (May and July), $-20°$ (January and November), $+11°$ (April and August) and $-11°$ (February and October). Thus we were able to simulate the direction of the sun relative to the Globe for each of the hours of the day for every month of the year. By rotating the model on the table we were also able to test the degree of insolation for various orientations of the building, but here we are interested only in those for the historical bearing of $48°$ (plate 23).

24   Sunlight penetration of the Globe's galleries at 3.0 p.m. on 11 June, looking west.

The photographs show the model as seen from above, and the hours illustrated, from 1.00 p.m. to 4.00 p.m. GMT, have been chosen to cover the afternoon performance times. After 4.00 p.m., even at midsummer, very little direct sunlight penetrated the theatre on this orientation, and because very little entered it at any time of the day between October and February, these months have not been included. Of course much depends on the details of the structure of the model chosen for the experiment. The Bear Gardens Globe model represents the thatched first Globe of 1599, scaled at a diameter of 96 ft with a frame height of 33 ft to the plates. Its stage extends to the middle of the yard, and is partly covered by a Heavens and hut whose design is based not on Norden but on the de Witt drawing of the Swan and Visscher's etching of the Globe. We should now, if the arguments presented in the previous chapter are correct, revise this structure a good deal, converting it to a single ridged roof with its gable end brought forward to the front of the stage. It would have cast a rather larger shadow than is shown in the photographs.

We may assume that the time of perfomance was usually in the afternoon, beginning at 2.00 p.m. and lasting until 4.00 or 5.00 p.m. During these afternoon hours the whole stage of the first Globe was in shade, even at the time of year (11 June, old style) when the sun was highest in the sky. It appears from the photographs that a major effect of the roof's design (and therefore presumably one of its major purposes) was to keep direct sunlight away from the acting areas. The placing of the stage cover not only ensured

94

25   Sunlight penetration of the Globe's galleries at 3.0 p.m. on 11 June, looking south.

that the stage itself remained shaded, but also kept any patches of direct sunlight well away from it, even though some of the audience consequently had the sun in their eyes. Plates 24 and 25 show the insolation of the galleries at mid-performance (3.00 p.m.) on St Barnabas' Day, 11 June, old style, the midsummer solstice. One may only speculate about the reasons for this peculiar disposition of the playhouse, but Nicholas Hilliard, who painted in the jewel-like linear Elizabethan style, would hardly have approved. In his *Art of Limning* he declared that his models were best displayed in open sunlight, and seemed to equate subdued light not only with 'shadowe' or *chiaroscuro* moulding of forms but also with questionable morality:

If a very weel favoured woman stan[d] in place wher is great shadowe, yet showeth shee louly, not because of the shadow, but becausse of her sweet fauor consisting in the lyne or proportion, euen that littel which the light scarsly sheweth greatly pleaseth, mouing the desier to see more, ergo more would see more; but if she be not very fayre together with her good proportion, as if to palle, too red, or frekled etc., then shadowe to shewe her in doeth her a fauore. Wherfore I conclud great shadowe is a good signe in a pictur after the life of an ill cause . . .[16]

Without accepting the ethical drift of Hilliard's argument we might agree that the shade of the Elizabethan stage could well assist a certain kind of illusionism, softening boys' faces into women's, and lending or taking away the years from an actor's appearance.

Direct sunlight on the stage, or even a more intense but diffused front

95

lighting, would have picked out the actors against a darker background and possibly given stronger contrasts of light and shade. Yet, as Graves has noted,[17] these effects would have been quite uncontrollable, and even the wittiest actor seeking to exploit them by improvisation would have been hard put to it on a breezy summer's afternoon with scudding cumulus clouds cartwheeling the beams of the sun. Such would have been the difficulties had the stage been built in the northeast quarter of the yard in order to enjoy a maximum of afternoon light. Some idea of the effect may be gained from the photographs in plate 23 if one imagines that the stage had been built at the side opposite to that actually shown; only rarely would the entire stage have been lit (perhaps at 2.00 p.m. at midsummer), the height of the main frame ensuring that various amounts of shade would normally invade it and always cover it altogether by late afternoon.

The Globe's orientation permitted sunlight to play across at least part of the auditorium during the performances, but always kept the stage itself in shade. At midsummer, when most direct light penetrated the galleries, the altitude of the sun was highest, and so furthest from the actual line of sight of the spectators as they looked down from the upper benches towards the stage. At times of the year when the sun was lower in the sky, and therefore more likely to shine from an angle close to that of the spectators' gaze, it penetrated correspondingly fewer bays of the frame, as may be seen from a comparison of the March/September column with that for midsummer. Thus the more acute the problem the fewer the audience members affected, until by late afternoon at the equinoxes only a few in the topmost gallery had the sun uncomfortably in their eyes. In the winter months remarkably little direct light penetrated even here.

The photographs also show that at the hour of the start of performances the sun stood more or less directly over the centre of the stage roof as viewed from the yard, an effect which was accentuated by the presence of the gnomon-like finial on the louvre shown in the second Globe as depicted by Hollar and the flag staff at the first as depicted by Norden. At midsummer the sun at 2.00 p.m. stood some 2° to the right of this mast; in May and July it stood directly over it; in April and August it appeared 4° to the left, and so progressively until at midwinter it was 20° to the left. These variations mean that there could hardly have been a tradition of beginning the play at a time determined by reference to the sun's alignment with the building, but the roof was so placed that the sun stood over some part of it at 2.00 p.m. throughout the year, and for most months marked the progress of the afternoon (and so of the play) by passing over it from left to right.

The underside of the 'shadowe' was painted in a representation of the Heavens. It is unfortunately impossible to be sure of the design, though the sheer size of the cover – equal to that of the stage beneath it – will have influenced the nature of the scheme. At the Rose it may have boasted the signs of the zodiac, for they are mentioned in *Titus Andronicus*, entered by Henslowe in his *Diary* as a 'ne[w]' play in 1594.[18] Titus persuades members of his family to shoot arrows into the air, bearing messages to the gods:

Tit.	Now Maisters draw, Oh well said *Lucius*:
	Good Boy in *Virgoes* lap, giue it *Pallas*.
Marc.	My Lord, I aime a Mile beyond the Moone,
	Your letter is with *Iupiter* by this.
Tit.	Ha, ha, *Publius*, *Publius*, what hast thou done?
	See, see, thou hast shot off one of *Taurus* hornes.
Mar.	This was the sport my Lord, when *Publius* shot,
	The Bull being gal'd, gaue *Aries* such a knocke,
	That downe fell both the Rams hornes in the Court . . . (IV, iii, 63–71)

To treat such passages as this as veritably describing the playhouse structure is obviously risky, for one does not know where to leave off. Do the Ram's horns really fall into the court? Only common sense can tell us where to draw the line, and one supposes not; but it is certainly tempting to admit Hamlet's words about 'This Majestical Roofe, fretted with golden fire' as giving, under the guise of metaphor, good information about the Heavens at the Globe. They identify the 'canopy' of the 'Roofe' with the sky in an optimistic way: the theatrical Heavens is a celebration of what is ordered and lovely in the firmament. The possibility that it represented a full cosmic display rather like that of the Calais theatre must therefore be considered, though we should bear in mind that the Heavens appears usually to have been a substantial tiled roof, probably ceiled with plaster below the joists, and little resembling the canvas and rope structures of the temporary banqueting houses. It may have presented an image of the sky itself as well as the stars and planets. The roof's large area overall may suggest that the decoration was concentrated in one part of it, but the canvas ceiling at the Banqueting House in Whitehall was even larger, and 'great spaces' of it had been painted in 1581 as 'the cloudes with starres, the sune and sune beames', together with the Queen's arms, all richly gilded.[19] If this roof was vivid enough to stay in people's memories, it did not last long in concrete reality. Within three years the fabric had been restrained, nailed with 'hoobie nailes' and painted 'in sondrie kindes of coulours with Diamondes frutage and other kinde of woorke . . . in water coulours'.[20] Perhaps the 'other kinde of woorke' was sky painting; in 1603–4 a new canvas ceiling was sewn and strained, 532 square yards in all, and painted with 'worke called the Cloudes in distemper'.[21] On a smaller scale such ceilings were not uncommon. The poet Henry Vaughan describes one in the Globe tavern early in the seventeenth century as 'painted over head with a Cloudy Skie, and some few dispersed Starres . . .'.[22] At Theobalds in 1592 there was a curious ceiling that seems to have had some of the qualities of a planetarium:

97

it contains the twelve signs of the zodiac, so that at night you can see distinctly the stars proper to each; on the same stage the sun performs its course which is without doubt contrived by some concealed ingenious mechanism.[23]

For all the obvious deliberation with which the 'shadowe' was orientated in relation to the sun, there is no evidence that the public theatres shared this kind of scientific interest.

Indeed it may be that the theatrical Heavens, as it developed in the last years of the sixteenth century, was an altogether less pictorial decoration than was usual in the festive halls at Court. Direct evidence about its design is very scarce, but a few allusions in plays performed in the early years of the seventeenth century suggest that its treatment was architectural rather than painterly. Shakespeare, for reasons that are unlikely to have been wholly free from theatrical allusion, caused Othello to swear by 'yond Marble Heauen' (III, iii, 467), and Timon, delving for roots in the first Globe's stage, imagines it to be opposed to 'the Marbled Mansion all aboue' (*Timon of Athens* IV, iii, 194). The Heavens ceiling in the public theatres was probably made of plaster rather than canvas, for at the Fortune the stage as well as the gentlemen's and twopenny rooms was to be ceiled with lath, lime and hair. According to the Elizabethan proprieties this work should have been performed by members of the London Plasterers' Company, whose charter, confirmed in 1597, gave them the exclusive right to fashion material that included hair as well as the bricklayers' ordinary mortar of lime and sand. Possibly Street subcontracted the plastering, or he may have taken it on himself illegally. Hamlet's use of the specialized word 'fretted' in connection with the cover may indicate that it was a flat ceiling compartmented into decorative panels by means of interlacing ribs, a method of articulation at which the plasterers of Elizabethan and Jacobean London excelled. Richard Dungan, who worked on the Whitehall Banqueting House of 1606–9, was paid 'for fretts & other worke done at Knoll',[24] where the quality of his craft may still be seen. Similarly, in 1601, John Cobb was rewarded for 'frettishing' the ceilings of the great chamber and long gallery at St John's College, Cambridge,[25] and in 1578 Sir Thomas Cecil wrote of 'the fretting [at Burleigh House] which is a lingering and a costly work'.[26] Sir Henry Wotton would later praise the 'Plastique Art' of 'gracefull fretting of roofes',[27] and there remain in and about London several fine examples of such work. Fragments from Essex House, Putney (*c.* 1596) are at the Victoria and Albert Museum, as is the more complete enriched pattern of intersecting squares and quatrefoils that survives from the Old Palace at Bromley-by-Bow.[28] A splendid composition at Canonbury House, Islington, includes moulded medallions of Alexander, Tarquin and Lucrece and illustrates a persistent classicizing tendency in the decorative schemes. In a huge neighbouring room the portrait busts represent Tarquinius Priscus, Aegeria, Julius

98

Caesar, Alexander the Great, Titus Vespasianus, Jovinianus, Augustus, Hersilia Sabina, and Crispina Augusta, all set among enriched intersecting ribs, and dated in a central panel, 1599, the very year of the Globe.[29] Many of these ceilings, which were made for substantial citizens as well as royal patrons, give evidence of having been assembled from a common series of moulds, and some share common patterns of geometrical setting-out. That at Bromley-by-Bow repeats forms found at Canonbury House, and they appear again at the Vicarage, Tottenham, built for a barber-surgeon in 1620.[30] The setting-out in the first-floor ceiling at Canonbury House is identical with that of a ceiling at Broughton Castle, Oxfordshire, also of 1599,[31] and details of strapwork and foliage from Bromley reappeared on the soffit of a beam at Bury Hall, Edmonton (c. 1615). All these ceilings – and a good number more in the provinces – consist of a flat field interlaced with moulded ribs in a geometrical design. The panels are enriched with conventional motifs such as sprays of flowers, wreaths or cherubs' heads, but often there are more particular images, a three-masted ship, or a series of medallion heads. At Knole in the Cartoon Gallery the ribs are serpentine and form ogival compartments adorned with English flowers: the pink, the rose, the lily, honeysuckle and columbine. Usually the intersections of the ribs are marked with bosses, and from the more important ones hang moulded pendants.

Elizabethan ceilings of this type were sometimes whitened, but commonly they were painted in colours. Thomas Joyce, for example, was paid 116s. for 'colouring the fret in the Privy Chamber' at Woodstock in 1593–5,[32] and occasionally traces of the original paint have been discovered on surviving examples, beneath coats of limewash. The bosses and pendants might be gilded, so that the whole work presented a brilliant array of colour and texture to the observer in the room below. It seems unlikely that the Heavens at the Rose or the 'shadowe' at the Fortune were merely whitened, and in *Cymbeline* Shakespeare suggests something of the richness of effect in a contemporary theatre, either the Globe or the Blackfriars, when Jupiter descends from his 'Marble Mansion'. His subsequent ascent to what he calls 'my Pallace Christalline' is observed by Sicilius:

> The Marble Pauement clozes, he is enter'd
> His radiant Roofe . . .   (v, iv, 120–1)

Doubtless the Sharers could not have afforded gilded work at the Globe in 1599, and the whole ceiling would have been painted to imitate marble and other rich stones. Nevertheless the possibility that the bosses at the junctions of the 'frets' or intersecting ribs were gilded cannot be altogether discounted. Hamlet's majestical roof is fretted with 'golden fire', and there are many references to the stars in the Heavens couched in terms that suggest such a scheme. At the Fortune, for example, whose design was based on that of the first Globe, the '*3. King*' in Dekker's *Whore of Babylon* turns his eyes to heaven in anguish:

> Can yonder roofe, thats naild so fast with starres,
> Couer a head so impious, and not cracke?[33]

No surviving Elizabethan plaster ceiling gives an adequate idea of how the planetary or zodiacal theme of the Heavens might have been carried out by the craftsmen of the London school. It seems likely that a formal system of moulded panels may have been inserted into the compartments defined by the ribs, each containing a sign of the zodiac or the representation of a planet, possibly in mythological form. Between them the gilded or flame-coloured bosses and pendants might have been shaped to represent stars. The marble, or even azure, finish of the compartments and ribs would indicate a schematic idea of the firmament rather than a picture of the real sky, with its clouds and sunbeams. Elizabethan and Jacobean plasterers usually maintained pattern books in which the various devices in their repertory were recorded: there is extant an excellent one that once belonged to the Abbott family in Devonshire,[34] but none survive from the London company. Some evidence of the type of appearance they might have sought to imitate is however to be found in the work of contemporary sculptors, and especially in the visual flourish created by the great stone testers of their funerary art. For it happens that during the period of the building of the Bankside theatres the business of providing carved marble monuments had become something of a monopoly of the craftsmen – chiefly Dutch in origin – of what is often called the Southwark School.[35] In earlier years immigrants like William Cure the elder had produced work of great refinement in a Renaissance mode; later their techniques coarsened and their play with coloured marbles became more ebullient as they came to command a wider and often less discerning market. By the end of the century their workshops were busy with commissions at every level from the most modest wall-bracket to monstrous tombs like that of Sir Christopher Hatton in St Paul's. Those of Queen Elizabeth and Mary, Queen of Scots at Westminster are similarly ambitious, and possibly give some hint of the kind of decorative style that might have been imitated – in painted wood and plaster – at the playhouses over the river. Garret Johnson's tomb for the fourth Earl of Rutland, in Bottesford Church, Leicestershire (1591), shows details of carving, in its richly coloured Corinthian columns and entablatures, that call to mind de Witt's description of the Swan. There is no evidence that the craftsmen of the Southwark School had anything directly to do with the painters and plasterers of the Elizabethan playhouses, but so far as the latter used the techniques of illusion to present an appearance of marble they are unlikely to have ignored the local models whose production they could witness every day in the streets about them.

The playhouse Heavens came into being as a result of the need to provide a roof all over the stage. Its main business was practical, but its introduction caused some rearrangement of the tiring house; the tall turrets of the early theatres were superseded at the Rose, the Globe and the Fortune by integral roofs of the kind illustrated by Norden, and the tiring house was constructed beneath them, contiguous with the stage. Because these parts were placed in the south-west quarter the new roof adequately sheltered the stage from the prevailing winds and shaded it against the afternoon sun, providing comfortable accommodation for those whose vanity and purses prompted them to sit where they were most obviously on view. Above them the great expanse of the ceiling was decorated, probably within a finely executed framework of moulded plaster ribs, with panels and medallions representing the zodiac and the planets. In its innovatory pragmatism as much as in its decorative style the Heavens was the child, not of the half-forgotten pageants of mediaeval times, but of the Elizabethan age itself. Its design may have been related to that of the polygonal frame, but in a way quite different from that found in the Calais round house. There the programme of the roof may be said to have shaped the frame, the repeatedly fourfold pattern of the *mappa mundi* and cosmic display being projected into the sixteen-sided figure of the building. At the earliest public playhouses the polygon was established without the agency of a programmatic ceiling; the Roman associations of the arena design, untrammelled by the symbolism of the elements and the constellations, could speak more clearly.

When the Theater, with its Roman name and configuration, was reborn on Bankside in 1599 its new stage roof and decorated Heavens ceiling had the potential to charge the amphitheatrical form of its galleries with a new meaning, and indeed its name was aptly changed to the Globe. But this new identity did not indicate that the rebuilt playhouse had become a fully realized cosmic theatre. The decoration of the Heavens was too subordinated to the general architectural scheme to dominate the stage with insistent skyey influences. As at the Rose, which was similarly equipped, the playwrights sometimes alluded to the plaster zodiac and the painted planets and stars, and occasionally included such images in a larger universal theme, but none treated them as a continuing or unavoidable emblematic presence. They could be ignored just as easily as they could be invoked, and in general they were left alone, as a neutral architectural ceiling over the stage. What remained was a theatre suited more for human action than for divine interventions, but one that could readily assume a cosmic significance when required. Some thirty years after the Globe was built, not far away in Kent, the antiquary Henry Oxinden made himself a round house of pleasure on top of a hill. People must have remarked on its odd shape, for he composed a few lines of verse to defend his choice of the plan:

A Qua're why I made the house on the top of the Hill round?
Tell mee how Henry in thy minde it came
Vpon the Hill thy House so round to frame
Answere
I imitated the great Architector, Loe
Both Earth, & Heauen, hee hath framed soe.[36]

Almost all round buildings could be similarly justified, though with varying degrees of conviction. At the Globe the new plaster Heavens, painted to resemble marble and adorned with its mouldings of the zodiac, the stars and the planets, made a similar identification possible but by no means necessary. The wooden O might sometimes become a little world beneath its '*brightest Heauen*'; but more often it remained an *amphitheatrum* of timber posts and wooden boards, a theatre meant for human pageants.

7
The Elizabethan Banqueting House, Whitehall

The Elizabethan public theatre, with its yard half open to the sky, lay partly exposed to the vagaries of sunshine, wind and rain. Henslowe's *Diary* tells us that performances took place at the Rose on all the days of the week save Sundays, and never is there a hint that they could be rained off, or abandoned like cricket for bad light. Webster complained of the 'blacke' theatre and sparse audience at his *White Devil* when it was first performed at 'so dull a time of Winter',[1] but the play went on in spite of the unappealing conditions. Eventually – by the time of the Restoration – the habit of acting by daylight in this fashion fell into disuse, and theatres were enclosed more or less adequately against the elements. Indoor stages had always been customary at Court and in the great houses of the shires, as well as in guildhalls and inns throughout the land, and it was this type of theatrical arrangement – rather than the open courtyard type – that shaped the subsequent development of English theatre design. In the sixteenth and seventeenth centuries such auditoria were smaller than the great frames of the public playhouses, their stages more compact and their lighting (by candles) more intimate. The most famous of the so-called 'private' houses was the Blackfriars, designed by James Burbage for the Lord Chamberlain's Men as early as 1596–7, though not used by them until a dozen years later. Other enclosed playhouses were built in imitation of the Blackfriars, but all of them appear to have owed something of their design to the theatrical arrangements that had for generations been made at the royal palaces, whether for masques or for the performance of plays by the professional acting companies. The most remarkable of these Court theatres, and by far the largest, was the Banqueting House in Whitehall. Erected in 1581, it long survived its initial function as a place of entertainment for the French commissioners and the object of their embassy, the hopeful Duc d'Alençon. In chapter 2 we noted Holinshed's description of it as having been built of 30 principal masts, each 40 ft high, spaced about 10 ft apart so that the perimeter measured 332 ft. The plan was a 'long square', in Holinshed's regrettably imprecise phrase. But there are a few indications in later documents that suggest what the layout might have been. The most striking is the provision, in 1605, of a mobile stage 40 ft square, designed to roll forwards on wheels as part of the spectacular display of *The Masque of Blackness*.[2] The Banqueting House must have contained a space uncluttered by structural posts at least 40 ft wide and considerably more than that in length. It is sometimes said that no contemporary representations of the building survive, but in fact we have no fewer than four, all the work of John Norden. We first see it in two plans of Westminster published in 1593 as part of the *Speculum Britanniae*.[3] One of these was engraved by Pieter van den Keere and shows the Banqueting House occupying the southwest corner of the palace court, between the Palace and Holbein gates (plate 26). The area immediately east of the Banqueting House was surrounded by 'tarrises', or galleries raised on posts, and was sometimes called the 'Chapel Court' or 'Sermon Court' after the outdoor pulpit erected at its centre. All this is clearly illustrated by Norden, and beyond the further 'tarris' stands the Banqueting House itself. It appears to be an aisled hall, though only the eastern aisle is visible. It is lined

26   John Norden, 'Westminster', from *Speculum Britanniae The First Part . . . Middlesex* (1593), detail showing the Banqueting House at Whitehall.

27 John Norden, *Civitas Londini*, detail showing the Banqueting House at Whitehall.

with windows, and above it the central part of the building rises to a greater height, likewise showing signs of fenestration. The roof has a longitudinal ridge, and may be hipped at the northern end; the southern end is obscured by some neighbouring chimneys. The survey of Middlesex in which the map appears was issued with a variant print, a woodcut based either on the engraving or on Norden's original drawing.[4] This shows all the same features as the first, more crudely realized but sometimes all the clearer for that. A curious tower-like object engraved by van den Keere at the northeast corner of the building appears to be an external stair turret. Again the 'tarris', aisle and hipped roof are all visible. In a revised map of Westminster which appears in the *Civitas Londini* (1600) the Banqueting House has shrunk, and is shown less high than the nearby Holbein gate. Its aisled form is obscured, and there is no hipped roof. But at the southern end a gabled bay rises as high as the main part of the building. And one last glimpse of the roof appears in the *Civitas Londini* proper, beyond the Great Hall at Whitehall and immediately to its left (plate 27). The Banqueting House here is large, and has a ridged roof apparently punctuated with two chimneys; but the panorama offers no further information about it.

These pictures suggest an aisled building, well fenestrated. The roof may have been hipped, and there may have been an extended bay close to the southern end. The central part, if it was to take the great stage for *Blackness*, must have been at least 40 ft wide. In 1603–4, when the ceiling was repainted, the account was for 532 square yards of work.[5] If we assume that this area covered only the central nave, it would be roughly consistent with a rectangle 40 ft wide by 120 ft long (or $533\frac{1}{3}$ square yards). We have Robert Smythson's survey drawing of the first Jacobean Banqueting Hall,[6] which replaced the Elizabethan one, and this measures 120 ft long internally, with a central nave about 39 ft wide between the centres of its columns. It seems likely that the Jacobean building took the main dimensions of its plan from its predecessor, and that the Elizabethan structure was also 120 ft long. If it was 332 ft all round, as Holinshed claimed, it would then have been only 46 ft wide and the aisles impossibly narrow. It is not possible to reconcile all these figures, but a ground plan rather like that shown in Smythson's survey seems not at all unlikely.

The ceiling was, as we have noticed, originally a magnificent affair of cloud-painted canvas, adorned with evergreens and gold-spangled fruits. The canvas walls were painted to resemble rusticated masonry outside, and

Figure 8   The Whitehall Banqueting House (1581): an aisled hall or basilica. Axonometric diagram.

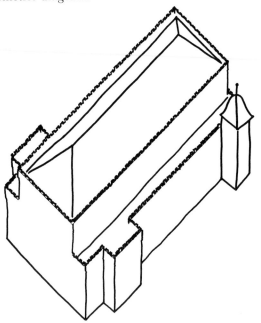

inside ten steps of degrees flanked each of the long walls. So flimsy a structure could hardly have endured, and there are signs even in the earlier records of some more substantial systems of construction. In the Declared Accounts for 1582–3 we find that the Sergeant Painter, George Gower, was paid 'for layinge all ye windowes, and Joul pillers in white leade, oile, and russet'.[7] A jowl post is one with an enlarged head, capable of supporting beams or bressummers converging on it from different directions, and the presence of such pillars in the Banqueting House implies that the mast and canvas system of construction was supplemented by a more conventional timber framing, consisting perhaps of a gallery structure over the degrees, reached by the external staircase shown by Norden.

Above the level reached by the degrees and by any gallery, the walls were pierced by 'Clerestorie light*es*' framed up by the carpenters, part of the 292 lights noticed by Holinshed. A clerestorey window, in Elizabethan usage, is simply one constructed in the same plane as the wall, and the word cannot by itself be taken to show – as modern usage would – that the central part of the hall was higher than the aisles, as in a Roman basilica. Nevertheless that is the form recorded by Norden. The 'two great Baywindowes' for which carpenters were also paid,[8] and one of which seems to appear in Norden's map of 1600, suggest the model of a Tudor hall, these large windows serving to light the dais at the upper end. The 'Clerestorie light*es*' are probably to be identified with the 'lxiij great casement*es*' which were painted in white lead in 1582–3.[9] The floor of the room was of deal boards planed smooth enough for dancing. It was at first-floor level, for in 1596–7 three partitions were erected underneath the building 'to devide the rooms for the newe librarie'.[10] In 1581–2 carpenters were paid for 'Makinge upp of Scaffoldes under the Banquettinghouse for ffrenchmen',[11] perhaps in the same basement but possibly against the western wall outside.

Holinshed stressed the rapidity with which this temporary building was put up, the work being completed in three and a half weeks. When the French commissioners arrived the Banqueting House was ready for them, and Elizabeth 'with amiable countenance and great courtesie receiued them' there, 'and afterward in that place most roiallie feasted and banketted them'.[12] But the masque that was supposed to have been performed was at first cancelled and then perhaps transferred to the Great Hall. John Rose the property maker was paid 46s.8d. 'for the tymber and workmanship of A mounte to take it agayne into his owne hand*es* because it was not vsed', and there was also much activity in cutting paper patterns for the costumes. 'A paire of winges of Estrichfeathers to have ben vsed in the maske' was paid for, and altogether £38.15s. spent on 'The chardges of the work*es* begonne & lefte vnfynished for the receauing of the ffrenche Comissioners.'[13] But the pasteboard lion and dragon prepared for the Banqueting House turned up again in the Revels Declared Accounts for 1581–2:

to Iohn Rose for a Mount with a Castle vpon the toppe of it a Dragon & a Artificiall Tree by great – C^{li}
To him for a artificiall Lyon & a horse made of wood – vij^{li}.[14]

An entry in a warrant of 1 April gives a little more detail of the kind of thing intended:

The Mounte, Dragon w*ith* ye fyer woorkes, Castell w*ith* ye falling sydes Tree w*ith* shyldes, hermytage & hermytt, Savages, Enchaunter, Charryott, & incydentes to theis. – CC markes.[15]

Two entries in these documents concern branches and garnishings for the Hall, and it seems likely that the masque, intended at first for the Banqueting House, was eventually performed in the Great Hall. Whatever the design of the new building, a production originally intended to be mounted in it could evidently be transferred to a traditional Tudor hall without too much difficulty.

In the following year there began a series of changes at the Banqueting House that account for its long life. In the Declared Accounts we read of payments made for work

in qu*a*rteringe up of ye sides thereof, and closing diverse plac*es* of ye same with boordes, aswell for ye plumbers woorke of pipes, Cisterne, and other piec*es* there imploied, as also to defend ye plaster caste on ye said sides from the violence of whether, workinge of ye battilment*es*, ioisting, and boordinge of longe gutters for avoidaunce of Rayne, makinge of a longe partition at ye farther ende next ye Quenes gallerie, quartering, and puttinge in of interlesses, and other timber about ye Porche, Lathinge and laying the Walles with lime and heare, and stikinge on of Plaster, the better to Receive ye Painters woorke.[16]

The Banqueting House emptions for this year include £53.15s.7½d. for boards and £37.12s.8½d. for nails. The side walls with their windows were strengthened with quarters, or studs, and extensively boarded. Presumably the stone-painted canvas was removed, for the walls were now plastered with lath, lime and hair. This new surface, the conventional covering of a timber frame, was then painted by George Gower and his men:

for paintinge of all ye outeside of ye banquettinghouse walles cont viij lx viij yardes square, with oile cast on ye said woorke after ye p*er*fectinge thereof . . .[17]

Some work was also done on the roof, part of which was boarded, and £82.10s.3d. was spent on lead for the new gutters and down-pipes. Evidently rainwater had begun to spoil the canvas walls of the original building. Nearly all the work in this year was devoted to strengthening and protecting the house and its 'Porche', with the result that what had begun as a temporary structure of masts and canvas became a more permanent one with timber walls boarded and covered with plaster, and with adequate protection against rainwater. It appears that the rain had spoilt the battlemented parapets, for as well as 'workinge of ye battilment*es*' the Works accounted for 'castinge an oile coulo*ur* on the boorded Roofe, and inside of ye battilment*es*'.

The interior of the house remained much as before, with its ranges of degrees, the wooden dancing floor between them and a stage or halpace at the southern end for the queen. Now, however, 'a longe partition' was introduced 'at ye farther ende next ye Quenes gallerie' and, perhaps associated with this joiners' work, five new wainscot doors were provided, four of them 7 ft high by 4 ft 2 ins broad, the fifth 6 ft 6 ins by 3 ft. The chamber was furnished with various joined forms, deal tables for the banquets and enormous framed cupboards for the display of plate. One has the picture of a grand aisled hall set up for masquing, with a central floor overlooked by tall ranges of degrees and perhaps galleries too, the upper end arranged as a stage (the Works had been responsible for 'Reringe of a platt with Shoores under the same [and] enclosinge upp thendes':[18] the raised 'theatre' of the French account).[19] From the beginning, therefore, the Banqueting House was a type of theatre, built in the tradition of Henry VIII's Disguising Theatre at Greenwich, and intended for dancing and revels quite as much as for the serving of food.

At Greenwich in 1527 these two functions had been separated, so that in the Banqueting Hall the walls were kept clear of seating and lined with tapestries and serving tables, while the adjacent Disguising Theatre was equipped with degrees (or 'stages') to either side:

this chambre was raised with stages. v. degrees on euery syde, & rayled & cou*n*tre-railed borne by pillars of Azure, full of starres & flower delice of gold, euery pillar had at the toppe a basin siluer, wherein stode great brau*n*ches of white waxe, the degrees were all of Marble coler, and the railes like white marble . . .[20]

An Italian visitor, Gasparo Spinelli, observed that there were three 'ordeni' of degrees to either side of the room, providing comfortable seats, each row having a rail all along it for the spectators to lean on.[21] The term *ordeni* may imply orders or storeys of galleries, but the posts seem not to have been superimposed. Each supported a silver basin with candles, and the arrangement was probably like that which Holinshed describes at Greenwich a few years earlier, on 7 May 1520, when the great chamber was prepared for the performance of a comedy by Plautus. On that occasion there were 'great lights . . . set on pillors that were gilt, with basons gilt, and the roofe was couered with blue sattin set full of presses of fine gold and flowers.'[22] In the 1527 Disguising Theatre we may suppose that Spinelli's account is the more correct in mentioning three rows to either side, for the audience was divided accordingly by rank. Part way down the room – Hall says 'in the middest', and Spinelli 'Alli dui terzi della sala' (Two-thirds of the way down the room) – stood a great arch, reaching from one side to the other and consisting of a single span ('un arco d'un volto solo') painted in gold and bice and topped by busts of classical heroes. The king sat on a halpace presumably facing this handsome composition. The performers entered in front of it, first from one side and then from the other, to initiate a dialogue about love and riches. Failing to resolve their debate, the principals each called in three knights, one set of whom attempted to penetrate the arch while the others resisted. As they fought a gilt barrier fell down spectacularly from the soffit of the arch between them. Another barrier fell to mark the conclusion of their trials, and when they had all departed an old man stepped forward to point the moral of the show:

Then, at ye nether ende [i.e. opposite the king, and so beyond the arch], by lettyng doune of a courtaine, apered a goodly mount, walled with towers and vamures al gilt, with al thinges necessarie for a fortresse, & al the mount was set ful of Christal coralles, & rich rockes of rubie cureously conterfaited & full of roses & pomgranates as though thei grewe: on this rocke sat eight Lordes appareled in cloth of Tissue & siluer cut in quater foyles, the gold engrailed with siluer, and the siluer with gold, al loose on white satin . . .[23]

The mount with its fortress and seated masquers was revealed by a falling curtain beyond the great arch in a theatre equipped with degrees and a dancing floor. At Whitehall in 1581 there was no arch, but the rest of the room followed the Disguising Theatre pattern, even if its decoration was markedly less lavish. And within two years a certain amount of new work was undertaken at the Banqueting House which, though not very explicitly described in the Declared Accounts, may have brought its auditorium to conform more closely still to the Greenwich pattern. As usual there were small maintenance tasks: the floor was mended with deal boards and its joists were 'furred', or wedged to bring the surface level.[24] A brick wall was built on either side of the stone doorcase at one end of the building. In 1583–4 also 'ij^o borded particions' were made 'under ye Bankett house'. But a more arresting entry concerns 'Quarteringe about Tharch of the Banquett house'. Hitherto we have heard nothing of any arch in the building, but among the Taskwork entries for this year we find that George Gower was paid 'for xxviij yeardes of other sortes of payntinge worke with ij^o Personadges done about the Arches & Pillers of the Bankett house at ix^d ob le yearde square – xxij^s ij^d'. The turner Richard Dickenson received 23s. apiece for carving six beasts, and Gower was further paid 'for layinge the postes Rayles and Ballesters in oyle Colours and the vj Timber Beasts – x^li'. These posts and rails are presumably those of the galleries we have already postulated, supported by the 'Joul pillers'. The beasts are a decorative motif that was found everywhere at Whitehall, inside and out, and may have appeared almost anywhere about the building. But the arches and pillars are puzzling, especially because one arch had quartering around it and was presumably therefore a substantial timber-frame structure. The painting included two figures or 'Personadges', and it may be that they flanked a wide arch of the sort that had divided the Greenwich Disguising Theatre. 'Personadges' commonly decorated the supports of a scenic frontispiece in Italian practice, and when the visiting artist Constantino de' Servi designed one for Campion's *Somerset Masque* in the Jacobean Banqueting House in 1613, the Sergeant Painter was paid 'for payntinge of a great arche with two spandrelles, two figures and two pillasters on either syde for the maske'.[25] The record of 1583–4 alludes to arches in the plural, but in noting that one of them was quartered suggests a composition like that of a triumphal arch, with one large central opening flanked by smaller ones to either side, the whole adorned with the 'Pillers' mentioned in the account.

Originally constructed as a temporary hall for dancing, the Banqueting House had been rendered solid, its walls framed and plastered, its roof made adequate with boards and lead. And now it would seem that the Works were converting it piecemeal into a theatre proper. The Declared Account for 1584–5 contains a long special entry for 'The Bankettinge howse' from which we may extract the following:

makinge of iij Rounde Skaffoldes and setinge them up in the same howse, Nailinge up Deales at the upper ende thereof Takinge downe a baye of Tarris nere y[e] greate Chamber dore to give light to the wine Cellor, Makinge newe postes railes and ballasters settinge them up, boordinge sondrie places with boordes on the Tarris & Bankettinge howse, makinge a waye for the plumber, and mendinge the Roofe in sondrie places, Cuttinge downe the olde ivie from the roofe, Ceelinge, and strayninge the Clothes to painte the same, layinge of Leade about the ballasters over the Tarris . . . at the Bankettingehouse Ende, round about a rounde windowe and other places where neede was, also sowdringe sondrie faultes in the gutters there . . .[26]

Some of this work had to do with the terrace to the east of the building, and the provision of daylight to the cellar. The greatest part concerned the ceiling, for which new canvas was purchased, presumably for use in patching and making good. The Taskwork entries indicate the nature of the new work:

Lewes Lizarde and his Companie painters for newe paintinge all the Bankettinge howse Celinge overhead upon the Canvas in sondrie kindes of coulours with Diamondes frutage and other kinde of woorke, in all for doinge the same in water coulours, with xvj^d for hoobie nailes for y[e] strayninge of their clothe – xxx^{li}.

The ends of the chamber were decorated in a different style:

More to him [Lizarde] by greate for paintinge a greate border at y[e] upper ende of the Bankettingehowse, beinge the whole breadth of the same howse, and filled with the Queenes Armes and Badges, the some of – $iiij^{li}$
More for paintinge the other ende of the same howse in like maner with the Queenes Armes & Badges by greate y[e] sume of xl^s.

If the lower end of the room already possessed a fixed arch decorated with 'Personadges' the space available for Lizarde's work would be limited to the area above the opening, and we notice that his painting there cost only half the amount required for the 'greate border' at the upper end.

The ceiling had previously been adorned with wicker pendants and hanging towsions of holly and ivy. Now all this was cleared away and new pendants were installed, made of wire and garnished with 'archden plate and other flowers': 25 great ones, 28 somewhat smaller, and 24 ordinary. In addition there were 28 'creaste towsions' fashioned in a similar way, and 44 'single towsions'. The work was under the general supervision of George Gower, the Sergeant Painter, who spent 40 days on it.

The most radical change was possibly the introduction of 'iij Rounde Skaffoldes' into the auditorium. Unfortunately the cursory entry in the account is all that we have to go on, but they are unlikely to have been altogether circular and may have formed a segmental or semicircular *cavea*, providing a U-shaped range of seating around the central dancing floor. If so, the whole room, with its newly painted ceiling, its architectural arch flanked by 'Personadges' and pillars, its degrees flanking the walls and its triple round scaffolds will have constituted a Court theatre on the Italian model. Or perhaps not. The arch and personages may have been another kind of decoration altogether, the round scaffolds possibly something other than seating, and the Banqueting House little more than its name implies. This earliest of English U-shaped auditoria must remain no more than an hypothesis until more reliable evidence about it emerges.

In the following years there were only minor works, mainly repairs 'where it rayned in' and 'framinge and settinge up of new prickpostes under the same Banquethouse' (1592–3);[27] there were more partitions in the basement, framed and plastered (1597–8);[28] and 'two greate tables' were made by the joiners. There is no notice of any major alteration, or any changes to the seating arrangements, until 1603–4, when the house was once more renovated at the initiation of the new reign. The first item relating to the Banqueting House in the accounts of that year is a reference to the auspicious business of 'making and bourding a bottlehouse under the Banquetting house for the Lord Chamberlaine for the king'. The canvas ceiling was repaired, resewn and restretched, and Leonard Frier, the new Sergeant Painter, painted it with 'V^{c}xxxij yardes square of worke called the Cloudes in distemper'. The old queen's arms were replaced at the front and rear of the auditorium: 'for of [*sic*] lxxij yardes square at the endes being the kinges Armes Pillasters &c at xiiij^d the yarde square – iiij^{li} iiij^s'. In addition, 14 'Braces' were painted, presumably a decorative as well as a practical part of the structure.[29]

The house was still in this condition when *Othello* was performed in it on 1 November 1604. Almost immediately afterwards enormous new works were undertaken in preparation for the first of the Jacobean masques, Ben Jonson's *Masque of Blackness*:

settinge upp of a greate stage in the bankettinge house xl[ty] foote square and iiij[or] foote in heighte with wheles to go on, makeinge and settinge upp two particions there xlviij foote longe the pece with a retorne at one end, frameinge and settinge upp of an other stage a great halpace and degrees in y[e] saide bankettinge house for people to sitt on to see maskes and showes before the Kinge and Queene with paintinge the roofe overheade with Cloudes and other devices . . .[30]

The presence of the vast mobile stage, 40 ft square and on wheels, indicates – as we have seen – that the Banqueting House must have possessed enough floor space clear of columns to permit its movement. Possibly the two 48 ft partitions with a return at one end were intended to fence off its runway down the room. Although the Declared Account is regrettably imprecise in its description of the devices, Jonson himself gives us a number of clues. But first we must recognize the quite remarkable parallelogram of forces which he invoked in the masque. The scene, once it was revealed in the lower or northern end of the building by the parting of a painted curtain, consisted of a mechanical sea in front of which Tritons and sea-maids were seated. Here Oceanus spoke with Niger, the one originating in the west, the other in the east, both mounted on great mechanical sea-horses which writhed and sank in the waves. To the rear was a huge concave shell, rising and falling as if afloat on the waters, brilliantly lit. Beside it swam more sea-monsters with torch bearers on their backs, two apiece, while within the shell itself sat the twelve lady masquers, blacked up as Aethiopes. Behind all this, but visually united with it, lay a seascape painted in perspective, its horizon level with the king's eye as he sat under his canopy of state at the upper end of the room.[31]

To the north, then, the sea; and to the south the king, 'a SVNNE . . . / Whose beames shine day, and night, and are of force / To blanch an AETHIOPE, and reuiue a Cor's' (lines 253–5). Opposite the king, in the upper part of the house above the stage, the moon was to appear. And it was of course the moon that caused the tide to flow at the beginning of the masque, though she did not emerge from her 'cloudy night-piece' until the second of the evening's visual climaxes. The first was the opening moment, when the complex mechanical scene was first revealed, for then 'an artificiall sea was seene to shoote forth, as if it flowed to the land' (lines 26–7). The whole mechanical contraption, waves, Tritons, sea-maids and monsters, rolled forward on its wheels down the Banqueting House like a flowing tide, impelled by the lofty moon, as yet still obscured above. The rest of the masque put the advanced front of the stage to work as the boundary between the sea and the land. First the moon appeared in the upper stage, surrounded by the 'Cloudes and other devices' for which the Works would be paid: a throne of silver, a silver glory at her head, the blue silk of the heaven set with silver stars and lights. Hers was the force that had caused the tide to flow, bringing its freight of black beauties to the shore of Britain. Next, the masquers came forward from their shell two by two, stepping down from the stage onto the floor in front of the state. There they danced together, and were about to choose male partners from the audience when they were urged by a tenor voice singing from the stage to return to the sea. Resisting this 'charme', they danced several measures with their men, at the end of which they were once more 'accited' to the sea, this time by treble voices. But echoes located in 'seuerall parts of the land' (i.e. about the auditorium) wistfully mocked the singers. The moon spoke once more, and the ladies danced back towards the sea, remounting the stage and returning to their shell.

> Now DIAN, with her burning face,
> Declines apace:
> By which our Waters know
> To ebbe, that late did flow.   (lines 354–7)

So the 40 ft stage rolled back again, as – we may suppose – the moon vanished once more among the clouds.

Jones's first attempt at the unified setting for a masque combined the old form of the wheeled pageant, grown to giant proportions, with the newer perspective system which required a precisely calculated station point in the auditorium for the prime observer. It borrowed something of its form from a Florentine entertainment,[32] and some of its perspective theory from Serlio or another Continental handbook. For the occasion the auditorium itself was reshaped with new degrees and a halpace designed to elevate the king to the correct height for viewing the foreshortened scene. The old round scaffolds were replaced with others, presumably straight, and it is likely that the quartered arch with its two personages went too, there being insufficient space behind it for the great stage on its runway. In the quarto text of 1608 we are told that the initial scene was a landscape 'of small woods, and here and there a void place fill'd with huntings'; this cloth is then reported to have fallen. But the manuscript of the masque says that it opened 'in manner of a Curtine', and one eyewitness recorded that the performance began with the 'drawing of the trauers'.[33] A curtain capable of being drawn will have needed a border above it to conceal its wire and pulleys, and it is possible that Jones provided a new one well forward of the location of the old.

For *The Masque of Blackness* Jones animated the Banqueting House with forces like those of the cosmos itself. The king beneath his state conventionally personated the sun, a power whose central control was recognized in the text. Aethiopia, the moon, emerged in the 'heauen' clad in silver light, a reflection of the sun's radiance, while beneath her the great rolling stage of the sea first flowed and then ebbed in time with her ascendancy. The masquing theatre had for a moment become a working model of the nearer cosmos; in this it echoed once more the great banqueting houses of Ardres and Calais, with their elaborate canvas roofs painted with the elements, the planets and the stars. But like theirs its glory was fleeting. The old Elizabethan Banqueting House, enough of a theatre to have provided the setting for performances of plays and the first of the Jacobean masques, had come to the end of its days. Even while *Blackness* was in production, George Weale, the Clerk of Works, was busy 'drawinge of the ground plott of parte of Whitehall for the newe intended buildinge of the banquettinge house with the gatehouse and raunge of buildinges on the west side of the Courte', and Robert Stickells his colleague was drawing the 'uprightes' or elevations from them.[34] In the following year Toby Samways was paid a lesser amount 'for his paynes in drawing the plott for the banquet house',[35] possibly working copies of his colleagues' designs, and a few months after the performance of *Hymenaei* on 5 January the bricklayers began their work on the new foundations. The 'old rotten, sleight builded'[36] house had by then been demolished.

→ this discrepancy resides in the far refer to Dessen Jonson & what says about masque text being different from actual performance

II SERLIAN THEATRES

8
The Christ Church theatre

If, as seems possible, the 'iij rounde skaffold*es*' installed in the Banqueting House in 1584–5 did constitute an auditorium of the U-shaped type that had occasionally been favoured in Italy, the likeliest source of its inspiration will not have been the Italian theatres themselves, but the woodcuts illustrating Sebastiano Serlio's *Il secondo libro di perspettiva* (Paris, 1545). The most remarkable of the segmental auditoria of Italy, the Teatro Olimpico at Vicenza, was first occupied by an audience only in 1585,[1] and Scamozzi's 'antique' scenic theatre at Sabbioneta was not yet built.[2] Generally the new scenic playhouses of the Continent retained the rectangular auditoria of earlier courtly entertainments, and Giorgio Vasari's theatre at the Palazzo Vecchio in Florence, constructed in 1565, carried on a tradition that was by then many years old. A proscenium border framed a perspective scene, and seating degrees were constructed straight along the remaining walls of the chamber.[3] Such a pattern had been seen at Lyons in 1549 and was later to influence Buontalenti's famous Medici theatre at Florence.[4] When Inigo Jones, informed by his extensive travels and reading, began designing temporary masque theatres at Court he reverted to this type, and may have done so already for *The Masque of Blackness*. But Jones was not at this time on the strength of the Works; he contributed to the courtly entertainments as a freelance, just as Ben Jonson did. The Surveyor was one of King James's Scotsmen, Sir David Cuningham, an office-holder with little record of architectural practice who left much of the design work to the Comptroller, Simon Basil. Basil succeeded to the Surveyorship itself in 1606, having already achieved two things of great importance for our enquiry: he had studied the architectural works of Serlio, and he had designed a Serlian theatre in the hall at Christ Church, Oxford, in August 1605.

The occasion was the annual Act of the university, when rhetorical exercises were held in a special auditorium constructed in St Mary's, the university church. Other ceremonies were customarily performed in connection with this event, and chief among them in 1605 was a sequence of plays produced at Christ Church. In this year James I and his court visited the university, and for three successive nights beginning on 27 August attended the plays. A theatre had been set up in the hall, not by the college itself but by the Royal Works, whose carpenters had been specially sent up from Whitehall:

Ffor the better contrivinge and finishinge of their stages, seates, and scaffoldes in Saint Maries and Christchurch, they intertayned two of his Majesties Master Carpenters, and they had the advise of the Comptroler of his Workes.[5]

The Cambridge visitor who made these attributions also recorded that the scenes and stage were constructed on the advice of 'Mr. Jones a great travellor', doubtless Inigo.

The plays were of an academic sort, at once learned and facetious. The three evening productions, in Latin, represented the whole range of the drama, for in accord with the ancient division found in Vitruvius and his Renaissance commentators the authorities had chosen a tragedy, a comedy and a satyr play. The satyr play, *Alba*, was performed first, on the Tuesday night; it was followed successively by the tragedy, *Ajax Flagellifer*, and the moral comedy, Matthew Gwinne's *Vertumnus*. All were staged at Christ Church, as was an English pastoral, Samuel Daniel's *Arcadia Reformed*, given on the morning after the main series had concluded. One of the Latin plays, *Vertumnus*, is extant and owes little to the classical Plautine tradition;[6] and a description of *Ajax Flagellifer* made by Isaac Wake, who had been among the audience, reveals it to have been a mixed affair with three stage settings which were changed during the course of the performance, much to the admiration of the spectators.[7] The satyr play, partly written by Robert Burton,[8] told the story of Pomona and her rival lovers, but it also had a magus in it, and '5. or 6. men almost naked' as well as 'Satyres', 'nymphes' and 'sylvanes'.[9] Like the *Ajax*, it seems to have been a formless, energetic romp.

Both Inigo Jones and Simon Basil responded to the challenge of these plays and their royal occasion by appealing to classical precedent. Jones, responsible for the stage and scene, resorted to Vitruvius for inspiration, providing a changeable set of updated classical *periaktoi* painted with perspective settings.[10] Basil was rather less adventurous. His drawing for the auditorium survives (plate 28),[11] and shows that he turned to a less learned but more immediately useful source in Serlio's *Architettura*. Here he found a series of woodcuts of a model scenic theatre, including three generic scenes which he passed over, choosing to concentrate instead on the plan and section of the auditorium (plates 29 and 30). He was, after all, responsible only for the house side of the theatre; the stage side could safely be left to Jones. His own drawing imitates Serlio in offering both a plan and a long section, and in showing a *cavea* of raked seating disposed in a U-shaped pattern.

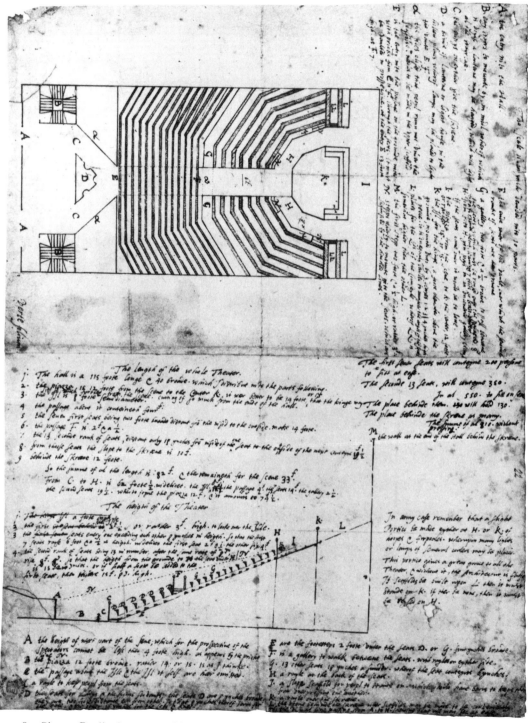

28 Simon Basil, theatre at Christ Church, Oxford (1605).

It had been Serlio's intention to press as much as he could of the form of an ancient Roman theatre into the narrow rectangular space afforded by a Renaissance courtyard or great hall. His scenes, which replace the ancient *frons scenae* with a perspective painted on receding wings, show how far the illusionist techniques of Italian scene painting had proceeded by mid-century under the guidance of such practitioners as Baldassare Peruzzi, Serlio's acknowledged master. But the auditorium stays closer to its ancient model, providing a semicircular orchestra surrounded by special seats for the noblest spectators. A full *cavea* of degrees sweeps round the orchestra on the side opposite the stage, so that five rows retain the semicircular plan. Beyond them a gangway and further arcs of seating are cut off to each side by the lateral walls of the court or hall, with the result that each degree is only a segment of a circle. All this is repeated in the Christ Church drawing, save that here the curves of Serlio's original have been replaced by a polygonal structure, doubtless with an eye to economy, straight boards requiring much less labour to prepare than composite curved ones. Serlio's range of seats extends as far as the requirements dictate and space allows, and to the rear there is room – expressed more clearly in the section than in the plan – for standing places for the 'plebe'. Similarly the Christ Church design makes provision for standing places at the rear of the hall, and this too is better seen in the section.

Marginal comments written on Basil's drawing also bear witness to its Serlian inspiration. The seating is arranged hierarchically, as it is in the *Architettura*, ranging from front benches for ladies and courtiers, through the group of thirteen narrower seats for the mass of the audience to the standing room or place for additional scaffolds marked at I and L in the section. The floor-level interval between the stage and the seating is repeatedly called the 'piazza', a term borrowed from the later editions of Serlio's work.[12] Even some of the dimensions appear to have been carried over directly from the source. Measured in terms of the squaring of the forestage, Serlio's orchestra is 24 units wide; at Christ Church the analogous feature is 24 ft across. The Italian's woodcuts are not explicitly scaled, but in his text he suggests that we take each of the squares as representing 2 ft.[13] By this scale his piazza is 12 ft deep and the forestage 4 ft high. So they are too in the Oxford drawing. Serlio's seats are 2 ft from front to back, and so are those in the front – and most important – range at Christ Church.

But Christ Church was no Italian *palazzo*, and James's Court had its own special requirements. The king's seat is placed on a foot-high central 'Isle' occupying most of what Serlio left as a half-round orchestra raised 'un mezzo piede' (half a foot) above the piazza level. The Isle is reached by three shallow steps which invade the piazza, and to either side this floor-level interval is further diminished by boxes for the lords of the Privy Council, an arrangement quite alien to Serlio's almost archaeological scheme. At every point, indeed, the Christ Church drawing is more practical and detailed than its Italian source. It is particularly concerned to give full information about the method of access by way of a lobby beneath the rear of the house. Stairs lead up to the highest levels from either side of the entrance, and a carefully judged *vomitorium* conducts the royal party and nobility directly towards the royal Isle and the *cavea* by means of a passage 'vaulted in prospectiue'. Serlio offered only the most perfunctory indications of how such things should be arranged, but the marginal comments show that the English designer was constantly aware of the actual problems faced by those who had to manage the assembly and dispersal of a large audience. The stairs in the back corners are 'easy stayrs to mounte by, in midl wherof which is voyde [the stairs indicated are open newel] a lanterne may bee hanged, which will light al the stayrcase'. For illumination in the main part of the lobby there is 'a kinde of lanterne or light house, in the hollow places wherof lamps may bee placed to light the vaute E. F.'. Even the possibility that the lords and ladies might lose their way among the props of the scaffold is foreseen: 'the sides closed that peopl runn not vnder the scaffolde. needles [studs or props] to bee made in the vpper scaffold.' The designer has noticed that the vomitory passage must be higher, for headroom, than the lateral access gangway under which it passes, and he makes the necessary detailed provision: 'G. a gallery two foote & a $\frac{1}{2}$ broade to pass betweene the seats. which must bee raysed ouer the passage ∞, 8 *ynches* to pass rounde about, leauing 7 foote at least vnder'.

The woodcuts of the *Architettura* appear, as they lie there on the page, to offer a definitive scheme for a scenic stage and neo-Roman auditorium, but in the text Serlio is always alive to the possibility of variation because of local conditions. At the suggested scale his plan indicates a width of 68 ft, but he describes as an alternative an auditorium he had designed at Vicenza, 60 ft wide by 80 ft deep.[14] We shall have cause to investigate this flexibility in Serlio's scheme in a later chapter; for the moment we need only observe that Basil entered fully into its spirit. As he worked on the drawing he saw that the depth of the piazza, taken from Serlio as 12 ft, needed to be increased. At first he wrote, keying his comment to the plan, 'I. the piazza from the scene, to K. the center, 12 foote.' Then he added, squeezing the words between lines previously inked, 'or rather 14. or 15.' In the list of items contributing to 'The length of the whole Theater' he gave a reason for his change of mind: '2. the piazza is 12 foote from the scene to the Center K. [Then, added later:] it wer better to bee 14 foote, / or 15 \ that the kinge may sit so much further from the scene. cutting of so much from the ende of the hall.' In order to give the king a proper view of the whole stage it seemed best, on reflection, to move his seat back three feet, and with it the plan of the rest of the auditorium, with the result that an equivalent three feet would be cut off the standing room at the rear. This move may have been intended to bring the centre K to a point 20 ft

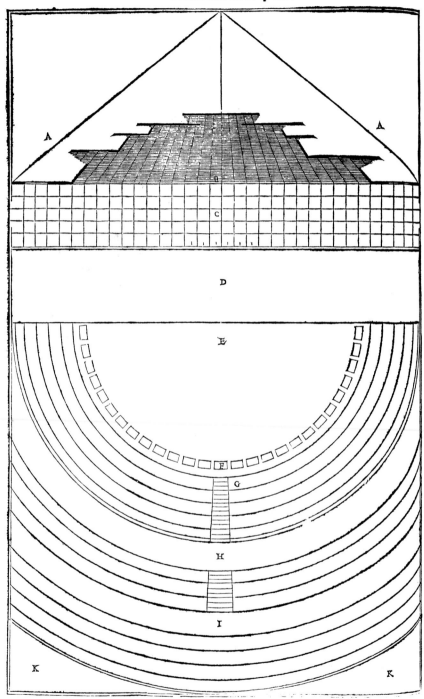

29   Sebastiano Serlio, *Il secondo libro di perspettiva* (Paris, 1545), theatre plan.

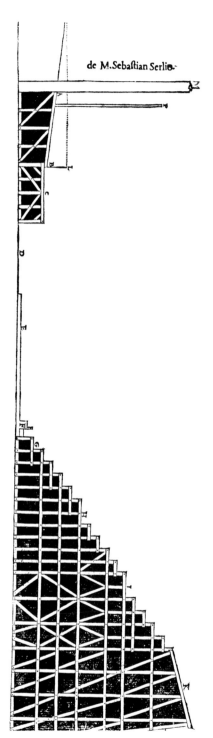

30   Sebastiano Serlio, *Il secondo libro di perspettiva*, theatre section.

from the scene proper (the sum of the 5 ft level forestage and the 15 ft piazza). If the king was positioned there the full width of the scene would have subtended an angle of 90° at his eye, the angle usually judged to represent a comfortable field of vision.[15] The shift appears to have had nothing to do with any more exacting theory of perspective than this: it seems clear, for example, that the king sat well below the level of the horizon established in Jones's scenes, even though *The Masque of Blackness* had earlier been staged with a due regard for such matters.

The question of the royal halpace, the most obvious addition to the Serlian model, caused the designer a good deal of trouble. The king's view of the scene had to be considered, but so did that of the people sitting on the benches. In the notes on 'The heigth of the Theater' we find '2 the first seat behind the Isle $2\frac{f}{2}$. or rather 3^f. high. to looke ouer the Isle', the latter clause a further change of mind. In the section 'the passage about the Isle & the Isl it self are heer omitted', though for what reason is not clear. The omission seems to have led to some confusion in the handling of the section, for while the depth of the piazza is correctly repeated from the plan the central part of the seating is brought forward 12 ft to its edge, with the result that the whole auditorium is shortened. But, for reasons which we shall discover in a moment, the upper range of seating is rendered some 2 ft deeper in the section than in the plan, and overall the auditorium is therefore given as only some 10 ft shorter than it should be. This confusion is carried over into a note on the length of the theatre:

From C. to H. is 62 foot $\frac{1}{2}$. uidelicet. the Isle $8\frac{f}{2}$ [*sic*] / 8^f \ the passage 4^f the / 7 \ seats 14^f. the gallery $2\frac{1}{2}$. the second seats $19\frac{1}{2}$. wherto joyne the piazza 12f, & it amounts to $74\frac{f}{2}$.

Not according to my arithmetic it doesn't. Basil seems to have been thrown into error by his need to include the Isle somewhat awkwardly in the Serlian scheme.

That the Isle caused difficulties for the draftsman is obvious enough, but there was worse to come. When the auditorium had been constructed in the hall a group of courtiers inspected it and found themselves in disagreement about the placing of the king's seat:

They (but especiallie *Suff*[*olk*]) vtterlie disliked the stage att Christchurch, and above all, the place appointed for the chayre of estate because yt was no higher and the kinge soe placed that the Auditory could see but his cheeke onlie. this dislike of the Earle of *Suff*[*olk*] much troubled the *Vicechancelor*, and all the workmen, yet they stood in defence of the thinge done, and maynteyned that by the art *p*erspective the kinge should behould all better then if he sat higher.[16]

There was a prolonged debate, in which the Chancellor himself – Thomas Sackville, Earl of Dorset, the part author of *Gorboduc* – supported the design provided by the Works. But this was Oxford, and a compromise emerged:

126

in the end the place was removed, and sett in the midst of the hall, but too farr from the stage (vizt) xxviij. feete, soe that there were manye longe speeches delivered, which neyther the kinge nor anye neere him could well heare or vnderstand.[17]

Quite what such radical surgery did to the original scheme we do not know. The drawing antedates it, but there is Wake's description of the auditorium in its revised state:

From the floorboards of the hall right up to the lofty trusses of the roof, great wedges (of degrees) were fixed to the walls in an arc. In the middle of the *cavea* the royal throne was set up for the princes, surrounded by a balustrade; flanking it to either side lay boxes for the nobles; the remaining space between the throne and the stage was set a little lower, for young women and ladies.[18]

Evidently the first range of seating, intended for the ladies, was taken down; the Isle was moved back into the space thus vacated, and new seats were constructed, doubtless parallel with the lateral walls, in the much enlarged piazza. The university, in the persons of the Chancellor and Vice-Chancellor, appears to have been alive to the experiment in neo-Vitruvian scenery and Serlian auditorium design, while the Court, despite their experience with *The Masque of Blackness* the previous January, sought to impose a more traditional pattern in which the monarch was set prominently in view.

Whatever became of his scheme in practice, one aspect of Basil's drawing deserves special notice. The rectangle within which the auditorium is planned is 4 ins by 8 ins on the sheet, representing, at the scale of 'an ynch deuided into 10 parts', 40 ft by 80 ft, an exact double square. These dimensions slightly regularize the actual requirements of the hall, for according to one of the notes 'the summe of al the length is . 82^f & ther remaineth for the scene 33^f', a total of 115 ft. The interior of Christ Church hall is indeed within a few inches of 40 ft by 115 ft, dimensions which Basil cites. Nevertheless some imprecision is introduced because the dimensions listed under the heading 'The length of the whole Theater' are measured radially between the arcs which have been scored on the paper as an underdrawing on which the polygonal arrangement of benches is located. Thus while the front benches are correctly 2 ft apart measured radially at the angles, they are something less than that measured straight across. The same variation applies to the Isle, the gangways and the rear degrees. The distance from the centre K to the back of the rear bench may therefore be correctly stated, as it is in the notes, as 8 ft for the Isle + 4 ft for the passage + 14 ft for seven seats + 2 ft 6 ins for the gangway + 19 ft 6 ins for the rear seats, for a total of 48 ft; but measured axially down the centre of the theatre the same interval is only 46 ft. The difference accounts for the 2 ft variation between the length of the auditorium as drawn and as noted. Far more important, it points up the regularizing impulse that lies behind the whole design. The width of the orchestra in Serlio's plan is 24 squares, and in the Christ Church drawing the analogous feature is 24 ft across. In Serlio this basic dimension is repeated in the width of the *occhio*, or gap between the front wings through which the perspective is viewed, and it is commensurately related to the piazza depth of 6 squares. Similarly in the Christ Church design the piazza's original depth of 12 ft is just half the 'orchestra' width of 24 ft; and this in turn is half the depth to the rear benches, measured radially, of 48 ft. Basil's auditorium, seen in this way – as indeed the author sees it in his own notes – is a regular piece of proportionate design. Even the width of the Isle, at 16 ft, is proportioned at one-third the depth of the seated *cavea*, and the width of the passage leading to it at one-eighth.

We shall have reason, in a later chapter, to observe that the Christ Church drawing is far from exhaustive in its borrowings from Serlio, but neither is its resemblance to the source superficial or merely approximate. It finds some of its dimensions there, and much of its system of proportion. In two respects it adds to Serlio. First, as we have seen, it tackles detailed problems of access and escape; and second, it provides a significant feature not found in the model, the 'Portico' which is raised at the rear of the *cavea*. Unfortunately the portico is not shown in the drawing, but it is specified in a long note:

In anny case remenber [*sic*] that a slight Portico bee made eyther at H. or K. of hoopes & firrpoales. wherupon many lights or lamps of seueral coulers may be placed. This portico giues a great grace to all the Theater, & without it, the Architectur is false. If scaffolds bee built upon L. then it must stande on K. if ther bee none, then it must bee reysed on H.

Clearly what is intended is a colonnade, or more likely – in view of the 'hoopes' – an arcade, which will close off the composition of the auditorium in a manner reminiscent of the theatres of antiquity. Such surely is the implication of the phrase that without it 'the Architectur is false'. The portico – what de Witt had called the 'porticus' at the Swan – is to be there for the sake of correctness, of truth to a classical ideal. It is a reminder to everyone who enters the building that there is such a thing as true architecture, and that this theatre is an example of it. The *cavea* is true both because of its fidelity to ancient theatrical models as interpreted by Serlio, and because it follows ancient example in matters of proportion.

The Christ Church design is the first adequately documented neo-Roman theatre in England. (It is, in addition, the earliest extant theatre plan.) But it was not altogether unique in its time, for in naming their 'Theater' in Shoreditch John Brayne and James Burbage had also appealed to classical models, the models that had previously inspired the banqueting houses at Ardres and Calais. Their amphitheatre was 'Roman' in association, and to some extent in spirit. It imitated an antique idea without archaeological precision. But Basil's commission was for an indoor theatre and he could readily turn to the pages of the *Architettura* to find the solutions to most of his problems of design. There the great semicircular *cavea* of antiquity had been restated in a manner fitted to a rectangular hall or court; the essence of the Roman form had been preserved, at least in the auditorium, and some indication given of a correct proportionality. The builders of the Theater, the Curtain and the Rose will have found Serlio less immediately useful for their purposes, if indeed they knew his work at all. But in their way they were engaged in a similar rediscovery of ancient forms suited to modern conditions, and they succeeded in setting the pattern for a greater theatrical age.

9
Serlio's theatre plan

When Simon Basil leafed through the pages of the *Architettura* he found that the theatre scheme was presented, not so much as a self-sufficient lesson in itself, but as a case history illustrating some of the more arcane problems of perspective. The First and Second Books had originally been published, in Paris in 1545, as works on this subject rather than on architecture proper, though of course it was seen as a necessary part of any architect's skill. The method of their discourse is to take the reader carefully through first principles, point by point, the text often indicating how the many diagrams are to be interpreted. By the time we reach the paragraphs on theatre design in the Second Book we have become initiates in this mystery of perspective: we know how to construct a squared floor, how to project its orthogonals to the horizon, how to erect verticals within the system and how to place them at measurable distances from the picture plane. The 'distance point' construction has become familiar, and we have been taught how to think in terms of a fixed and necessary station point. In short, we are ready to move from the simple case of a perspective composition made on a two-dimensional panel, as in a history painting, to the more complex one of a scene constructed in three dimensions, but foreshortened. Here Serlio's text leaves the reader to work out what he can from the illustrations, turning instead to an altogether less geometrical account of the parts of the stage and auditorium, the magnificence with which they can be presented, the visual content and construction of the three generic Scenes, and the means by which all can be lit. The geometry of the stage is touched on, but lightly; that of the auditorium is hardly treated at all. Yet the woodcuts continue the instruction in perspective with which the book began, and do so in meticulous detail. The reader, however, must find all this out by independent study, using the principles already learned.

The more difficult lesson in perspective we may safely leave until later; for the moment we are concerned only with the evolution of Serlio's auditorium design (plate 29). It is, as he tells us, intended to include as much as possible of the theatre of the ancient world within the straitened confines of a modern *grande salle* or palazzo courtyard:

and for that a man can hardly finde any Halls how great soeuer, wherein he can place a Theater without imperfection and impediment; therefore to follow Antiquities, according to my power and abilitie, I haue made all such parts of these Theaters, as may stand in a Hall.[1]

Serlio thinks of the ancient *cavea* form as being only partly realizable in a rectangular space, and at the front of the auditorium given in his plan there is a neo-Roman semicircular 'orchestra' surrounded by a full semicircular arc of wooden degrees. Here the senators sit on seats below, and ladies of rank occupy the degrees behind them. Beyond this fully expressed half-round the outer access passages and seats become only segmental in plan, as the sides of a complete *cavea* are cut off by the lateral walls. Even so, the curve of the seating retains something of the Roman form, and successive rows can be extended backwards as far as space will permit:

The places marked K. [on the plan] must bee made so great backward as the Hall will afford, which is made somewhat slooping, that the people may see one ouer the others head.[2]

In the section Serlio shows the rearmost standing room carrying much further back than in the plan, with the incidental result that in the original edition his block is a little larger than the leaf on which it has to print, so that the woodcut is mercilessly topped and tailed. This capacity to admit variation shows how flexible is his attitude to the ancient model: he will do what he can to imitate it, but only within the necessary constraints imposed by contemporary ideas of the theatre.

In matters of theory Serlio held the text of Vitruvius in high regard; higher, indeed, than the actual monuments of antiquity. Digging and measuring among the excavated ruins of the Theatre of Marcellus in Rome, he found evidence that 'the Dorica Cornice, although it be very full of members, and well wrought, yet I found it to differ much from Vitruuius instructions'.[3] He observed that the 'wonderfull works' of the Greeks were now alas 'almost all spoyled and cast downe', and the Roman workmen had sometimes been 'licencious' in their departures from the established canons of design. But Vitruvius, who had studied the Greeks, could be relied on. The various measured plans and elevations of ancient theatres which appear in Serlio's Third Book must therefore be seen as concrete manifestations of the purer idea which is expressed in Vitruvius's Fifth. For it is here, after the preliminary discussion of the best favoured site and the longer exploration of the theme of harmonics and the transmission of sound, that the Roman turns to a canonical prescription of the plan.

The plan of the theatre itself is to be constructed as follows. Having fixed upon the principal centre, draw a line of circumference equivalent to what is to be the perimeter at the bottom, and in it inscribe four equilateral triangles, at equal distances apart and touching the boundary line of the circle, as the astrologers do in

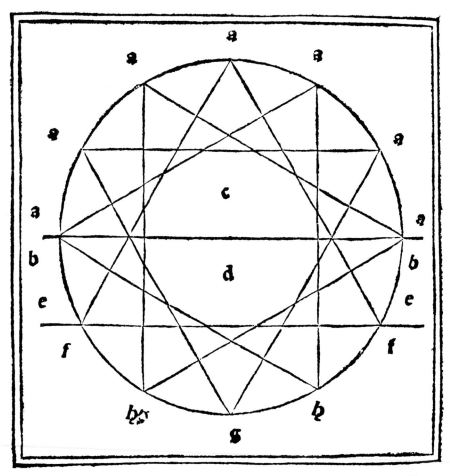

31   Vitruvian diagram of a theatre. Vitruvius Pollio, *Architectura libri decem* (Lyons, 1523).

a figure of the twelve signs of the zodiac, when they are making computations from the musical harmony of the stars.[4]

The introduction of the zodiac here seems merely incidental, and its peculiar relevance to the business in hand is not explained. There was, however, always a touch of the Platonist in Vitruvius, no matter how practical and concrete his particular advice, and it seems that he assumed, almost so easily as to find further explanation unnecessary, that a monumental public building like a theatre would require a cosmic as well as a human and physical rationale. We who have read of the ceiling at Calais and the Taurus in the Heavens at the Red Bull know how widespread that assumption has been in history, but we shall find little warrant in Vitruvius for making a great fuss

132

about it. His diagram (plate 31) is based on that of the so-called triplicities, a demonstration of the network of affinities and oppositions that astrologers thought energized the belt of the zodiac. But Vitruvius, having accepted this cosmic model, made nothing further out of its astrological possibilities. He used it instead simply to govern the proportional setting out of the stage and *cavea*. The perimeter of the circle defined the limits of the orchestra. The diameter located the front of the stage, whose depth to the *scaena* was yielded by the distance between the diameter and the base of one of the triangles lying parallel to it. Since in fact this distance was half the radius of the circle the diagram itself was of small consequence: the same result might have been obtained, as it was in most parts of the design, simply by appealing to the diameter of the orchestra as a standard measure. The stage depth in the Vitruvian scheme is one-quarter the width of the orchestra. The astrological diagram is more fully exploited in the advice to place the *cavea* stairs at points around the orchestra defined by the angles of the triangles. Seven sets, including those coinciding with the diameter of the circle, are to lead up to the first cross aisle. Beyond that the relevance of the diagram becomes more obscure, as the higher steps are laid out at intervals between the lower ones. The remaining five points of the twelve-point diagram locate the stage entrances: a central 'royal door', two to the flanking *hospitalia*, and two more along the surface of the *scaena* roughly indicating passages of entrance. With this unmysterious twelve-point arrangement Vitruvius comes to an end of his exploitation of the astrological model. The remainder of his canons of proportion derive from fractions of the orchestra width or, in matters such as the size of the degrees or the height of the stage, from common necessity as dictated by the size of the human body.

When Alberti turned to the design of ancient theatres in his *De re aedificatura* (c. 1450–72) he offered a summary of much of the Vitruvian argument, but left out all reference to the astrological diagram. He began with a brief historical and typological survey, then proceeded to an account of the parts of a theatre, carefully distinguishing – as Vitruvius had done – between the Roman and the Greek. A more detailed description followed, in which Alberti sometimes slipped into a prescriptive rather than an historical mode. Of the *cavea* he wrote:

I shall here describe one of these Structures which I think the most compleat and perfect of any . . . The first or lowest Seat must not be upon the very Level of the Area, but be raised upon a Wall . . . from the Top of which Wall the Seats must take their first Flight: And in the smallest Theatres, this Wall must never be less than seven Foot high . . . Among these Seats, spaces must be left at certain Distances for Passages into the middle Area, and for Stairs to go up from thence to those Seats . . . Of these Passages there should be seven principal ones, all directed exactly to the Center of the Area, and perfectly clear and open, at equal Distances from each other; and of these seven, one should be larger than the rest, answering to the middle of the

Semicircle, which I call the Master Entrance . . . Opposite to the Front of the Theatre was raised the Stage for the Actors, and every thing belonging to the Representation, and here sate the Nobles in peculiar and honourable Seats, separate from the common People, or perhaps in the middle Area in handsome Places erected for that Purpose. The *Pulpitum* or Stage, was made so large as to be fully sufficient for every thing that was to be acted upon it. It came forward equal to the Center of the Semicircle . . .[5]

Here much of the form of the Vitruvian layout is retained. The stage comes to the diameter of the orchestra, and seven entrance passages radiate through the seating degrees, evenly spaced. When he turns to the design of the stage and its entrances Alberti echoes the five-point system without any further appeal to an organizing geometry. The justifying astrological diagram has altogether disappeared, though it returns briefly, with no canonical or proportionate authority, in his description of the Roman circus:

Some tell us, that this was built in Imitation of the heavenly Bodies; for as the Heavens have twelve Houses, so the Circus has twelve Gates for Entrance; and as there are seven Planets, so this has seven Goals, lying from East to West at a good Distance one from the other, that through them the contending Chariots may hold their Course, as the Sun and Moon do through the Zodiac; which they did four-and-twenty Times, in Imitation of the four-and-twenty Hours.[6]

This system has no application to the theatre proper.

What, then, are we to make of Serlio's determination to include as complete a realization of the ancient theatre as he could within the confines of a modern hall or courtyard? It would not, I think, be altogether absurd to read his Comic Scene (plate 44) as offering in some sense – a highly compromised one – a version of the five-point *scaena*, radically transformed into a perspective vista. Here, after all, is a central portal akin perhaps to that described by Vitruvius, though hardly intended to be a practical stage entrance. The stage plan shows gaps behind the front wings large enough for such access, and it would be possible to interpret these as equivalent to the *hospitalia* passages of the Fifth Book. In the original edition of the Serlian scheme two further doors of entry are marked at either end of the level forestage, like those to either side of the *scaena* according to Vitruvius. Vitruvius was also the authority for the triple division into Comic, Tragic and Satyric Scenes, but neither of the latter is shown in Serlio's woodcuts with the level forestage of the first, and neither therefore complements the entries through the scene with others in front of it. Only the Comic Scene shows even the loosest analogical kinship with the principles of the antique *scaena*.

In front of the forestage Serlio provides a floor-level *proscenio* or *piazza della scena*, a feature unknown to Vitruvius but necessary in a theatre equipped with a large unified perspective scene, to prevent the audience from sitting too close to the stage. It also had its uses in a Renaissance theatre for the sort of dancing that involved members of the audience. In the auditorium proper there is a semicircular orchestra, or raised *piazza del Teatro*, with seats for the most important spectators placed along its perimeter. If the stage be considered, as it properly should, to include the *proscenio*, its front, lying on the diameter of the orchestra, agrees with the observations of Vitruvius and Alberti. The five rows of seating up to the first cross aisle constitute a compact antique *cavea*, but are entirely uncomplicated by the geometry of the twelve-point diagram. Only a central stairway is marked, or indeed required. The six other sets of steps which both Vitruvius and Alberti described as radiating through the *cavea* have disappeared. The whole width of this front section of the house equals that of the *scaena*, as it often did in the theatres of antiquity, and as it does in the woodcuts of the Theatre of Marcellus and that at Pola included in Serlio's Third Book. But like these the scenic theatre plan departs from Vitruvian guidance in failing to make the *scaena* twice as wide as the orchestra. Beyond the cross aisle the *cavea* is truncated to either side for practical reasons of space; and Serlio thinks of its rearward extension as adjustable to need, not defined by a proportionate or geometric construction. There is no *porticus* to close off the composition and work its acoustical magic on the actors' voices. In short, the theatre plan shows an auditorium which owes surprisingly little to the details of the Vitruvian text, and almost nothing at all to the famous astrological diagram. Yet its antique provenance is clear enough. A simpler and more commonly used auditorium plan would have placed the degrees along the three walls, leaving a rectangular floor at their feet, to be occupied by a *palco* for the noblest of the spectators. In choosing the semicircular and segmental form Serlio aimed to reproduce something of the design of the ancient theatre, but his attitude to Vitruvian authority was far from servile.

Not long after the publication in Paris of *Il secondo libro di perspettiva* Daniele Barbaro's edition of Vitruvius appeared in Venice, with illustrations by Andrea Palladio.[7] A certain ambiguity in the original Latin text led Palladio to draw the astrological diagram in his illustration of the Roman theatre to include the whole round of the *cavea*, not just – as Vitruvius had probably intended – that of the orchestra. The enlarged scale of the diagram relative to the plan led to a doubling of the depth of the stage, which now equalled one half, instead of one quarter, the width of the orchestra. By extending it to include the whole of the *cavea* plan Palladio was able to use the diagram to locate the first cross aisle, which he neatly centred along a series of its intersections (plate 32), but it now retained only the loosest connection with the placing of the five stage entrances. Where Vitruvius had not given canonical observations about the outward extent of the *cavea*, Palladio contained it within his circle, which also defined the depth of the portico behind the scena. His preliminary drawings for the Barbaro illustration are extant, and much less vigorously schematic than the woodcut

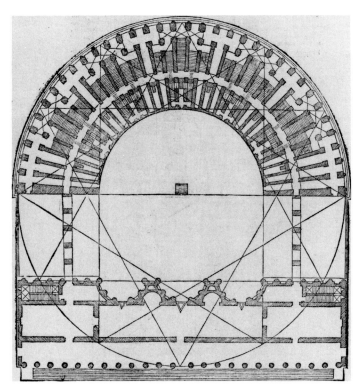

32   Andrea Palladio, Roman theatre scheme in Daniele Barbaro, *M. Vitruvii Pollionis de architectura* (Venice, 1567).

that was actually published, even while broadly agreeing with it. They show a thoughtful imprecision where the woodcut has hardened into dogma.[8]

Serlio's theatre plan represents a practical modern compromise, flexible, undogmatic. Yet it is firmly within the orbit of Renaissance design. In particular it follows the straightforward principles laid down in the second chapter of Vitruvius's First Book: Order, Arrangement, Eurythmy, Symmetry, Propriety and Economy. With respect to the last, the theatre will be made of wood, and no larger than the budget allows. Yet it will also be magnificent: 'the more such things cost, the more they are esteemed, for they are things which stately and great persons doe, which are enemies to nigardlinesse'.[9] The first four principles may profitably be taken together, for they are all aspects of Order, which 'gives due measure to the members of a work considered separately, and symmetrical agreement to the proportions of the whole'.[10] Arrangement is the fitness and elegance of the whole work, expressed by the technical means of the ground plan, elevation and perspective rendering. Eurythmy has rather to do with the right correspond-

136

ence between the parts of the work, which must be related according to a system of Symmetry. In ordinary modern English the word symmetry usually means a balance in composition, centred on one or more axes, so that parts of a work are exactly similar and mirror each other. Vitruvius' definition of the term is quite different:

Symmetry is a proper agreement between the members of the work itself, and relation between the different parts and the whole general scheme, in accordance with a certain part selected as standard.[11]

Serlio's theatre auditorium is of course 'symmetrical' in the modern sense, but it also shows the expected agreement between the parts denoted by the proper meaning of the word. The 'certain part selected as standard' constitutes a unit of measurement, in terms of which all the remaining parts of the work may be measured too. Where a building makes extensive use of the orders, as in the case of temples, the thickness of a column is commonly taken as the repeatable module; but it might equally be some other essential part, and Vitruvius cites the examples of the hole in a ballista and the interval between the tholepins (or rowlocks) in a ship. The last example is particularly apt because it reminds us of the human scale which such thinking seeks to preserve in everything built. The distance between the oars of a trireme is dictated by the size and reach of the unfortunate who is required to do the rowing. Equally the columns of a temple, though of infinitely varied scale, could be thought of as preserving the proportions of height and girth found in various types of human frame. In the Fourth Book Vitruvius tells how the Ionians developed rules for the orders: the Doric originally proportioned as a man's foot is to his height, 1 : 6; the Ionic made more slender to repeat the same proportion for a woman, 1 : 8; and the Corinthian the same, but with a taller capital.

To this way of thinking, proportionality is nowhere more readily and more obviously seen than in the human frame. 'In the human body', wrote Vitruvius, 'there is a kind of symmetrical harmony between forearm, foot, palm, finger, and other small parts; and so it is with perfect buildings.'[12] Later, in the Third Book on temples, he returned to this theme:

For the human body is so designed by nature that the face, from the chin to the top of the forehead and the lowest roots of the hair, is a tenth part of the whole height; the open hand from the wrist to the tip of the middle finger is just the same; the head from the chin to the crown is an eighth, and with the neck and shoulder from the top of the breast to the lowest roots of the hair is a sixth; from the middle of the breast to the summit of the crown is a fourth . . . The length of the foot is one sixth of the height of the body; of the forearm, one fourth; and the breadth of the breast is also one fourth. The other members, too, have their own symmetrical proportions, and it was by employing them that the famous painters and sculptors of antiquity attained to great and endless renown.[13]

We may be sceptical, sitting on a bus and scrutinizing our fellow passengers, about all this human regularity, but of course Vitruvius was not thinking of a particular citizen's less than perfect frame. He had in mind a well-proportioned type, not an individual, and already was guilty of planting the proportions he then went on to educe. The thought here is not without its delusions, but it was none the less influential for that.

Serlio was no more than conventional for his age in accepting the Vitruvian view of symmetry with little explicit reserve if a good deal of flexible inventiveness in practice. The language of the orders, as understood by most architects of the period, was one of proportional relations. Usually the language was expressed in its own, specifically architectural, terms: the proportion of the column, of its intercolumniation, its entablature and so forth. If pressed, a working builder might remember the legendary origin of his science in the study of the human body, but he would be unlikely to dwell on the matter. Architecture had established its own canons of order, and indeed in the work of such theoreticians as Cesariano and Palladio it elaborated others developed from Pythagorean theories of number, and especially from the musical consonances.[14] But for an understanding of Serlio's theatre plan we need look no further than the simpler precepts of Vitruvius, among them the insistence on the human origins of symmetry.

The plan's unit of measurement is not explicitly stated, but in beginning his discussion of the Scenes Serlio calls attention to the scaling possibilities of the squaring of the forestage: 'suppose that each Quadran containeth two foote on eyther side'.[15] These squares lead directly to those that run, acutely foreshortened, through the raked area of the scene, whose scaling they therefore dominate, as we shall see in a later chapter. By their measure the forestage is 34 units wide by 5 units deep. One of the main principles of symmetry – that the parts should be measured by units of the same system – is therefore honoured. We notice the same thing if we take the depth of the whole auditorium from the front of the raked scene to the back of the furthest degree: a distance of 40 units, or 80 ft at Serlio's own suggested scale. Similarly the orchestra, measured between the front risers of the degrees that surround it, is just 24 units wide. So is the distance between the front wings on the stage, the so-called *occhio* through which we see the foreshortened area. The location of the wall behind the stage is not given in the plan, but we can take its depth by means of compasses from the profile: the match is not very exact, but it is approximately 11 units from the stage front, or 17 from the diameter of the orchestra.[16] Thus the whole stage end of the house, including the *proscenio*, occupies a double square, 34 units wide and 17 deep. The front part of the auditorium – that which is described in a full semicircle – has a radius of 17 units.

It was Serlio's habit, when surveying the ruins of antiquity, to use the unit of measure that he supposed to have been employed by the original builders.

In this way he was able to express their detailed symmetry in the same terms by which they had been designed. His illustrations of the Pantheon are accompanied by a ruled bar giving the size of the antique unit of measurement:

This is the old Romish Palme, which is deuided into twelue fingers, and each finger is deuided into foure parts, which are called Minutes, by the which measure this present Figure, with all the parts following, was measured.[17]

The same unit serves for the Temple of Bacchus, but Vespasian's Temple of Peace is presented in terms of the ell, divided into 12 'ounces'.[18] Several other ancient measures are provided, but for the theatre and amphitheatre at Pola Serlio gives 'a moderne or vsuall foote' as the standard, apparently because the construction was 'measured [i.e. designed] by one that had more vnderstanding in casting, then in measuring',[19] and therefore lacked the systematic proportions that might have revealed the nature of the original standard unit. Accordingly Serlio has been forced to use his own modern unit, one that naturally fails to 'fit' the dimensions of the ancient site. Fortunately, however, he provides bars to accompany the illustrations of Pola, and from them it appears that the unit in question is the standard Venetian foot of the sixteenth century, given here as 171.5 mm to the half foot. In the later editions of the *Architettura* a special page of standard measures is given, and the Venetian half foot is illustrated: '*La metà del piede moderno, ouero Venetiano diuiso in oncie sei, e minuti trenta*' (half a modern Venetian foot, divided into six inches, or thirty minutes).[20] This is evidently the unit of measure used for the scenic theatre plan in the original edition of the Second Book. Here 30 squaring units along the forestage cover 171.5 mm: each square is one Venetian minute wide, and the scale of the drawing, at the suggested 2 ft to the square, is accordingly 1 : 120.

More important, however, than the discovery of the scale is the new recognition that this plan, like those of the ruins of antiquities in the Third Book, is proportioned throughout according to a standard of measurement proper to the work. Most of the major dimensions in the woodcut are expressible in Venetian *minuti* as integers: 24 *minuti* for the orchestra, 34 for the width of the house, 40 for the depth of the auditorium, and so on. We have noticed that it is a characteristic of Vitruvian thought to seek to relate the dimensions used in a building to those of the human frame. In part this is a matter of sheer necessity, for certain elements of a structure will have to retain a human scale for quite practical reasons, no matter how monumental or heroic the size of the whole. In theatres, as Vitruvius observed,

There are ... some things which, for utility's sake, must be made of the same size in a small theatre, and a large one: such as the steps, curved cross-aisles, their parapets, the passages, stairways, stages, tribunals, and any other things which occur that make it necessary to give up symmetry so as not to interfere with utility.[21]

In Serlio's design the height of the stage is limited by the height of a man: 'First, you must make a Scaffold, which must bee as high as a mans eye will reach, looking directly forward.'[22] This provision seems to have nothing to do with the perspective arrangements of the scene, and it is possible that another Vitruvian precept is the source:

The height of this platform [i.e. the stage] must be not more than five feet, in order that those who sit in the orchestra may be able to see the performances of all the actors.[23]

Again the depth of the seating degrees, at one minute on the page or 2 ft as scaled, echoes a dimension given by Vitruvius:

The steps for the spectators' places, where the seats are arranged, should be not less than a foot and a palm in height, nor more than a foot and six fingers; their depth should be fixed at not more than two and a half feet, nor less than two feet.[24]

An ancient Roman foot, as illustrated by Serlio in the Third Book (for example, on fol. 47[a]) was about 0.85 of a modern Venetian one, so that the figures just quoted for the degree depth would range between 1.7 and 2.1 Venetian feet. In adopting 2 ft as his standard Serlio was following the ancient authority in terms of actual dimension; but he went further and made this unit – one with a properly human basis, so to speak – the fundamental measure of his theatre. The house is designed according to the age-old principle of putting bottoms onto seats.

Nor does the human proportionality of the theatre end with the repeated unit of its *symmetria*. We have observed that the plan seems to borrow remarkably little from the astrological diagram with which Vitruvius proportioned his exemplary theatre. Serlio's reticence here is not surprising, for the geometrical construction of the diagram, consisting as it does of equilateral triangles inscribed within a circle, produces ratios which, if followed with a pedantic thoroughness, are expressed in such figures as $1 : \sqrt{3}$ or $1 : \sqrt{2}$. These values are irrational, not expressible (except in a few special cases) in whole numbers; they are consequently inimical to the *symmetria* of repeated units to which both Vitruvius and his Renaissance follower were generally wedded. Vitruvius avoided the problem by exploiting only one actual ratio from the diagram – that between the radius and the distance from the centre to the base of one of the triangles – and that happened to be the perfectly rational $2 : 1$. For the rest he contented himself with following the twelve-point directions given by the figure, a quite different matter from its ratios of quantity. Some of his Renaissance interpreters went further and located parts of their illustrative theatres on various intersections of the diagram in such a way that irrational ratios were involved. We have noticed that Palladio, in his illustration of Barbaro's commentary (plate 32), located the cross aisle in the *cavea* at a point defined by the diagram but irrationally $\frac{1}{\sqrt{2}}$ of the whole radius away from the centre. Yet even he seems to have made no further use of the diagram's many proportional possibilities. It appears that the usual way of dealing with the irrational ratios contained in the geometrical construction was to ignore them. Palladio's whole *cavea* is thus made exactly twice as wide as his orchestra, the depth of the *scaena* equals the orchestra radius, and so on. Except for the case of the cross aisle, only the rational proportions inherent in the diagram are used.

Yet Serlio, for all his ignoring the twelve-point directionality of the Vitruvian scheme, appears to have adopted just this same $\sqrt{2}$ proportionality for the first cross aisle that we found in Palladio. The radius to the front of the aisle is 17 of his square units, while that of the orchestra is 12. These figures are in mathematics not quite related as $\sqrt{2}$ is to 1, but in practice they are identical with that ratio (they represent 1.417 : 1, as against the true value of 1.414 : 1). Evidently Serlio picked on a set of numbers that would express the essentially irrational $\sqrt{2}$ relation in terms of integers, so that he could combine the geometric way of setting out with the commensurate. The same specific numbers had been used by Cesariano to illustrate the proportions of an atrium generated from the square by means of the diagonal.[25] He gave the square as 12 by 12, and the diagonal as 5 units more, so that the whole plan was proportioned 12 : 17. Similarly Barbaro, in a recondite array of elaborated simple ratios, included the numbers 12 : 34 as one of the proportions that were capable of delighting the senses, calling it 'duple undecupartiens duodecimas'.[26] For Cesariano the $\sqrt{2}$ ratio was capable of expression in at least one pair of integers, and these are the ones used by Serlio in the theatre scheme. This way of having his cake and eating it too presumably accounts for the peculiar dimensions of his theatre as set out in the plan. The 80 ft length, from scene to back wall, is neat and regular, and coincides with the dimension of the theatre which Serlio mentions having designed at one of the Porto palaces at Vicenza. But the 68 ft width is a strange dimension to give an exemplary design. The Vicenzan theatre alluded to in the text was 60 ft wide, just three-fourths of its length, but 68 ft bears no similar proportionate relation to a length of 80 ft.

Yet it is as well to remember that Serlio considered the backwards extension of the plan as a flexible matter. More standing room might be added as required, and the section is designed with one more degree than the plan, and with an overall length well in excess of 80 ft. The clue to the meaning of the curious 34-unit width of the house emerges when we consider the full half-circle of the first group of degrees in association with the stage as the core which properly expresses the idea of the theatre. Here is the rectangular stage end confronted by the half-circle of the house side in the familiar Roman figure of the D-shape. The whole is scaled to be inscribed within a 34-unit square. The back wall, whose position must be transferred from the section, is approximately 17 units from the front of the orchestra;

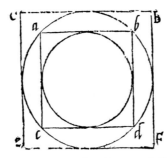

33 Sebastiano Serlio, *The First Booke of Architecture* (1611), *ad quadratum* diagram.

the semi-circle of degrees has a 17-unit radius. Within this marriage of square and circle lies the 24-unit orchestra, with the 24-unit wide *occhio* opposed to it. These are related to the larger square and circle in the ratio 1 : $\sqrt{2}$.

Already, early in the series of demonstrations that constitute the course of the First Book, Serlio has led us to contemplate the proportionality of a figure which combines the square and the circle in much the same way as this theatre plan (plate 33):

If within a foure square you make a Circle which toucheth the foure sides of the said foure square, and without the said foure square an other Circle which toucheth the corners marked A.B.C.D. Then the outmost Circle must bee once as great againe as the innermost: and then if about the greatest Circle you make another foure square as C.D.E.F. then the two foure squares must in like sort be once as great againe as the other.

If we were to consider the theatre plan as an example of this quadrate diagram we should find the side walls of the house located on the lines c–e and b–f, the wall behind the stage on c–b, the front of the orchestra on the diameter parallel to *a–b*, the orchestra on the smaller circle and the rear of the front *cavea* on the larger.

Clearly Serlio found something attractive in this geometrical regularity, and we shall do well to ask what caused him to embrace it so thoroughly. We find a clue in the passage in the First Book that immediately precedes the quadrate demonstration. A square has just been defined in terms of its construction out of 'foure euen long lines'. The diagonal is so called 'because it deuideth the foure corners into two euen parts'. One notices the repeated use of the word 'even': Serlio is interested in the simple equality of one part of a figure to another. He then goes on to introduce the aim of the construction-al geometry that forms the next part of his exposition:

Now when a workeman hath seene a forme of some of the most necessary Superficies, hee must proceed further, and learne to augment or diminish the same, and to turne them into other formes: but yet in such sort, that they may haue euen parts in them.[27]

The 'euen parts' that he now proceeds to demonstrate are even in area. The first stage is to show how to double the area of a square by forming another on the basis of its diagonal:

And first, if out of the length of the Diagonus aforesayd, by the adding of three other euen long lines, hee maketh another foure square: that foure square shal be once as great againe as the first . . .[28]

Then follows the proof, and after it the squares and circles diagram with its accompanying text. And now for the first time the architect allows himself a practical application of so much theory:

By this also, the projecture or the foote of the Bases of the Thuscane Columnes or Pillars, and also the bredth of the fundation of them vnderneath by Vertruuius declared, is set foorth.[29]

There is no need for us now to follow Serlio's argument through the successive pages of more and more complicated demonstrations. He has already shown the character of his work. From the most basic elements of geometry it moves by way of drawing-board constructions to the transformation of one figure into another proportionally related to it. The next stage in his discourse puts the matter exactly:

The workeman must yet proceed further, and learne to know how to change a Triangle into a Quadrangle, and also at last bring it to a right Quadrate, to the which I will set downe diuers formes.

The aim in this case is to keep all the various shapes equal in area, and several demonstration diagrams follow; but it might for other purposes have been to increase or diminish a given area by a determined proportion, and several folios are devoted to the theory and practice of similar triangles. Every step of the argument leads on to the next, but also calls for a particular architectural application. The quadrate method gives the proportion between the diameter of a Tuscan column and its base; the transformation of triangles to squares permits the measurement of area on the site; the geometry of similar triangles allows the architect to scale up or down in proportion; and so on.

The study of geometry leads to practical ends, among them the proportioning of buildings according to simple numerical ratios. A little later in the First Book Serlio offers seven 'Quadrangle proportions . . . which shal best serue for the vse of the workeman', principally for planning rooms; among them are the square, the square-and-a-quarter, the square-and-a-third, and so on up to the double square. Each is proportioned according to a straightforward ratio: $1:1$, $4:5$, $3:4$, $2:3$, $1:2$. Among them, however, is one that is different from all the others, for its larger side is equal to the diagonal of a square raised on the shorter:

The fourth, is called Diagonea, of the line Diagonus: which line diuideth the foure square Quadrate crosse through the middle, which Diagonall line being toucht from vnder to the end thereof vpwards with the Compasse, and so drawen, will shew you the length of the Diagonall Quadrangle: but from this proportion there can bee no rule in number well set downe.[30]

In fact the proportions of such a rectangle are $1 : \sqrt{2}$, or $1 : 1.414$, just the same irrational proportion that Serlio employed in the theatre plan, in the knowledge that in most cases 'from this proportion there can bee no rule in number well set downe'. Why, then, did he use it? And why did he include the *ad quadratum* diagram so boldly at the foot of the very title page of the First Book when it was originally published?

It was, of course, a much used proportion that had the authority of centuries of actual practice behind it.[31] It lent itself to work with compasses on the paper and with masons' lines on the building site. It appears in the twelfth-century additions made to the d'Honnecourt manuscript as the best method of setting out a cloister within a square yard, and it was extensively used – for good practical reasons – in mediaeval construction. Its appeal to Serlio, who was no pedant in his view of antiquity, might simply have been its traditional ubiquity. But there may be more to it than that.

Here I must crave the reader's patience yet again for another consultation with Serlio's mentally active text. Towards the end of the First Book, after so much discussion of the transformations of squares and triangles, there comes a series of ordinary practical hints: how to make a column fit firmly on its base, how to design urns, how to interconnect a floor out of short joists. All make some use of the geometrical principles previously introduced. The last of them concerns the design of a church door.:

If a workeman will make a Gate or a Doore in a Temple or a Church, which is to be proportioned according to the place, then he must take the widenesse within the Church, or else the bredth of the wall without: if the Church bee small, and haue Pilasters or Pillars within it: then he may take the widenesse betweene them, & set the same bredth in a foure square, that is, as high as broad, in which foure square, the Diagonall lines, and the other two crosse cutting lines will not onely shew you the widenes of the doore, but also the places and poynts of the ornaments of the same Doore, as you see here in this Figure [plate 34]. And although it should fall out, that you haue three doores to make in a Church, and to that ende cut three holes, yet you may obserue this proportion for the smallest of them. And although (gentle Reader) the crosse cutting thorow or deuiding is innumerable, yet for this time, lest I should be too tedious, I here end my Geometry.[32]

Serlio signs off a little too hastily, as was his custom. But Rudolf Wittkower has contributed a useful analysis of this design. Adding his own key-letters, he observes that Serlio

completes the central bay, in which the door should be placed, into a square (by drawing a line parallel to the base), draws the diagonals (AB, CD) and erects from

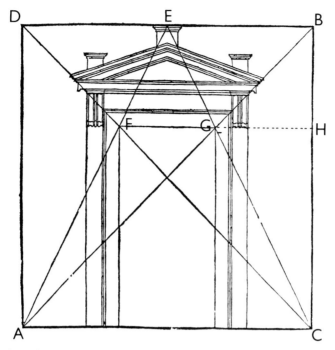

34   Sebastiano Serlio, *The First Booke of Architecture*, temple door design, with key letters added.

the two corners of the base an isosceles triangle (AEC). The intersections between the diagonals and the sides of the triangle (F, G) mark the height and width of the door. The drawing seems to suggest a geometrical procedure, not very different from the 'ad quadratum' method practised during the later Middle Ages. In both cases the geometric pattern leads to the arithmetically irrational focal points in the design (point F, for instance, divides the $\sqrt{2}$ diagonal CD as well as the $\sqrt{5}$ line AE into one part and two parts). But in Serlio's case the geometrical scheme is posterior rather than prior to the ratios chosen for the door. His design was evidently the result of commensurable divisions of the large square. The door itself is a double square, its width and height in the light are related to the side of the square as 1 : 3 and 2 : 3, the frame of the door and the height of the pediment are related to the width of the opening as 1 : 3 and 1 : 2 respectively, and so forth. Thus an interrelated series of ratios of small integral numbers is really at the basis of Serlio's design. 'Mediaeval' geometry here is no more than a veneer that enables practitioners to achieve commensurable ratios without much ado.[33]

In its use of the diagonals of a square the method has some affinity with the mediaeval *ad quadratum* construction, as Wittkower observes, and it would readily be understood by masons accustomed to setting out their work by means of the geometrical manipulation of waxed lines. But the scheme is also an extension of ideas about the transformation of squares and triangles discussed earlier in the text. If we extend FG to intersect BC at H, we shall readily see – trained as we are by our reading of the First Book – that the triangle CFH is similar to the triangle CDB. Since DE = EB, FG must be equal to GH. One side of the diagram mirrors the other, and it follows that FG is equal to one-third of DB. Similar thinking will lead to the conclusion that the door's open space height is equal to 2FG. Thus although the method of construction, with its $\sqrt{2}$ and $\sqrt{5}$ values, is 'innumerable', the result to which it leads, in Serlio's constructive geometry, is expressible in the ratios of small integers, $1:2$, $2:3$ and so on. Wittkower believed that this commensurate proportioning was prior to the geometric construction, whose purpose was simply to be of use to masons trained in the mediaeval tradition. But in fact the use of geometrical constructions to produce ratios expressible in integers has been the habit of the First Book throughout. Its marriage of geometry and simple proportion is no shotgun affair, but the product of a long and intimate relationship, devotedly pursued.

Nevertheless Serlio has the 'workeman' in mind, and his geometry is actually useful in the setting out. Much the same is true of the theatre plan in the Second Book. The scale as given in the six-unit bar marked off on the forestage appears to be conceived in terms of the Italian *pertica* (or perch) of 6 ft. The orchestra, at 48 ft wide, is 8 perches, a measure readily determined with a traditional mason's line marked off in perch intervals. The workman seeking to realize Serlio's plan on the ground of a courtyard might begin with the circle of the orchestra, whose radius is 4 perches. Tangential to that he will erect a square, using his lines to determine its trueness by checking that the diagonals are equal. Now he can run a further circle through the corners of the square, to mark the round of the limits of the semicircular *cavea*. This will also yield the width of the theatre as given in the plan.

The *ad quadratum* system by which the plan is developed certainly possessed characteristics that made it practical in the workman's hands. But it is possible that its proportion in this particular version – essentially irrational but in practice commensurate – enshrined a more profoundly humanist principle. We know that the simple proportional relations of Renaissance architecture found their deepest, if half forgotten, justification in a theory about the proportionality of the human body. The ratio of column height to thickness repeated the relative dimensions of a man's or a woman's foot and height, and further development of the orders followed a series of simple proportions of the same type that Vitruvius had observed in the typical human body.

Therefore, since nature has designed the human body so that its members are duly proportioned to the frame as a whole, it appears that the ancients had good reason for their rule, that in perfect buildings the different members must be in exact symmetrical relations to the whole general scheme.[34]

Most of these 'exact symmetrical relations' involved ratios of small integers, such as 1 : 2, 2 : 3, or 3 : 4. But there was one special case to which Vitruvius himself gave particular emphasis:

Then again, in the human body the central point is naturally the navel. For if a man be placed flat on his back, with his hands and feet extended, and a pair of compasses centred at his navel, the fingers and toes of his two hands and feet will touch the circumference of a circle described therefrom. And just as the human body yields a circular outline, so too a square figure may be found from it. For if we measure the distance from the soles of the feet to the top of the head, and then apply that measure to the outstretched arms, the breadth will be found to be the same as the height, as in the case of plane surfaces which are perfectly square.[35]

This notion of the *homo ad circulum* and *ad quadratum* seems to have appealed to thinkers of the Renaissance, if we are to judge by the frequency with which editors of the Vitruvian text called on their woodcutters and engravers to illustrate it. Sometimes they showed the two figures separately, one a naked man with his arms outstretched horizontally to either side, inscribed within a square; and the other, bounded by a circle, a man with legs wider apart and arms stretched up a little to the level of his head. Frequently they wrenched the poor fellow this way and that to make him fit, as in the illustrations to Fra Giocondo's Vitruvius (Venice, 1511) and Francesco Zorzi's *De harmonia mundi* (Venice, 1525).[36] Occasionally, as in Francesco di Giorgio's manuscript on human proportions in the Laurentian library,[37] the figure is graceful but the square less than true. Some illustrations bring the two figures together in one diagram, as in Leonardo's famous version. And some contrive to show the manikin in a square inscribed within a circle, as in Cesare Cesariano's Vitruvius (Como, 1521)[38] (plate 35).

To those of a mystical cast of mind the idea of man's circularity led by easy stages to his identification with the shape of the cosmos, and the manikin was whipped into astrological shape in such works as H. C. Agrippa's *De occulta philosophia* (Cologne, 1533) or Robert Fludd's *Utriusque cosmi historia* (Frankfurt, 1619).[39] But this side of the argument seems to have little enough to do with Serlio's interest in it. He designed his theatre *ad quadratum*, not so much because he saw it as a little world, but because his preconceptions as a Renaissance architect led him to exploit a proportional resolution between the perfect shapes of the circle and the square, a resolution which such writers as Cesariano had taught him was already complete in the form of the human body.

Similar preoccupations led Alberti to propose the round plan for churches, and to demonstrate how other centrally designed shapes might be developed from the circle. In his Fifth Book Serlio followed him, leading off his discussion of temples with the observation 'for that the round forme is the perfitest of all others, therefore I will begin with it'.[40] Drawings for two round

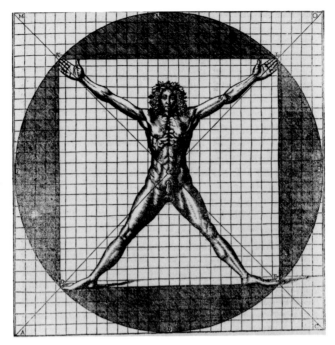

35 Cesare Cesariano, *M. Vitruvio Pollione de architectura* (Como, 1521), the *homo ad quadratum*.

churches follow, and are succeeded by an oval and six centrally designed schemes derived from the circle and the square. All these buildings are free-standing, raised clear of their surroundings on an elevated base. They can express the idea of geometrical perfection without compromise. None faces the special problem of the theatre plan: how to reconcile the semicircular *cavea* of the ancient model with the rectangular hall or courtyard of the modern palazzo. And it is in response to this challenge that Serlio invokes the *ad quadratum* resolution of the perfect but incompatible figures of the square and the circle. The central, fully expressed, part of the theatre is bounded by a square 34 units wide. The stage fills its width, and the last degree of the semicircular seating follows the perimeter of a circle inscribed within it. The front of the orchestra lies on its diameter. A square inscribed within it delimits the width of the *occhio*, and within this a further circle marks the boundary of the orchestra behind the senators' seats. The six units marked off as a scale bar at the centre of the forestage front indicate the numerical unit with which the whole scheme begins, the $\sqrt{2}$ proportional series being $6 : 8\frac{1}{2} : 12 : 17 : 24 : 34$.

The plan of the auditorium is not the most important part of Serlio's total theatre scheme. Much of his interest lies in the development and content of the three generic Scenes. But I hope that enough has been said to indicate the nature and thoroughness of the woodcut's proportionality, and of its origins in Vitruvius. Serlio seems to have had no time for the complex astrological diagram with its twelve-point directionality. Such thinking was more appropriate to the vast open theatres of antiquity than to the Court theatres of the Renaissance, however lavish in scale. We are offered rather a design that reconciles the newer type of unified scenic stage with a deliberately antique auditorium, one whose measurements derive moreover from the scale and proportion of the human body. The stage height and seat depth are dictated directly by this scale, and the latter becomes the repeated unit by which the whole is measured. The stage and *cavea* are related as the square is to the circle, and this relation too was characteristic of the human frame, at least in the opinion of some of Vitruvius' distinguished Renaissance interpreters. The theatre design in the Second Book was enormously influential in England, especially through its readily imitable scenic constructions, but also through its auditorium planning, as the Christ Church drawing shows. It governed the design of many of the Court theatres of Inigo Jones, their auditoria as well as their scenes, and there is, as we shall see, some reason for believing that it helped to shape even the commercial playhouses, both public and private, of Elizabethan and Jacobean London.

10

This goodly frame: the public theatres

I have been arguing in earlier chapters that the wooden frame of the Elizabethan public playhouse was a three-storey galleried structure built to a polygonal plan whose firmly integrated design owed much to a popular conception of the ancient Roman theatre. Like the banqueting house at Ardres, it was built 'comme du temps passé les Romains faisoient leur théâtre'. It is a little disconcerting therefore that the one public playhouse for whose plan we have detailed information provided in a contemporary document is the least obviously reminiscent of amphitheatre design, no matter how broadly understood. The Fortune playhouse, built in 1600 in general imitation of the Globe, differed from its model in being planned as a square rather than a polygon. It is hard, on the face of it, to conceive of a square playhouse having much to do with a Roman amphitheatre design, but then it is almost as hard to see how it could have had much to do with the polygonal Globe. Yet the contract between its owners and its carpenter, Peter Street, insists on the point:

the said howse [the Fortune] and other thinges beforemenconed to be made & doen To be in all other Contrivitions Conveyances fashions thinge and thinges effected finished and doen according to the manner and fashion of the saide howse Called the Globe.[1]

Many special variations from the model are required by the contract – the plan shape being only the most important – but the parties to the agreement apparently found the general idea of likening their square house to the Globe not disconcerting at all, but of immediate practical use. We shall not go far wrong if we follow their example.

For the square of the Fortune's plan might profitably be considered merely a very simple polygon. A square building can be as centrally planned as a round one, and indeed Alberti, while favouring the round shape above all others for churches, puts the square before the polygons in his list of desirable alternatives.[2] It too is a 'perfect' shape, like the circle itself, and Serlio includes several temple designs derived from the square in his Fifth

150

Book. It is surely significant that when Philip Henslowe and Edward Alleyn looked for a simpler – and presumably less expensive – alternative to the difficult polygonal framing of the Globe and similar prototypes they chose the one right-angled figure that was also centrally planned. They could, had they considered the example of the Blackfriars, have opted for an auditorium that was longer than it was broad, as many a theatre designer since their time has done. Neither is the square a plan that will have been suggested by the inn yards. The recently altered Boar's Head theatre at Whitechapel was almost square, but it had been shaped ingeniously out of part of the original inn yard, which was far deeper than it was wide. According to Herbert Berry other Whitechapel inns had yards of similar proportions, if smaller in dimension.[3] The shape of those at the Cross Keys and the Bell remains unknown. Among the theatres whose plans are recorded, the square Fortune is not quite unique, for the Red Bull was fitted up in the 'square court in an inn',[4] but it is unusual enough to warrant special notice. It differed from the Red Bull in being a purpose-built structure whose designers could presumably have chosen another shape if they had wanted. Like the Theater in Shoreditch it represents a deliberate architectural idea.

And the contract shows that it was, like Serlio's auditorium, designed *ad quadratum*. I have explored this matter at some length in *The Quest for Shakespeare's Globe*[5] and shall now be as brief as my argument allows. At first glance the plan dimensions mentioned in the contract appear to offer a commensurate design of a kind we might expect to come from the hand of a neo-Vitruvian. The timber frame is 80 ft each way overall, made of three storeys of galleries so arranged that the yard between them is 55 ft square. The proportion of yard size to plan size, 11 : 16, is hardly of the sort that might recommend itself to an Alberti or a Serlio, but it is at least conceived in commensurate terms. The elevation of the yard measures 33 ft to the plates, the whole consisting of 1 ft for the foundations, and 12 ft, 11 ft and 9 ft for the three floors of galleries. The total of 33 ft suits well with the 55 ft width of the yard, in the ratio 3 : 5. The nice regularity is obscured a little by some jettying inwards of the upper galleries, but in general the design shows a careful regard for the demands of what Serlio would call 'numerable' quantities.

These are, however, for the most part surface-to-surface or 'superficial' dimensions that are required for the purposes of a contract, in whose language they appear as 'lawfull assize'. A carpenter, thinking in terms proper to his craft, would measure such a building between the centres of its timbers, not between their surfaces. If we assume provisionally that a post was 1 ft thick, we may take it that to Peter Street a square framed structure measuring 80 ft superficial would be 79 ft by centres. Similarly, the yard would be a foot larger, 56 ft by centres for 55 ft superficial. In seeking to set out his foundations, and to calculate the size and number of the structural bays, these dimensions between centres will have been at the front of Street's mind, rather than the 'lawfull assize' specified in the contract. And they are related fairly accurately by the $\sqrt{2}$ ratio characteristic of *ad quadratum* design: 79 ft $\div \sqrt{2} = 55.9$ ft, or a little over 55 ft 10 ins. Of course these figures would vary a little according to the precise thickness allowed for the posts. An 11 ins allowance would provide dimensions of 55 ft 11 ins for the yard and 79 ft 1 in for the outer wall, virtually an exact $\sqrt{2}$ proportion.[6]

Nevertheless Street used traditional surveyors' implements and techniques for setting out the Fortune's foundations. He will not have possessed a modern tape measure, marked off in feet and inches, and although he would have been perfectly capable of setting out an 80 ft square with the aid of his lines and a carpenter's 10 ft rod we have to allow for the fact that he came to this playhouse after working on the dismantling of the Theater and its reassembly as the Globe. He was enjoined generally to imitate the Globe in his work on the Fortune, and it would not be surprising if he used setting-out techniques at the latter which he had developed while working on the former. It would be impossible to set out a great polygonal frame, probably of as many as 24 sides, simply with the aid of the *decempeda* and a carpenter's square. Obviously the Globe, like the Theater, had been set out on a circle, or two concentric circles for the gallery fronts and perimeter wall. The frame of the Globe, shaped of necessity by a geometrical construction, presupposed an exact centre. And so of course did that of the Fortune.

For not only was the building 'sett square and to conteine ffowerscore foote of lawfull assize everye waie square withoute and fiftie fiue foote of like assize square everye waie within', but it incorporated the centre into the design. The stage was to 'conteine in length ffortie and Three foote of lawfull assize and in breadth to extende to the middle of the yarde'.[7] The galleries on every side were specified as 12 ft 6 ins deep at ground floor level, so that the yard was certainly concentric with the perimeter; the centre was also marked by the centre of the stage front. The width (what the contract in Elizabethan parlance calls the 'length') of the stage at 43 ft seems a curiously arbitrary size, related neither to the commensurate superficial dimensions of the frame nor directly to the centres dimensions used by Street. In fact, however, its size gives us our best clue to the development of the whole plan.

The builder's most useful measuring instrument for large dimensions was the surveyor's line, marked off with knots at 1-rod intervals. Surveyors commonly used the line (waxed to prevent shrinkage) to measure the area of land, a feat which they were taught to accomplish by systems of squaring and triangulation.[8] Lines – and subsequently chains – were usually three or four rods long, and it happens that the altitude of a 3-rod equilateral triangle is very close to the width of the Fortune's stage: 49 ft 6 ins $\times \frac{\sqrt{3}}{2} = 42$ ft $10\frac{1}{2}$ ins. To set out the foundations of the Fortune carpenter-fashion, Street would begin with a 3-rod square. Within this he would peg out two 3-rod equilateral triangles, from the apexes of which he would drop perpendiculars – I speak metaphorically, all this happening on the level ground – and drive in pegs at the end of each line. Through these he would construct another square incorporating the first but enlarging it: the new dimension would be about 56 ft $1\frac{1}{2}$ ins. He would check its trueness by testing the equality of its diagonals, establishing its centre in the process by marking the point where they crossed. Through it he could run a line to indicate the forward extent of the stage, whose width was already defined by the diagram he had created. Finally, in order to mark the extent of the outer walls he could run a circle from the centre, touching the corners of the 56 ft $1\frac{1}{2}$ ins square. At each quadrant he would drive a peg, subsequently making a large square concentric with the other through the points so marked. Its size would be 56 ft $1\frac{1}{2}$ ins $\times \sqrt{2} = 79$ ft 4 ins. If we suppose that posts 10 ins thick were used at the Fortune, as they were to be at the Hope in 1613, these dimensions came to within 2 ins or so of the figures that must have governed the scheme in Street's mind, and yet they have been arrived at exclusively by the manipulation of surveyors' or carpenters' lines without benefit of any anachronistic tape measure.

The elevation of the playhouse, at 33 ft, was just two rods high to the plates, and checkable by means of the surveyor's line. It was also, as we have seen, proportional to the 55 ft superficial width of the yard. The Fortune contract, it now appears, defines a building whose proportions testify to an order of constructive design far removed from the *ad hoc* improvisations of Oliver Woodliffe at the Boar's Head. Its concentric square plan, developed *ad quadratum*, produces a coherent entity, indeed a strikingly proportionate one when set against Elizabethan buildings generally. A useful comparison may be made with the gatehouse which Henslowe and Alleyn contracted with Street to build at the Bear Garden in 1606. Like the second Globe, this structure was erected on the reusable foundations of a previous building which Street was required to demolish before he began.[9] His new gatehouse therefore shared the plan dimensions of the old, 56 ft by 16 ft superficial. Street was to deliver to Henslowe and Alleyn 'a platt maide of the said frame', from which the proportionate elevation might be deduced by a skilled workman, though some dimensions were given also in the clauses of the contract. The new building was to be 24 ft to the plates, the third storey being partly built up into the roof with dormers. A measure of 24 ft is $1\frac{1}{2}$ times the width and $\frac{3}{7}$ the length of the plan, rationally proportionate to both. The building was to be decorated with 'twoe carved Satyres', like those specified for the posts at the Fortune,[10] and this classical theme in the entrance bay was continued on its gable, where 'one piramen with three piramides' were to be provided. A 'piramen' was a classical pediment, and the 'piramides' were doubtless finials in the shape of obelisks.

These somewhat perfunctory applications of classical forms were matched by the commensurate overall proportioning of a building actually 'framed with crooked postes and bolted with iron beltes thorough the rafters': the reduction of native techniques and design to a 'Renaissance' order is far from complete, and the character of the structure, with its 'clerestorye' and 'splay' windows, its dormers and its jettying remains firmly native. But the Fortune was a larger and more complex affair, and the conclusions of our analysis point to two separate sources of its unusual coherence. The *ad quadratum* proportioning is probably the result of the application of a traditional carpenter's method, without regard for any special value in the ratios this produced. But the concentric square plan with its emphasized diameter is another matter: its simple eloquence asserts the kinship with the polygonal or 'round' building on which its design was generally to be based. The square here is the most elemental of polygons, and the Fortune's design a restatement of the 'round' theatre programme in transformational terms that would be thoroughly understood by anyone capable of manipulating builders' lines to produce an *ad quadratum* construction.

That Peter Street had already demonstrated his prowess with the lines there can be little doubt. He had been employed to dismantle the Theater with such care that its timbers could be reassembled as the Globe. He must have measured its vast polygonal frame with a view to preparing the new foundations on Bankside, made just the right size to accept the translated timbers, and as the new building went up he must have checked and rechecked its dimensions. The foundations that he supervised on Bankside survived the fire of 1613 and were reused for the second Globe, defining its floor plan in size, shape and proportion, just as the old Beargarden gate-house had strictly governed the site dimensions of the new. We have Hollar's drawing of the second Globe to show that its frame was proportioned *ad quadratum* and measured about 100 ft superficial in external diameter, the yard within being 69 ft across.[11] These were the dimensions to which Street built at Bankside, and which he had found already established in Shoreditch: they appear to have been the standard measurements of the Elizabethan public theatre frame, departed from only in special cases such as the smaller Rose and the square Fortune.

A polygonal frame 100 ft in diameter would strike a carpenter, more used to measuring between post centres than their surfaces, as being properly 99 ft across, the larger figure representing 'lawfull assize'. The Globe was often described as 'round', although common sense and Norden's *Civitas Londini* combine to suggest that it must in fact have been polygonal. A structural frame of timber cannot be made truly round without great expense and the weakening of the fabric; the first Globe appears to have been a fairly cheap building and it is most unlikely that the Sharers' scarce money would have gone into so fruitless an enterprise as making their wooden O altogether without angles and straight faces. The building was surely a polygon, as Norden observed, but one of many sides, as he did not. A many-sided polygon would be set out on the ground within a circle marked with a builder's line and pegs. In the case of the Globe, which measured 99 ft between centres, the circle would have a radius of 49 ft 6 ins, or 3 rods. An inner circle reduced from the larger one by *ad quadratum* means would measure 99 ft $\div \sqrt{2}$, or 70 ft, and the yard would be 1 ft less superficial. The most natural width for a rectangular (half-square) stage extending to the centre of the yard would be 49 ft 6 ins, for this would be the size of a square inscribed within the 70 ft circle.

If the Fortune and the Globe resembled Serlio's theatre scheme in being designed *ad quadratum*, that is partly because the London builder's practice shared some common theoretical ground with the Italian's text. Serlio's academic tradition and Street's craft were both deeply rooted in the quite ordinary practice of land surveying, with its attendant command of Euclidean geometry. Parallels to the early chapters of the *Architettura* may be found in several English surveyors' textbooks of the sixteenth century. In these the familiar problems of reducing irregular areas to square dimensions by means of their resolution to regular forms involves precisely the same geometry of transformation that so concerns Serlio in the First Book. Edward Worsop, in a dialogue on the techniques of surveying, regrets that England had no civic geometers, as many European cities did:

Masons, Carpenters, Joyners, Paynters, clockmakers, Inginors, and such others vnto whose faculties most needefully appertaine the knowledges of making squares, roundes, triangles, and many other figures, with their transformations according to any proportion assigned resort vnto these professors and Geometers, to learne certaine grounds, & chiefe mechanicall rules.[12]

The list of craftsmen here is an indication of how widespread the appetite for applied geometry might be; although it was most fully and often treated in surveyors' handbooks it pervaded much of Elizabethan design. Radolph Agas, promoting the use of the theodolyte and its attendant geometry, observed that it might serve the needs of 'Surueighors, Builders, Imparkers, Gardners, Planters and such like',[13] while Gervase Markham published a book of knot garden designs many of which were developed on *ad quadratum* principles.[14] In it he advised the reader how to set out the borders and beds by means of the same line and peg technique we have supposed that Peter Street used at the theatres, in the process 'making squares', as Worsop said, 'roundes, triangles, and many other figures, with their transformations'. The principle of geometric transformation, which is at the heart of Serlio's First Book, is one above all of practical utility.

But it also has a more theoretical, even a mystical, side. The surveyor's professional need to reduce a field to square proportions in order to state its area bears some similarity to the heady Pythagorean reduction of numbers to the cube. Alberti believed that the cube, whose root is 1, generated

155

numbers; Cornelius Agrippa followed Plato in the *Timaeus* in identifying Earth with the cube because it was said to 'contain the first cube of eight solid corners, twenty-four planes and six bases'.[15] Other Renaissance thinkers developed such ideas to what may seem to us indulgent and fantastic limits, contriving to find evidence of the cube in everything that God or man had touched. Vitruvius, in a famous passage from the Fifth Book, had given some warrant for applying the idea even to the structure of literary works:

Pythagoras and those who came after him in his school thought it proper to employ the principles of the cube in composing books on their doctrines, and, having determined that the cube consisted of 216 lines, held that there should be no more than three cubes in any one treatise.[16]

These words, though they do not seem to have been taken as a constructional guide by the author himself, were seized on by Cesariano and Barbaro in their commentaries on the text, and substantially developed.

We need not, in the present discussion, follow in the footsteps of Vitruvius' more dazzling commentators. Serlio, whose work is before us, was comparatively restrained in his pursuit of the Pythagorean content of the *Ten Books*, and had little enough to say about the cube, whether geometric or numerical. But he did wax eloquent on the subject of the square:

Among the quadrangular forms I find the rectangle the most perfect. And the more the rectangle moves away from the perfect square the more it loses its perfection, even though it is bounded by a line of the same length.[17]

This passage opens a discussion of the relative areas of squares and oblongs, the square being 'most perfect' because for a given perimeter it encloses a greater area than any other rectangular figure. The longer and narrower the rectangle, the smaller the area it encloses and the more it departs from the perfection of the square: a square 10 ft each way is 40 ft around and encloses 100 ft^2, while a figure 18 ft by 2 ft, equally 40 ft around, encloses a mere 36 ft^2. This demonstration, says Serlio, will be of sovereign value not only to the architect, but to merchants as well. And so delighted is the author with the principle that he likens the departure of the rectangle from the square to that of the human soul from God:

Thus we see what power the more perfect forms have, as against the less perfect; and so it is in Man, who, as he advances mentally towards God, who is perfection, enjoys a fuller wellbeing. And the further he departs from God, delighting in earthly things, the more he loses that primal innocence originally granted to him.[18]

In practical terms this adulation of the divinely inspired square means that room proportions may be expressed in such terms as 'a square and a quarter', 'a square and a third', and so on. The further the room in question lies from the main purpose of the building, the less it need approach the proportions of the square, so that a hierarchy of forms underlies the development of architectural plans. Rooms longer than a double square, for example, are not to be found in the remains of antiquity, 'unlesse it bee in Galleries, Entries and other to walke in . . . but such as are wise will not passe such lengths in Chambers or Halles'.[19]

It is not surprising, then, to find that the semicircular *cavea* and stage of Serlio's theatre scheme are inscribed within a square. The theatre is itself a hierarchy of a social as well as a geometrical kind. The seats around the orchestra and in the semicircle of degrees are reserved for the noblest spectators, while further out, beyond the limiting square where the seating becomes segmental, are places for the less important, with standing room for the 'plebe' beyond. In these further reaches there is, as it were, no geometry: the radius to the back degree, at 29 units from the centre, completes the auditorium depth of 80 ft alluded to in the text, but has no relation to the proportionate system that encloses the stage, and in any case is flexibly extendable in the manner illustrated in the section. The theatre proper, one might say, is confined within the stage and the front range of degrees and contains the perfection of both the square and its inscribed circle. It is at once stable and a model of society, of the circles people move in. The geometry of the scenes will preoccupy us in another chapter, but their generic range from Tragic to Satyric encompasses the full scope of the drama, while above them elaborate mobile sky effects are envisaged that will complete the model cosmos.

So much for the Italian, with his acknowledged veneration for Vitruvius and the works of antiquity. What of Peter Street the Elizabethan builder of the Globe and the Fortune? He will certainly have been familiar with the kind of transformational geometry to be found in Serlio's First Book, for it was the foundation of the surveyor's craft, of which any builder must have possessed some knowledge. All the textbooks, from Richard Benese's *Maner of Measurying* (1537) to John Norden's *Surueiors Dialogue* (1610), were chiefly concerned with the practical application of Euclidean geometry, but not infrequently we find chinks in the armour of utility through which it is possible to see something of the assumptions, frequently neo-Platonic, that underlaid the businesslike pragmatism. Unfortunately Peter Street wrote no such book, but the Fortune contract, in specifying a concentric square plan with an acknowledged and emphasized centre – the location of the stage front – commands geometrical analysis by the very terms in which it is conceived. The frame of the theatre is proportioned *ad quadratum* for ordinary technical reasons of construction, but these reasons do not preclude others, more speculative or philosophical in kind. The systems of design that developed the plan of the Fortune are generally the same as those that shaped Serlio's theatre scheme: the careful respect for the square, and the related preference for the *ad quadratum* method of proportioning. In both cases, though with widely differing results, the irrationality of the $\sqrt{2}$

dimensions is smoothed into neatly commensurate ones. In the case of the more explicit Serlio we have been able to pursue the matter further and find that the square is venerated for Vitruvian and neo-Platonic reasons, being identified both with God and – in the Vitruvian *homo ad quadratum* – with man. Furthermore the Serlian theatre is specifically intended to repeat or invoke the form of the Roman theatres of antiquity, of which it is something of a shadow, much as a rectangle is a debased departure from a square. Within the narrow confines of a modern rectangular space only part of the work can be realized: 'The greater the hall, the more nearly will the theatre assume its complete form.'[20]

With Street only the terms of the contract are explicit. Were we to have his views on architecture, even such a glimpse as that contained in Robert Stickells' quirky memoranda on the subject, we might be able to look more deeply into the contractual arrangements with Henslowe and Alleyn, in search of their intellectual programme. Robert Stickells, a mason who later became Clerk of Her Majesty's Works at Richmond, must have moved in some of the same circles as Peter Street, and in September 1595 he had put pen to paper to note down some of his observations on proportion:

For the byldinge of an howse of state, then to shewe by the quantite of the grownd delyevred, howe hie I may bylde that I byld not to hie, nor to loe, &c.

And that by that quantite of grownd before rehearsed, the offices or Roumes beinge contrived by due preporction, then by the breadthe, the heathe may be geven that the lyght, shalbe no more, nor no less then nede shall Requiere, &c.

Then havenge the heathe of the storries, to showe howe greate or howe thicke the wales or postes shalbe, that the shall not be too begge, nor to lettell, &c.

Thes things consisteth in man hime self, for that man is the proporctinall & Resonable creatuer, & therfor whatso is done witheowt thes Rules of proporction, is but unsearten matter, the seartayn have ther true quantites & measueres, & the unsearten, ar delivered throwe Ignorance, &c.

Thear ar too sortes of byldenges, the on in sence; the other withowt sence; The antikes in sence; the moddarn witheout sence; Because it is from cirkler demonstrac-tion, witheowt sence; for that no cirkell Riseth in evenness of nomber, the antikes allwayes in evennes of nombre be cauese the ar derived from an Ichnographicall ground; it the unevn may be broght into proporctions, as well as the even, &c.

Ther is no mor but Right & wronge in all thinges whatsoever, The sqear Right the cirkell wronge, &c.[21]

Some of these principles are familiar to us: right proportion, used in judging the elevation of a building from its plan length and breadth, is commen-surate and rational, in part because 'thes thinges consisteth in man hime self'. Man is both reasonable and proportionate, and so must his building be. The distrust of the circle is a consequence of identifying right design with com-mensurate proportions, for elevations derived from the use of the compasses will not rise 'in evenness of nomber' but in irrational ratios such as $1 : \sqrt{2}$.

Here, fully developed, is the language we need to analyse the design of the Fortune, though not of course the particular critical position. Stickells, faced with the 'Plott' that once accompanied the Fortune contract, might well have approved of its commensurate plan, and perhaps also the 33 ft elevation. He would presumably have resisted the *ad quadratum* proportioning precisely because of its 'cirkler' method; at least he might have done had he seen such a drawing before 26 November 1597, when he set down another note on similar matters. He had evidently been giving them a great deal of thought, and either sought or was seeking advice from people who ought to know more about them:

Propoctions propounded unto the
Learned & skilfull;
Feirst, it wold be known [whether] the woorkes, moddarn; or the woorkes Antiques, is of most Effecte, & which of them, Contayn most Truthe; theay both consest in all thinges livnge & being seprated; the one is sencable, the other insencable, no sencles thinge can be perfet, before by lif it be maid perfet.

There follow three questions about the just height of a building on a given area of ground, its storey heights and the thickness of its walls or posts. A fourth point concerns the just proportions of the parts of a 300-ton ship. Then Stickells adds a concluding note:

I shewe thes propoctions to the ende I wolde have them exzamond, proved, & tryed, by the Learned & Skilfull; & for thes propoctions Ill make perfet demonstraction; fore that I see all Buildenges, grownded upon the emperfect sence, the bookes of, Architecktur, victriuces & all thoos Authers have, taken the wronge sense; ther in wardes woorkes are dead when theay shewe no lif in ther owtward Doweinges.
Robert Stickelles[22]

Now it would seem that 'lif' is the essence of right design, and the 'insencable' proportions allegedly espoused by Vitruvius '& all thoos Authers' are dead without it. There is perhaps no warrant here for identifying the 'lif' of the later memorandum with the 'cirkler' mysteries of the earlier, but to do so may help us to interpret the Fortune contract. For here is a building ostensibly commensurate, and therefore possibly 'insencable' in plan, yet animated by a 'cirkler' *ad quadratum* system of proportioning. The superficial dimensions of the frame are related through their commensurate nature to one view – a Vitruvian one – of man as a 'proporctinall & Resonable creatuer'; but the traditional geometrical system with its pegs and three-rod lines produces a further set which evoke the proportionality of man in another, and equally Vitruvian fashion, as the *homo ad quadratum*. The two kinds of ordering, of *symmetria*, are combined in the height of the elevation, which is straightforwardly commensurate with both the width of the yard and the rod unit used to develop the *ad quadratum* scheme.

One would dearly like to have some word directly from Peter Street that he was disposed to think in the same theoretical terms as Robert Stickells. They were contemporaries, both deeply involved in the crafts of building, both practical men of their time. Stickells was something of a factotum: not only did he become the Clerk of Works at Richmond soon after he drew up the second memorandum, but he designed a demountable pinnace, did work for the ingenious Sir Thomas Tresham at Lyveden, and was sent to clear rocks from Dover Harbour, adopting the procedure of attaching barrels to them with chains at low tide, then floating them clear during the flood.[23] In 1604–5 he was paid for preparing 'uprightes' for a design for the new Banqueting House at Whitehall – the successor to the building of 1581 – from a plan by George Weale.[24] He is therefore at least a candidate for the attribution of part of that anonymous building, and we note that his memoranda were especially concerned with just this matter of the development of an elevation by just proportion from a plan, what he called deriving it 'from an Ichnographicall ground'. The interior elevations of the Banqueting House, when built to these designs, were striking enough to catch the attention of the one observer who left a general account of the building, the almoner of the Venetian embassy, Orazio Busino. He found

a large hall . . . arranged like a theatre . . . While waiting for the king we took pleasure in admiring the decorations, in observing the beauty of the hall, with two orders of columns one on top of the other, their distance from the wall the full width of the passage, the upper gallery supported by Doric columns, and above these the Ionic, which hold up the roof of the hall. It is all of wood, including even the pillars, carved and gilt with great skill. From the roof hang garlands and angels in relief. There were two rows of lights, which were to be lit at the proper time.[25]

The Doric and Ionic orders called forth the best from the craftsmen of the Works, but even they were not sufficiently equipped for such a task, and they turned to one of their acquaintance among the London builders to find the necessary specialized tools. The arrangement is recorded in the Declared Accounts of the Office of Works for 1606–7:

Peter Streete for the lone of v^e great pumpaugurs for boringe the great Collumbes in the Banquettinge house at iiij^s the pece – $\underline{xx}^s$ [26]

The augers will have been used to bore out the core of the columns so that as they shrank they would not split.[27] Street provided some of the implements by means of which Stickells' designs were realized, and it is possible therefore that the two men knew one another. The transaction is of small consequence in itself, but it does illustrate the dependence of the Whitehall administration on the supply of technical prowess and specialized skills available in the city of London and its surroundings. Simon Basil, by now the Surveyor of the Works and responsible for overseeing the job at Whitehall, must have known Street; and Basil in 1605 had been the author of the definitively

Serlian theatre scheme set up in the hall at Christ Church. Might Street, one wonders, have known Serlio too? Such craftsmen were not ignorant of Italian and French sources, however illiterate they might be when it came to signing documents. A memorandum in Sir Edward Pytts's will records that 'John Chaunce [Sir Edward's mason and surveyor] hath in his keeping one booke of Architecture of myne which he hath promised to deliver unto me' – doubtless, as Sir John Summerson has remarked, Serlio, Shute or de Vries.[28] Serlian details, and some plans and larger schemes, were everywhere in Elizabethan architecture, especially in the larger country houses. Sometimes it might be the whole plan that derived from the *Architettura*, as at Wollaton (*c.* 1580–8), where the great central hall and corner towers echo an original design based on the Poggio Reale in Naples which Serlio had published in his Third Book.[29] In elevations we find a rough Serlianism in the porch at Kirby (begun in 1570), and something more refined at Wothorpe, where windows in the octagonal corner turrets are taken from a woodcut in the Fourth Book.[30] As early as 1540 the artificers of Henry VIII had celebrated his brief union with Anne of Cleves in a painted ceiling at St James's whose compartments were taken directly from a block in this same Book, which had been published as the *Regole generali di architetura* in Venice in 1537.[31] There were Serlian chimney pieces at Wollaton and Hardwick, at Burghley and later at Bolsover.[32] One piece of design of a Serlian character, the Gate of Honour at Caius College, Cambridge, was taken only indirectly from the *Architettura*, being based on a festive gateway for a royal entrance into Antwerp in 1550.[33] Nevertheless the Gate shows the high regard in which Serlio was held by its originator, Dr John Caius, and it effectively reproduced in miniature a complete Serlian façade taken from the Fourth Book.[34] But perhaps most telling of all these borrowings from the *Architettura* is in the roof of the great hall at Wollaton. Here a false hammerbeam system is suspended from a flat ceiling of timber which spans the 32 ft width of the room and is constructed according to the interlocking grid pattern which Serlio illustrates at the end of the First Book. This device was the work of Robert Smythson, who often resorted to the *Architettura* among the other pattern books with which he was evidently well equipped.[35] A similar structure appears to have been intended by Robert Stickells in the crossing of the lodge at Lyveden New Build, for which his own schematic drawing is extant (plate 9).[36]

All the more notable surveyors of the period were well acquainted with Serlio. Simon Basil, Robert Smythson, Robert Stickells and John Thorpe are surely representative of their class, and it would be surprising if a carpenter such as Peter Street, a major figure in the Carpenters' Company and an accomplished London builder,[37] were very different from the rest. If he did know the *Architettura* he will have recognized the antique quality of Serlio's practical theatre auditorium, and will have found in the same volume a number of surveys of Roman theatres. He will also have found, in the illustrations to the geometrical instruction of the First and Second Books, a condensed survey of matters with which his own training and experience had made him familiar. He will therefore have been well equipped, both by training and by disposition, to interpret the theatre designs as they were meant to be interpreted, and to appropriate their lessons for his own purposes.

But Street was not the originator of the Elizabethan playhouse design. The Burbage sons claimed that their father 'was the first builder of playehowses',[38] though that honour ought strictly to go to his partner, John Brayne, the projector of the Red Lion. Whether Burbage and Brayne had read their Serlio we do not know, but they were both intelligent people of substance, committed over many years to the business of constructing and running playhouses. There is reason to believe, as we shall find in chapter 12, that when Burbage designed the Blackfriars in 1596–7 he was influenced by what he found in the Second Book of the *Architettura*; moreover it seems certain that the Theater as much as the Globe was designed *ad quadratum*, for the latter was in essentials a reconstruction of the former on a different site, and repeated its proportions. The documents from which we learn what little we know about the playhouses are generally legal or fiscal in character, and not surprisingly fail to record less tangible matters; even the contracts of the Fortune and the Hope are workaday papers, giving no sense of an intellectual programme behind the practical clauses. Yet the round plan of the majority of the playhouses certainly reminded visitors of the Roman amphitheatres, and a glance at the tall, tower-like rounds which often stood for the ancient theatres in contemporary woodcuts and book illustrations makes it clear that the kind of structure recorded by de Witt was a good deal more like the popular idea of an ancient theatre than a knowledge of the real thing would lead us to suppose. What Serlio offered Street, and before him such theatre builders as John Brayne and James Burbage, was not so much a pattern book of playhouse design as confirmation of the value of seeking to reproduce the ancient forms in a modern context. Serlio sought to express, in courtyard and great hall, the *perfetta forma* of his model, or at least as much of it as his space would allow. In the Third Book he offered his survey plans and elevations of the remains of Roman theatres alongside the other wonders of the old world. An Elizabethan, poring over these careful architectural drawings, would find little enough of direct use to him but a great deal of suggestive encouragement.

To de Witt, our fullest commentator on the Elizabethan public theatre buildings, the matter was clear: he thought that the Swan resembled Roman work, and labelled his drawing accordingly. In 1600 another traveller recorded that one of the Bankside playhouses at least was a *theatrum* constructed out of wood, in the manner of the ancient Romans.[39] It seems clear that the architectural idea, the programme, of the public theatres derived from the Elizabethans' understanding of antiquity. But not, one would suppose, much else. The details did not follow a genuinely Roman pattern, but they did broadly conform to the scheme passed down to Brayne and Burbage from the festive tradition of the Calais and Ardres round houses.

I I
The Court theatres

Serlio's theatre scheme is a characteristic product of its age. Its main purpose, in the continuing argument of the *Architettura*, is to illustrate a particularly difficult aspect of perspective, a necessary discipline for the architect of a major Court, whose tasks would include the preparation of scenic stages. Much of the discussion is therefore about the construction of the scenes, for it is these that embody the special rules for compressing a three-dimensional stage structure within a shallow space. But the discussion is concerned too with the aristocratic magnanimity of a Court theatrical occasion. The theatre is to be a showplace for largesse and magnificence. No expense should be spared in the pursuit of these ends, and Serlio imagines a richly adorned stage glittering with coloured lights and resplendent with noble architecture. He has less to say about the auditorium, but his plan and section of the theatre quite clearly indicate that he thought it worthy of the devoted attention of the designer. For just as the noblest of the scenic designs contains the triumphal arches, the temples and obelisks of antiquity, so does the auditorium evoke the idea of the ancient Roman *cavea*. The new scenic and perspective stage is to be viewed from seats arranged like those of the Theatre of Marcellus, in a semicircle ranged about an orchestra. In a non-scenic playhouse this arrangement would have the virtue of focusing the audience's attention on the forestage or orchestra, but in Serlio's scheme the stage is backed by a huge unified perspective setting, and the pattern seems curiously inept. A large part of the audience would have only the most strained and unsatisfactory view of the scene. The power of the ancient building form, it seems, with all its cultural associations and long history, cannot easily be dismissed. It happens, of course, that the semicircular form is suited to the typical Court notion that no one should sit with his back to the occupier of the prime seat, and it may be that the persistence of the rounded auditorium even in scenic theatres during the sixteenth and seventeenth centuries has a good deal to do with this convention. And it is true that Serlio's arrangement, though inconvenient for those seated at the sides towards the front, does position a large number of seating places towards the back of the *cavea*, where they are behind the prime seat and yet face the stage.

The persistence of the neo-Roman auditorium was doubtless due to the habit of Renaissance Courts of seeing themselves as resurrections of an ideal antique state, but Serlio's book was not without its influence too. Scamozzi's *teatro all'antica* at Sabbioneta, built in 1588, erects a semicircular *cavea* of degrees before a raked stage of the Serlian type, the two elements separated by a piazza and the whole designed *ad quadratum*. Here the inconvenience of placing so many of the audience sideways to the scene was originally reduced by the expedient of returning the forward degrees towards the auditorium walls, so that the *cavea* was bell-shaped rather than half-round. Its 'Roman' character was – and is, for the theatre still stands, though with reconstructed scene and degrees – accentuated by a colonnaded portico at the back, each column surmounted by statuary, and by illusionistic wall paintings which represented the Campidoglio and the Castel S. Angelo.[1] Perhaps the most notable of these U-shaped auditoria is that of the vast Teatro Farnese at Parma,[2] but more modest ones had been built elsewhere. At Piacenza, for example, a permanent theatre erected for a troupe of actors in 1592, the Teatro delle Saline, partly foreshadowed its shape;[3] and there exists a plan of the temporary stage made in a Sala Grande 'over the wine cellar' at Ferrara in 1565 for the marriage of Alfonso II, showing a perspective scene of *periaktoi* faced with U-shaped seating. Here, however, the orchestra floor was set out with 15 rows of benches directly facing the stage.[4] Gian Battista Aleotti, the designer of the Farnese theatre, will doubtless have seen the house at Piacenza, and indeed in 1605 designed the Teatro dell'Accademia degli Intrepidi at San Lorenzo in Ferrara, perhaps with the Sala Grande scheme in mind. His plan is extant, and shows a semicircular *cavea* with returned front degrees on the Sabbioneta pattern and backed with a colonnade of 20 columns, behind which are a few extra segmental degrees. Between the *cavea* and the stage is a piazza of the Serlian type, and on the stage itself is a Tragic Scene of angled wings.[5]

Few of these Italian humanist theatres had much influence on English builders, for the simple reason that few English builders travelled. Inigo Jones saw Palladio's Teatro Olimpico at Vicenza, and made notes of his visit;[6] but he was an exception to the general rule: there is, for example, no evidence that Simon Basil ever left England. Yet in 1605 Basil designed a theatre for Christ Church that was in its way as complete an expression of the Serlian pattern as any of the Italian theatres. He worked from the text of the *Architettura*, not from firsthand acquaintance with the buildings of Vicenza or Ferrara, and the thoroughness of his attention to Serlio indicates how far it was possible to go on book-learning alone, tempered of course by extensive local experience. Even Jones, who in 1616 began designing a series of Court playhouses and masquing rooms, is unlikely to have learnt many of his lessons from his French and Italian tours, if only because there were not many theatres for him to have seen. Most of his theatrical design technique must have been worked out from first principles where it was not taught in the pages of architectural treatises. That the visual inspiration for his scene designs came from printed sources has been proved by John Peacock, in a scholarly series of comparative studies,[7] as well as by Orgel and Strong in their edition of the drawings.[8] We can even trace the means by which Jones came by some of the engravings he used in his stage work, for he often approached the Florentine Resident in London, Amerigo Salvetti, for copies of the works that he had heard about from Florence. Salvetti records passing on a copy of *Le nozze degli dei* to him in 1638,[9] and soon afterwards we find Jones using the engravings of Alfonso Parigi's sets to shape his own for *Salmacida Spolia*, the last of the great Stuart masques.

Between them, Jones and his assistant John Webb designed several Court theatres in the seventeenth century. Good-quality plans survive for the Cockpit-in-Court at Whitehall (1629),[10] the Paved Court theatre at Somerset House (1632–3) and the hall at Whitehall fitted out for a pastoral, *Florimène* (1635).[11] In addition there is Jones's informative design for the Cockpit in Drury Lane (converted to its theatrical use in 1616) and a neo-Palladian scheme for a theatre by Webb whose occasion is as yet unidentified.[12] Every one of these designs surrounds a central orchestra with degrees, approximately in the Serlian manner; some have elevated galleries as well. The Drury Lane Cockpit has a rounded auditorium, and the Cockpit at Whitehall is polygonal. Webb's unidentified project derives its semicircular *cavea* directly from Serlio; but the other two theatres are rectangular, lining their degrees and galleries against the walls of the containing building. Jones's Whitehall Cockpit scheme reflects his knowledge of the Teatro Olimpico, for it too is a deliberately 'Roman' design with a *frons scenae* of five entrances and a polygonal but U-shaped auditorium. Webb had no direct experience of Palladio's building, but his unidentified project includes a pair of careful studies of the *frons* drawing that Jones had brought back from Italy,[13] and exemplifies the processes of copying, conversion and adjustment that both architects apparently brought to the ordinary conduct of their work. To the right of his sheet (plate 42) Webb set out the Palladian design, which itself consisted of two alternative schemes for the *frons* offered side by side. Webb copied them separately, the right side at the top of his sheet and the left at the bottom. From the upper drawing he carried elevational dimensions across to the left, and there developed his own version of the Italian *frons*, retaining its scale and some of its proportions, but radically altering its composition. From this elevation he scored a large number of lines down the sheet to the bottom of its left side, and there laid out the plan to match the elevation drawn above it.[14] The whole process was one of thoughtful development, based on a specific drawn source. It characterizes very clearly the deliberate method which Webb probably learned from Jones

166

himself, and illustrates the importance of graphic source material to the designer.

In each of these Court theatres many of the seats were placed sideways on to the stage. The two scenic houses – at the Paved Court and in the hall for *Florimène* – were specifically intended for the performance of plays by the queen and her ladies before an audience that included the king on his halpace beneath the state. No members of the audience were permitted to sit in front of this prime position and facing the stage, though many were ranged in degrees to either side of the orchestra, facing inwards towards the centre. Webb's drawing of the Cockpit-in-Court at Whitehall does not date from the original conversion of 1629 but from a refurbishment of 1660, and it may not show the original pattern of the seating; it does indicate that at the later date the degrees in the pit were angled so that none backed directly onto the royal box. Webb's Palladian theatre project has a semicircular orchestra surrounded by degrees drawn from the same centre. Only two or three of them have room to complete the half circle; the remaining dozen or so are segmental like the degrees beyond the cross aisle in Serlio. This solution, which Serlio had anticipated but also resisted because it compromised the full expression of the Roman *cavea* pattern, effectively solves the problem of the sideways seating, but only at the cost of greatly enlarging the orchestra in relation to the rest of the auditorium. The audience would get a more comfortable view, but they would be further away from the stage. But perhaps the most revealing of these theatre designs is Jones's plan of the Drury Lane Cockpit. Here the degrees range around a full semicircle, and are extended forwards on each side so that a high proportion of the spectators flank the pit, looking inwards to it. Some of them – in what we shall discover are the most exclusive boxes – actually flank the stage, and have an excellent view of the play; but even in the pit the benches are ranged in what is sometimes still called 'collegiate' fashion, facing one another instead of the stage. Here there is no royal box to govern the disposition of the auditorium with its protocol. It appears that the habit of placing the audience so that it looked as much at itself as at the play had its roots deep in our stage history.

Serlio's motive for shaping the main part of his auditorium as a full semicircle was his desire to imitate the Roman form. His compromise with modern conditions allowed him to extend his *cavea* backwards so that the upper degrees were merely segmental, and effectively faced the stage. Basil followed this pattern in the narrow hall at Christ Church, and Webb's drawing records that the Paved Court theatre achieved a similar end, though in rectangular form. Here the seating is divided into two parts. At the front is a fully expressed U-shape of six risers, while at the back eight further rows extend straight across the house from side to side. Both the *Florimène* scheme and the Cockpit-in-Court are content with a regular U-shape, the former right-angled and the latter polygonal. The Paved Court and *Florimène* theatres, as well as Basil's Christ Church auditorium, provide a seatless piazza between the degrees and the stage, but in both of the non-scenic Cockpits this feature is reduced to a mere gangway at the front of the orchestra, now reinterpreted as a seated pit. Webb's unidentified project has so large an orchestra that no piazza is necessary, the great majority of the degrees being well removed from the stage. As the Drury Lane Cockpit approaches the stage area it begins to differ radically from any Italian model, whether built or published, and follows instead the pattern evidently established at the Blackfriars by James Burbage, with seating carried all around the house and even behind the stage at the upper level. The Cockpit-in-Court, taking the Olimpico as its pattern, carries the degrees all the way to the return walls of the *frons*, though the presence of a forestage which extends between them from one side of the pit to the other makes for a very different interaction of stage and auditorium.

In some fashion all of these theatres show the influence exerted by Serlio's well-known text, whether in the symmetry of their design, the human scale of their proportioning, or indeed in their echoes, however distant, of an antique magnificence. The most obviously 'Roman' of them all, apart perhaps from Webb's unidentified project, is the explicitly Palladian Cockpit-in-Court at Whitehall (plate 36), converted by Jones from Henry VIII's lavish and festive building of *c.* 1535. Jones incorporated the original gallery that had surrounded this octagonal interior from its inception into a regular *cavea* of degrees that rose from the level pit floor – in this case, of course, the actual location of the cock-fighting pit – in a steepening progression to the perimeter walls. In plan these seats took up five of the eight bays of the structure. The other three were screened by a wooden *frons scenae* built to a novel semicircular plan that may have derived from an ancient *frons* reported by Serlio to have stood near Fondi in central Italy.[15] Its architectural treatment, however, was light and rather French in taste, similar to work that Jones was engaged in for the queen at Somerset House. Above the stage was a coved plaster ceiling, and the large open space over the auditorium, beneath the Tudor cockpit's elaborate glazed lantern, was covered with a retractable blue *velarium* of calico and canvas. Once one had entered by one of the pit doors, or high onto the top level of the degrees, little of the sixteenth-century original would be visible. Jones's classical organization was everywhere, as thin as a board or a piece of ceiling cloth, but effectively closing off the older building from view. The original posts supporting the great lantern would remind a spectator of what had been, but five of these were obscured by the *frons* structure, leaving only three to stand out in the auditorium.[16]

The Cockpit was, however, a conversion rather than a new project fully worked up according to the architect's principles of design. Webb's drawings of it show little of the rational method that informs most of Jones's original schemes, and in particular the geometry of the pit – which occupies the place of the Roman orchestra – seems to have been defined exclusively by the Tudor fabric of the old building. The classicism of the finished theatre was a matter of broad allusion and general appearance, not of fundamental method. It is a very different matter in the other extant sets of drawings that we have before us in this chapter. We have seen how the idea of the neo-Roman orchestra was adopted in the Court playhouses, where it resembled the dancing floors of the masquing houses and could usefully isolate the royal state in a position that was required for reasons of protocol. A cursory glance at the drawings might suggest that this floor was proportioned almost by accident, being defined simply as the space that was left over when the necessary degrees had been aligned along the walls of the building. Entries in the Works accounts covering the provision of seating for masques and plays give little warrant for believing otherwise. Often they mention nothing more than an apparently routine procedure, as for example at Whitehall for Chapman's *Middle Temple and Lincoln's Inn Masque*, designed by Jones in 1613:

in making ready the hall with degrees and galleries for a Maske to be performed before the kinge by the gentlemen of the Temple . . .[17]

We shall probably never know quite what such abrupt formulae actually covered. It is possible that they describe a customary procedure of improvisation to suit each occasion, and that most of the Court auditoria were *ad hoc* arrangements of degrees and platforms carted in and assembled without much attention being given to the niceties of architectural symmetry. Nevertheless the extant drawings prove that for some events deemed important enough to require a detailed theatre plan the proportioning of the 'orchestra' space was far from arbitrary.

Vitruvius, in his discussion of the setting out of a theatre, produces a scheme in which the width of the orchestra is taken as a standard measure from which many other proportions of the structure may be derived. Thus the whole width of the *scaena*, or stage, is to be twice that of the orchestra, while the height of the vomitorium openings is to be made one-sixth of its width, and so forth. Against this passage in his copy of the *Ten Books* Jones wrote:

noat that y^e Diamiter of the orchestra ruiles y^e measurey of all.

Serlio's theatre scheme, as we observed in chapter 9, agrees that the diameter of the orchestra is a governing measure in the development of the whole plan, but there it is related to the width of the stage in the *ad quadratum* proportion of $1 : \sqrt{2}$. As we review the five remaining sets of theatre drawings that date from the period before the Restoration, we shall discover that each one of them follows these precedents in making the orchestra width a significant, and usually a standard, measure. At the Christ Church theatre

36 John Webb, the Cockpit-in-Court, Whitehall.

the area analogous to an orchestra was 24 ft wide, or half the depth of the *cavea* as defined by the scored arc within which it is described in the drawing. The original depth of the piazza was half the width of the orchestra, the king's 'Isle' or halpace was two-thirds, and so on. The pit at the Cockpit in Drury Lane did not 'ruile . . . yᵉ measurey of all', but was related to the depth of the stage as $\sqrt{2} : 1$, the result, as we shall see, of an *ad quadratum* construction evidently derived from Serlio's procedure. Webb's plan of the Paved Court theatre has few noted dimensions, but the chief of them records the width of the rectangular floor at the foot of the degrees as 18 ft, or precisely half the whole width of the auditorium. Evidently the notation is to be read as an indication of the method by which the whole is designed. Similarly the rectangular floor in the hall at Whitehall as fitted up for *Florimène* is marked at a total of 15 ft 4 ins across, a figure that governs the entire development of the plan. And in his unidentified theatre project Webb names the semicircular area at the foot of the degrees, and carefully calls attention to its size:

43 : fo bredth of yᵉ Orchestra.

In a further note he records that this is the depth too of the whole *cavea* to the columns of the *porticus* at its back. Only the remodelled Cockpit-in-Court fails to provide an orchestra-like feature whose width is systematically related to the architectural development of the building; yet even here the pit is defined by the old Tudor walls whose proportions closely approximate an *ad quadratum* development from the square plan of the outer perimeter of the structure. This last can hardly have been a deliberate part of Jones's intentions, but all the rest show every sign of being deeply considered proportionate designs.

In Serlio's work certain plans are more suitable than others for particular uses, not because they 'look right' nor even because they work well, but for reasons that have to do with the comparative 'perfection' of the circle and the square. The theatre plan is a combination of square and circle, coordinated by means of the venerable *ad quadratum* method, and it may be that Jones and Webb used similar methods in their work for the theatre. Some aspects of the design of a playhouse, such as the height of the stage or the size of a seating degree, must be governed by the actual dimensions of the people who are to make up its audience and its players, and Serlio adopts as his repeated commensurate unit the size of a single seating degree. Even the standard measure of the orchestra is an integral expression of this unit, and we must find out whether the English theatres were similarly scaled to the human frame. In a later chapter we shall see that Serlio also incorporates the perspective world of his scenes in the same commensurate system that he employs in the auditorium, so that the space of the one is virtually continuous with that of the other. For him the whole theatre scheme, seating and stage alike, is a wondrous interpenetration of Roman magnificence and modern technique, all rooted in and governed by a constant respect for the human scale. Is there any evidence that Jones and Webb thought in similar ways in seventeenth-century London?

We may begin with the drawings of a playhouse that will be considered more fully in the next chapter, the Cockpit in Drury Lane (plates 37 and 38). This was a commercial house, built for one of London's most tenacious theatre managers, Christopher Beeston, in 1616. It was converted from a regular cockpit that had been established on the site some seven years before, and retained a good part of its originally round plan, extending it with an additional rectangular stage end to form a U-shaped plan. Jones's designs are carefully drawn to a scale of 1 : 88, and show that the 40 ft width of the old circular building was retained, though extended to 55 ft by the new stage end.[18] In addition there were stair turrets attached, one for the stage and one for the auditorium. The undistinguished brick shell of the building was therefore proportioned in units of 5 ft, but the interior – where Jones was freer to design in his own fashion – was organized according to a module of 18 ins. The stage was 24 ft wide by 15 ft deep, its central door of entrance was 3 ft wide, the main entrance door was 4 ft 6 ins wide, and so on. Of course not every part of the design was governed by either module – the stage was 4 ft high and the main stage entrance 8 ft tall, for example – but a good many were. Even the upper windows were 4 ft 6 ins wide, and the narrow slits below were 3 ft tall. The unit of 18 ins was also used for the depth of each of the seating degrees in the auditorium, fulfilling a role similar to that of its counterpart in Serlio. Much of Jones's design was thus developed according to the principle of symmetry, and the unit which is everywhere repeated in the drawings is rooted in the human scale. Furthermore the relation of the stage to the auditorium is laid out along the lines of an *ad quadratum* construction, for the width of the pit between the opposing gallery rails is about 21 ft 2 ins, and is defined by the circumference of a circle described around a 15 ft square. A modular armature of two contingent 15 ft squares therefore governs the most important spatial relationships of the house, as is illustrated in plate 39. In this way the 'irrational' diameter of the pit – or, in Serlio's terms, the orchestra – is made a part of the general symmetry (15 ft representing 10 units of 18 ins each).

In the next chapter we shall return to this notable design for one of the most busy and influential of Jacobean playhouses, but for the moment it will serve to notice the thoroughly humanistic modularity of the drawings. The seating degree unit is repeated throughout the design; the orchestra width, though not the standard for the scheme, is included in it through the neo-Serlian device of the *ad quadratum* construction; and the 'perfect' figures of the square and the circle are therefore implicated in the plan's development. When we turn to the extensive documentation of the Paved Court

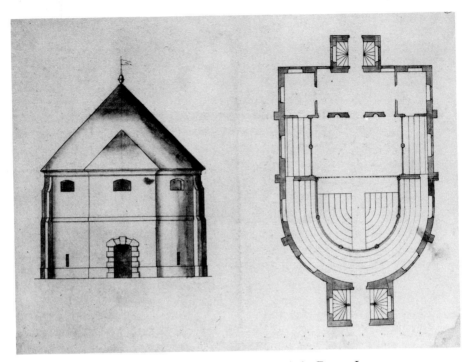

37   Inigo Jones, elevation and plan of the Cockpit in Drury Lane.

theatre we find that most of these characteristics are even more clearly expressed. The occasion for the building of the theatre was the performance – originally projected for the king's birthday in November 1632 – of Montagu's lengthy pastoral, *The Shepherd's Paradise*, by the queen and a number of her ladies. The production was to be more ambitious than was usual, and Jones was commissioned to design a standing scene for it, as well as a number of changeable backscenes. He had previously constructed many such scenic stages in various rooms at Somerset House, but for the present occasion it was decided to build a temporary theatre in the Lower, or Paved, Court of the palace, to the east of its main court. For this enterprise we have not only Jones's scenic designs, apparently in a complete set, but a generous entry in the Works accounts, a detailed plan by John Webb and even a page-long entry in what may be Jones's notebook concerning quantities and costs.[19] The building was erected, as was so often the case with the Court theatres, in something of a hurry. Late in the autumn of 1632 the carpenters were busy in the Paved Court, but they were quite unable to meet their first deadline of 19 November. The performance was several times postponed, in part because the ladies were not ready and in part because the theatre had not been finished. Eventually it was given on 9 January 1633, and the

174

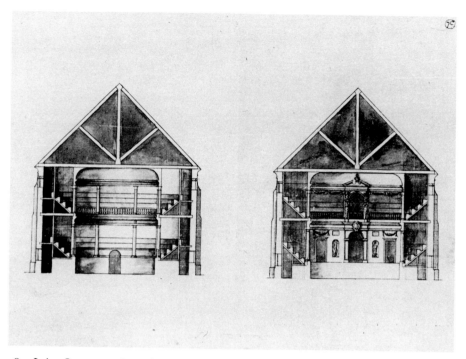

38 Inigo Jones, sections through the auditorium and stage of the Cockpit in Drury Lane.

auditorium was retained for a subsequent Shrove Tuesday masque (that year on 5 March) for which it underwent some fairly thorough modifications. The plan (plate 40) shows the first state of the building, before the alterations for the masque, and includes details of the stage as well as of the auditorium. The theatre was set up in the Paved Court so that its end walls were provided by the east and west walls of the permanent buildings; Jones had merely to provide the timber side walls 76 ft long and containing an auditorium 36 ft wide. The stage end was wider, at 51 ft, and was fitted with scenic equipment for running shutters along grooves and manipulating sets of relieves. There were degrees to either side of the house and at its west end, but there were at first no galleries. The construction was of fir and deal boards, the floor was boarded with split deal, and the roof was probably also of timber, for the accounts leave no record of tiles. After the production of Montagu's play the house was altered for the Shrovetide masque, and extensions were built to either side with galleries in them raising seats along the flanks of the auditorium. No records remain of any embellishments of the interior, save for the frontispiece design, the scenes themselves and mention of a blue cloth *velarium* over the main part of the auditorium.

The plan was drawn by Webb rather than Jones, and offers a thoughtful

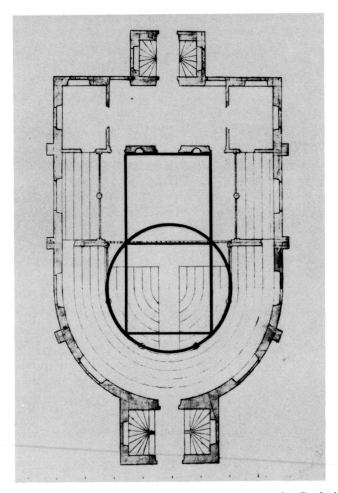

39 *Ad quadratum* relation of the stage to the auditorium at the Cockpit in Drury
Lane.

restatement of Serlian theatre principles in a Stuart context. One might
perhaps have expected the building to be a more or less *ad hoc* improvisation
in the space provided by the Paved Court, but the plan is anything but hasty
or casual in its approach to the problem of relating the scene to the auditorium, and of fitting the whole into the limited site. To be sure, the most
obvious characteristic of the Serlian auditorium – its semicircular *cavea* of
degrees – is here reduced to three sides of a rectangle, but the geometry by
which they are proportioned stems from the theatre design in the *Architettura*.
There is a Serlian 'piazza' between the seating and the stage, probably
intended here as a place for the ladies to perform. At the foot of the degrees is
a rectangular floor analogous to Serlio's semicircular orchestra, and like its

176

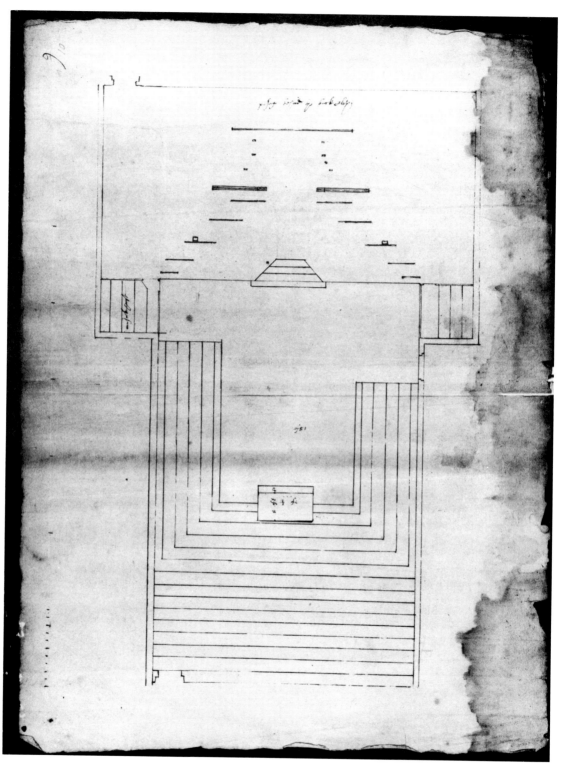

40 John Webb, plan of the Paved Court theatre, Somerset House.

progenitor it is scaled to a dimension that forms the basis of the design. Webb's plan is scaled, but includes also the single inscribed dimension of '18 fo' across the floor between the degrees. This figure is exactly half the whole width of the auditorium as measured between the centres of its timber walls and as recorded in the Works account:

a greate house of firtimber and Dealeborde in the paved Courte lxxvj fo: long xxxvj fo: wide and xxv fo: high with two outletts [i.e. extensions] at the end where the Sceane was . . .[20]

At 1 : 2 this proportion recalls Vitruvius rather than Serlio, but the Italian was chiefly concerned to compress as much as he could of a Roman *cavea* into his rectangular site, and resorted to the *ad quadratum* system to do so, so that his theatre is as wide as the diagonal of a square described around the orchestra. Webb also follows an *ad quadratum* scheme in his Paved Court plan, for the stage end of the house is 51 ft wide between centres, or 36 ft × $\sqrt{2}$. It seems likely that this proportion was derived originally from an *ad quadratum* construction centred at the middle point of the orchestra, but there is nothing rigid about Webb's use of the scheme; he extends dimensions derived from it to other parts of the house in a way that could not be controlled by the geometrical construction. The depth of the auditorium, for example, is also 51 ft as measured from the back wall to the stage front, but this longitudinal measurement is not centred on the mid-point of the orchestra. Furthermore the orchestra centre is just 36 ft from the back corners of the house, so that it is located at the apex of an equilateral triangle based on the back wall, a procedure that has nothing to do with the *ad quadratum* scheme, but follows quite precisely the method in the woodcut plan of the theatre in the Venetian edition of Serlio's *Architettura* published in 1551. There the centre of the orchestra is 34 units from each back corner of the plan, and the house is 34 units wide. In general the Paved Court plan is a free adaptation of the Serlian scheme, using many of its methods and translating its organization to a rectangular form. As a geometrical development on the sheet it looks more deeply into the Italian's way of proceeding in auditorium design than does the plan for the theatrical conversion of Christ Church hall in 1605, even though the immediate resemblance is less striking.

In Serlio the 2 ft depth of each seating degree is taken as the size of the modular unit from which the whole work is measured, and the human scale of the stage itself is established by erecting it as high as a man's eye, or $4\frac{1}{2}$ Venetian feet from the floor. The stage shown in Jones's elevation of the standing scene is only 18 ins high, and clearly has nothing to do with the Serlian model, nor is its arrangement of flat wings and backscene of shutters and relieves akin to the scheme in the *Architettura*. Furthermore Webb's degrees are smaller than Serlio's, and do not possess a full modular relation to the rest of the design. We can tell exactly how large they were by measuring off the whole block of eight of them at the back of the house against the scale: all the eight together take up 12 ft 8 ins, so that each one is 19 ins deep. The U-shaped *cavea* degrees around the orchestra are of a similar size, although the front ones and back ones at the sides are smaller than the rest. A measure of 19 ins has nothing to do with the size of the orchestra itself, nor with the *ad quadratum* system of proportioning, but it does represent a methodical division of the whole length of 76 ft, of which it is a 48th part. The degrees on the right-hand side range exactly to the halfway point of the length of the building; this side of the auditorium is again divided into three, with one part devoted to the degrees at the back of the house, and two parts to the U-shaped *cavea*. To the left there is room for the lateral degrees to be carried further towards the stage, and there the simplicity of the proportion is interrupted. Nevertheless it appears that Webb arrived at the size of each degree by a process of subdividing the major dimension of the theatre, a procedure that is quite the reverse of Serlio's. In the English design the degree dimension is subordinate to the proportions of the site; in the Italian it constitutes the unit out of which the whole structure is ultimately framed.

Webb's method was thorough, and clearly influenced by Serlio though by no means merely subservient to him; yet it may be that much of its force was lost in the event. A notebook crammed with entries on builders' rates and techniques for estimating survives at the Yale Center for the Study of British Art, and is possibly in Jones's hand. It contains a page full of jottings on the Paved Court theatre, and shows that in one interpretation at least the proportions of the building were altogether simpler than appears both in the declared Works account and in Webb's plan. According to the notebook the house was 75 ft long where the other documents give it as 76 ft; and it was 34 ft wide where they have 36 ft. The Works account, Jones's elevation of the frontispiece and the builder's notebook all agree that it was 25 ft tall, as the notebook puts it, 'from the ground [i.e. the floor] to the underside of the beames'. The scenic end was made wider by the presence of two 'outtletts', each 8 ft deep, so that it measured – in the notebook's terms – exactly 50 ft overall. If the stage was actually 25 ft deep, as appears in Webb's plan, then this end of the house was constructed as a perfect double cube, 50 ft × 25 ft × 25 ft. The auditorium was, in this version, 42 ft deep to the piazza, which itself must have measured 8 ft, for a total of 50 ft. When this part of the building was extended for the masque, with galleries in line with the 8 ft 'outtletts', it will have measured just 50 ft square. Perhaps Jones was less interested than Webb in the fine points of Serlio's theatre design. Certainly there is something almost perfunctorily direct about the measurements recorded in the notebook, though of course they are if anything more obviously symmetrical, and more devoted to the perfection of the square.

We cannot unfortunately make similar judgments about most of the theatrical preparations at Court, because so few of them are adequately

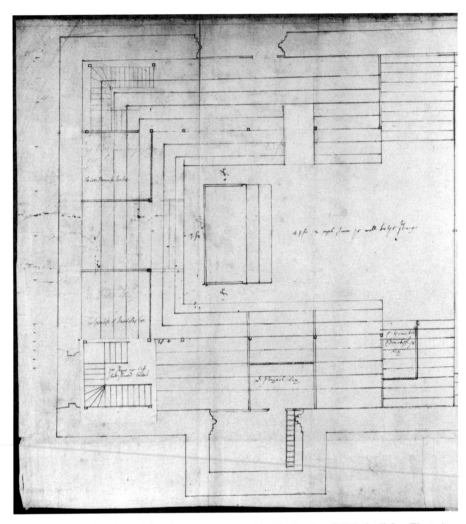

41   John Webb, plan of the theatre prepared in the hall at Whitehall for *Florimène*.

documented. In the case of *Florimène*, however, we have a large collection of drawings, both architectural and scenic,[21] and from them we can derive a fairly complete picture of how the hall at Whitehall was converted into a substantial scenic theatre. There is a large raked stage at the screens end of the room, with a scene consisting of four pairs of angled wings before a backshutter assembly and space for backscenes of relieve (plate 41, right). There is an upper stage for an appearance of deities towards the end of the play, and framing the whole scene is a large frontispiece over 30 ft tall and nearly 40 ft wide. In front of this is a forestage, apparently raked like the scenic stage beyond it, and standing 4 ft 6 ins high at its front. The audi-

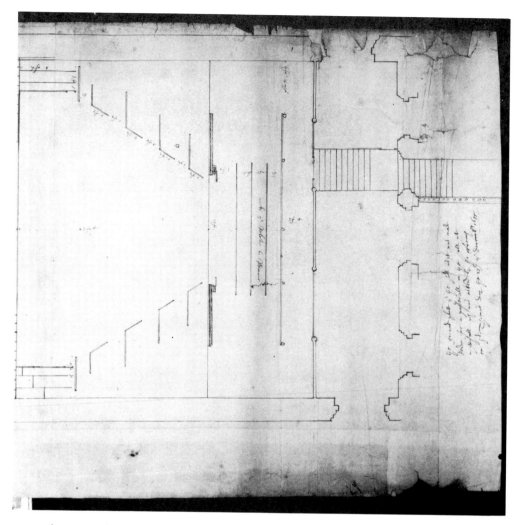

torium consists of a rectangular orchestra surrounded by degrees on three sides. At the end opposite the stage stands the royal halpace. The degrees rise towards the walls, three steps deep in the orchestra itself, with a further five steps behind the posts supporting a gallery which is not shown in the plan but presumably also has five steps of degrees.

The plan of the stage is inscribed with numerous dimensions, and is evidently a carefully considered adaptation of the Serlian model, with fore-stage, angled wings and backscene, the latter now developed into a cluster of moveable backshutters, profile relieves and a backcloth. The auditorium seems at first sight to be merely an improvised arrangement of seating set out in the simplest way, without much thought for the precisions of architectural design. Yet Webb's plan is carefully organized throughout. The orchestra is

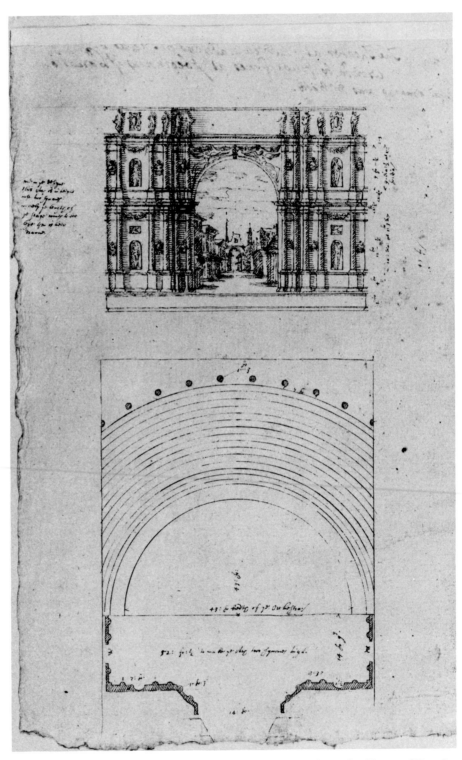

42 John Webb, unidentified theatre plan developed from the Teatro Olimpico.

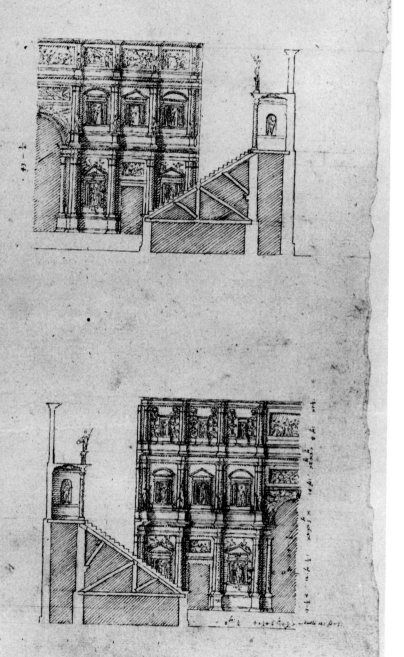

15 ft 4 ins wide (the sum of measurements inscribed across it at the halpace end) and 23 ft long from the front degree to the edge of the piazza where the U-shaped seating ends. Its floor is therefore proportioned exactly in the ratio 2 : 3. The width of the auditorium between the gallery fronts is also 23 ft. The stage end of the house is incorporated into this simple modularity, for the height of the frontispiece as drawn in the section of the scene[22] is 30 ft 8 ins, or twice the width of the orchestra; and the depth of the stage to the back-shutters is marked at '23 foott'. The height of the gallery in the auditorium is not known, but it is reached by steps with 23 risers. If each was the customary 8 ins, the whole flight would have reached 15 ft 4 ins, and it may be that the back of the upper gallery rose precisely halfway up the frontispiece.

Webb appears to have taken the 15 ft 4 ins measure from the bay size of the Tudor hall's brick and stone structure, which was a little over 90 ft long externally and built in six bays. On the face of it his organization of the auditorium therefore has little to do with the deliberately human scale adopted by Serlio. The depth of most of the seating degrees is an un-Serlian 18 ins, a standard, it would seem, in contemporary London playhouses, for we find it in the upper tiers of benches in the Christ Church plan, and again at the Cockpit in Drury Lane. Yet for Serlio the stage height had been established at the level of a man's eye 'looking directly forward', or 4 ft 6 ins Venetian above the floor, and the *Florimène* stage in both Webb's section and Jones's elevation of the standing scene is also 4 ft 6 ins high (though in English feet). In this case, moreover, the dimension is related to the equally human scale size of the seats (18 ins × 3 = 4 ft 6 ins) and to the 30 ft width of the scenic opening (18 ins × 20 = 30 ft). Webb also incorporates the proportions of the scene into those of the auditorium, so that both are part of the same modular system, just as in Serlio the squaring of the forestage by which the scene itself is proportioned repeats the dimensions of the degrees in the *cavea*.

Webb's project developed from Palladio's *frons* studies for the Olimpico was also a thoughtful scheme, though its occasion remains unidentified and the drawing may have been no more than an exercise (plate 42). The size of the theatre as planned to the given scale is altered radically in some written notations, an indication perhaps that this was a flexible theatre of the mind, and that no particular site was envisaged. The main influence on the design is certainly Palladio's drawing, whose handling of the architectural orders is closely followed in both manner and scale, but this is Palladio chilled into a staid impressiveness. No explicit provision is made for the circulation of the audience or the accommodation of actors, but as drawn to scale on the sheet the design is full of the type of simple symmetries we have noticed in the *Florimène* theatre. It employs a plan module of 3 ft 6 ins, so that the scaled width of the orchestra, 49 ft, is fourteen times the height of the stage front (3 ft

6 ins). The segmental degrees rise towards a portico of columns at the back of the house, and these are drawn on 7 ft centres; this is the dimension also of the prime bays in the *frons* structure. The width of the stage between the return walls of the *frons* is 56 ft by the scale (or sixteen times 3 ft 6 ins). The width of the arch scales at 18 ft, not part of the system, but Webb added a note that the width of the stage should be reduced by 3 ft 6 ins 'to make ye Arch two squares high'. If this reduction involved narrowing the arch to half its height it will have measured 14 ft across in the clear (or four times 3 ft 6 ins). As with the similar commensurate scheme at Whitehall in 1635, this appears to have little relation to the human scale. The degrees of seating are drawn a little unevenly, but fifteen steps take up 22 ft 6 ins, so that each is doubtless intended to be the standard 18 ins deep. But this figure is nowhere else expressed in the design; the orders in the *frons* are explicitly based on a column diameter of 1 ft 3 ins for the lower storey and 1 ft for the upper. The columns of the portico are likewise marked as 1 ft 3 ins in diameter. There is no evidence here of a careful development of Serlian principles of design even though the segmental auditorium and scene of angled wings clearly owe their origins to the *Architettura*, just as the great *frons* was developed from the Olimpico drawing. The project remains a literary, theoretical exercise, owing little to the auditorium and scenic arrangements of the Vicenzan theatre as it was built, and still less to the vigorous playhouses of contemporary London, to which we must now return.

12
The private theatres

So-called 'private' playhouses had been part of the London theatre world since 1576, when Richard Farrant set up the First Blackfriars in the old priory buildings and used it to accommodate the performances of the Children of Windsor and the Children of the Chapel.[1] It lasted only a few years, but just before his death in 1597 James Burbage converted another part of the priory, the Upper Frater, into a permanent playhouse intended for the Lord Chamberlain's Men. In doing so he set a pattern that was to influence at least two other important indoor theatres constructed in the following decades, though in fact his enterprise suffered an immediate setback and was prevented from opening. The new playhouse stood empty for three years before it was leased to Henry Evans for the use of the Children of the Chapel. Meanwhile a theatre had been established for the Children of Paul's somewhere at or close by the cathedral. It was an enclosed house like the Blackfriars, and appears to have had a round or semicircular auditorium.[2] In 1608 the boy actors at the Blackfriars got into serious trouble with the authorities and Henry Evans was forced to surrender his lease of the property. At last the adult players – by now renamed the King's Men – could move in, and there they established London's first fully professional indoor theatre, treating it as their winter location, with the Globe increasingly becoming limited to the summer season.[3] In 1616 Christopher Beeston, doubtless prompted by the success of the Blackfriars, converted the round cockpit in Drury Lane into his Cockpit playhouse, of which we have Jones's detailed drawings. A year or two earlier there had been a proposal to build a similar type of playhouse at Puddle Wharf, but nothing is known of the building's structure, beyond the likelihood that it was an enclosed house.[4] And scarcely more is recorded about the Salisbury Court, built in 1629, the last of the indoor theatres to be opened before the Commonwealth.[5]

Until the recent identification of Jones's drawings of the Cockpit the design of all these playhouses remained a subject for speculation, though much of it was mercifully very well informed. It is encouraging, for example, to compare Jones's plan and sections (plates 37 and 38) with the drawings of

186

the Blackfriars which accompany Richard Hosley's reconstruction in *The Revels History of Drama in English*.[6] Hosley's illustrations were made without knowledge of the Cockpit drawings, and yet the resemblance is close. Nevertheless there is a good deal of information in Jones's scheme that may, if carefully treated, lead us towards a fuller understanding of the indoor playhouses, even including the Blackfriars.

Several attempts at deducing the design of this most influential of the private theatres had been made before Hosley wrote his essay. A drawing by J. H. Farrar which was presented to a meeting of the English Association at the University of Aberdeen came to have enormous influence on our modern ideas about the playhouse.[7] Based on the researches of G. Topham Forrest, it showed a rectangular auditorium consisting of a level pit equipped with straight benches aligned parallel with the stage front. The elevated stage reached right across the large rectangular room, and along the lateral walls were ranged two levels of galleries jettying forwards into the auditorium. The frame of the drawing indicated that there was a similar disposition of galleries at the rear of the room, where the artist located his imaginary point of view. Beneath these galleries, rising from the level of the pit, degrees were ranged along the side walls, and presumably also at the rear. The galleries, shifting level in order to accommodate the height of the stage, continued over the stage itself, where spectators were shown viewing the performance from behind. At the centre of the first gallery was a curtained upper stage; the second gallery appears to have been too high here for utility, and became instead a decorative display of cartouches, obelisks and strapwork. Farrar's drawing is immensely appealing, and it formed the basis of a similar one published by Irwin Smith in his monumental study of the playhouse.[8]

The jettying of the galleries, a curious device for the interior of a building and one rejected by Smith, suggests that the Fortune contract was a potent influence in Farrar's scheme, for the galleries in that open playhouse were jettied forward ten inches to each storey. Irwin Smith likewise found that the dimensions of the Fortune were helpful in his reconstruction,[9] and more recently Richard Hosley has followed the same path, though he refers also to the arrangements made at Whitehall for *Florimène*.[10] All are agreed that the Blackfriars, being constructed in a large rectangular room, was itself a rectangular auditorium.

The playhouse was certainly erected in a chamber called the Upper Frater in the old dissolved Dominican Priory on the sloping land between St Paul's and the river. The theatre was reached by stairs and stood high up among the surrounding buildings. Something of a view of it may be seen in a drawing of St Paul's and the river by Hollar,[11] and it turns up again in the same artist's 'True and Exact Prospect' of the city showing it before and after the fire of 1666. Here, in the vista of the ruins, we can even catch a glimpse of

43A Wenceslaus Hollar, 'A True and Exact Prospect . . .' (1666), showing the Blackfriars theatre building before the Fire of London.

the rectangular interior of the Upper Frater (plate 43B), though there is no sign of the theatrical fittings. The theatre had long since ceased to be used for plays, and its interior had been converted into tenements.

The Blackfriars was the most influential of the private theatres of the early seventeenth century, but after 1616 it had a rival in the Cockpit in Drury Lane, sometimes known as the Phoenix. This playhouse was converted from a round cockpit built by John Best, Cockmaster to Prince Henry. From Jones's drawings (plates 37 and 38) it appears that the conversion was made by enlarging the original structure to form a U-shaped plan, the stage end of the house being located in the addition, and the auditorium occupying half of the old cockpit's round.[12] The circularity of the galleried auditorium was therefore partly a mere accident of the building's history, having been established for quite another purpose. Yet the shape of the original cockpit seems to have struck the new owner, Christopher Beeston, as being especially suited to development as a regular enclosed playhouse of the Blackfriars type. We shall come in a moment to this question of shape, and its significance in our theatre history, but first we must take notice of the many other ways in which Jones's Cockpit design resembles what we know about the layout of the Blackfriars.

The interior of the Blackfriars was gutted in 1649 by the Parliamentary troops, but the Cockpit, though similarly assaulted, escaped more lightly

188

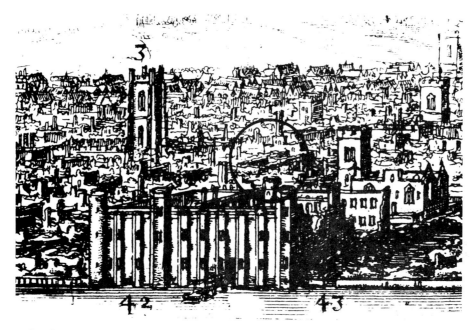

43B   The ruins of the Blackfriars after the fire.

and was repaired by William Beeston, Christopher's son.[13] It survived to the
Restoration and beyond, and was known to the antiquary James Wright,
who in his dialogue *Historia Histrionica* of 1699 surveyed the story of the
English stage, couching the work as a conversation between two enthusiasts.
Truman tells Lovewit about the old playhouses:

The *Black-friers*, *Cockpit*, and *Salisbury-court*, were called Private Houses, and were
very small to what we see now. The *Cockpit* was standing since the Restauration . . .
Lovew.   I have seen that.
Trum.   Then you have seen the other two, in effect; for they were all three Built
almost exactly alike, for Form and Bigness. Here they had Pits for the Gentry, and
Acted by Candle-light.[14]

Wright was born in 1643,[15] and cannot have seen a performance in either the
Blackfriars or the Salisbury Court, both of which were despoiled of their
theatrical fittings while he was still a child. As a young man, however, he had
lived in Silver Street where his father was the minister of St Olave's, and he
will have known the Cockpit at first hand during the period when it was
active with Davenant's operas. He was, therefore, in Lovewit's shoes rather
than Truman's, but he had talked to the old players and knew their stories.
Much of the information in the *Historia Histrionica* is secondhand, but it is
based on interviews with prime witnesses, and on most of the points that we

189

can check Truman lives up to his name. The private theatres were indeed smaller than the London houses of the close of the seventeenth century; they were lit by candles and they did have pits for the gentry. In 'Bigness' they do seem to have been similar, for the Blackfriars was made in a room 46 ft by 66 ft internally, the Cockpit measured 40 ft by 55 ft externally (excluding its attached stair turrets), and at the Salisbury Court a dancing room was built above the theatre 40 ft square, indicating that the auditorium itself was 40 ft wide, for it was placed on a site only 42 ft across.[16] These figures, though they are by no means complete, do support Truman's statement that the theatres were 'almost exactly alike' in size. And if for size, so also for form. If Wright's Truman is to be believed – and he is in the remainder of his story a generally reliable witness – then the Blackfriars resembled both the Cockpit and the Salisbury Court in substantial matters of design.

The Cockpit is shown in Jones's drawings as possessing two levels of galleries, an upper one supported on posts and a lower at the level of the rear of the pit, where the seats rise upward from the ground floor. We know that the Blackfriars was equipped with galleries, though their number is un-specified. In a deposition made in King's Bench in 1609, concerning a disputed bond, Alexander Hawkins read into the record the terms of the lease which Henry Evans had entered into with Richard Burbage when he took over the playhouse, which is then described in Latin, with a few English translations of some of the more pertinent terms. The property consisted of *'tocius illius magne aule vel loci anglice* Roome *cum locis anglice* roomes *super eadem sicut tunc fuerunt erecti ornati Anglice* furnished *& edificati cum Theatro Anglice* a Stadge *porticibus Anglice* Galleries *& sedibus'.*[17] In the English terms, the 'Roome' had certain other 'roomes' above it, and was 'furnished' with 'a Stadge', 'Galleries' and, we may add from the Latin, seats. It has sometimes been supposed that there were three levels of galleries, on the basis of two references in contemporary documents to audience members sitting 'in the middle region',[18] taken to mean the middle gallery of three. But 'the middle region' might very well have been some other part of the auditorium, and it would be unwise to base a reconstruction of the theatre on so flimsy a piece of evidence. All previous attempts to imagine what the Blackfriars looked like have assumed that the pit floor was level, not built up with degrees of seating. A schedule of the seating once attached to the Burbage–Evans lease, and perhaps also to Hawkins' recitation of it, is now unfortunately lost, and with it our hope of certainty in the matter. But if the auditorium did seat its highest-paying customers all on a level floor their sightlines would have been unnecessarily obscured, and they themselves will not have been quite as much on view as many of them would have liked. If the pit seats were tiered, as common sense suggests they must have been, then the lower gallery must have been elevated enough to look over them. In Jones's Cockpit design this simple solution leads to a further architectural felicity. The lower gallery floor is pitched at the same height as the stage, so that when the upper gallery extends over the stage itself it can clear enough headroom beneath without an abrupt change of level between one end of the house and the other. If we attempt to crush three storeys of galleries into an acceptable height at the Blackfriars – consistent, that is, with other extant examples of the Domini-can type of hall – the trick can only be turned at the expense of leaving the pit floor flat, and of admitting the architecturally unhappy dislocation of the gallery levels between the stage and house ends of the theatre. Jones's solution at the Cockpit may have been his own, or it may have reflected conditions that already obtained at the Blackfriars. The improbability of the flat pit suggests that the latter case is the more likely.

Hawkins' document also tells us that there was a *theatrum* or 'Stadge' in the theatre, and adds that in 1604 there were certain dilapidations in the flooring at the east end of it (*fuerunt in diversis partibus inde in decasu & minime reparata videlicet . . . in paviamento in orientali fine cuiusdam Theatri Anglice* the Stadge).[19] If the stage had an eastern end it will have run east and west across the room, whose longer axis ran north and south. In this way too it resembled the Cockpit, where the stage spans the shorter axis of the house. But the deposition is not an architectural document, and it fails to say anything further about how these parts of the theatre were related to each other. We must turn instead to more anecdotal evidence.

There are several mentions of boxes at the Blackfriars, few of them very specific.[20] But a newsletter written by the tattler John Pory in 1632 tells a dramatic tale which incidentally includes an account of how one of them was positioned in relation to the stage. The letter describes a current Star Chamber case involving Lord Thurles and a certain Captain Essex:

The occasion was this. This Captaine attending and accompanying my Lady of Essex in a boxe in the playhouse at the blackfryers, the said lord coming upon the stage, stood before them and hindred their sight. Captain Essex told his lordship, they had payd for their places as well as hee, and therfore intreated him not to deprive them of the benefitt of it. Wherevpon the lord stood vp yet higher and hindred more their sight. Then Captain Essex with his hand putt him a little by. The lord then drewe his sword and ran full butt at him, though hee missed him, and might have slaine the Countesse as well as him.[21]

It was possible for somebody sitting in a box to reach forward and touch a person standing on the stage, and then to suffer the peril of being run at with a sword, all the while without leaving his place. Such a box must have flanked the stage itself, and been pretty much on a level with it. Just such seating is shown by Jones at the Cockpit, on either side of the stage. Here again the Cockpit drawings conform to the pattern established at the Black-friars.

191

The Blackfriars documents make no mention of a tiring room, but there must have been a place in which the actors prepared themselves and from which they made their entrances onto the platform. Doubtless it was subsumed, in the Burbage–Evans lease, under the Latin term *theatrum*, in which case it will have formed part of the fitting out accomplished by Burbage in 1596. At the Cockpit Jones shows a range of three interconnecting chambers beyond the *frons scenae* at the lower level, and from the central one the actors made their entrances through three doors, the middle one larger than the others. In his meticulous study of the stage requirements of Blackfriars plays Richard Hosley concluded that the playhouse possessed three stage doors, the central one large enough to act as a 'discovery space';[22] indeed the first stage direction of *Eastward Ho* refers to the middle door as serving this purpose: '*At the middle dore, Enter Golding discouering a Gold-smiths shoppe.*'[23] Here is further confirmation that the Blackfriars resembled the Cockpit, and when we turn to the gallery over the stage we find much the same similarity. Some sort of stage action at this upper level is required in eight of the plays which Hosley identified as certainly presented at the Blackfriars, including several occasions when the actors appear at what is characterized, in dialogue or stage direction, as a window.[24] At the Cockpit Jones shows the stage gallery as filled to either side with seating degrees for the audience, except for a narrow section at the middle where no degrees are marked and the aedicule treatment of the *frons* suggests a window case. In locating seating in the stage gallery Jones agrees with what we know of the arrangements at the public playhouses, and conforms too to the pattern of the theatres shown in a vignette on the title page of Alabaster's *Roxana* (1632) and in the frontispiece of *The Wits* (1662),[25] both of which may allude in a general way to private playhouse conditions and depict onlookers seated here. The central part, framed with terms and surmounted by a broken pediment at the Cockpit, was generally used as a music room when not required for an upper stage, and at the Blackfriars many plays refer to the presence of the'*Musique aboue*'.[26]

In all these large matters, then, the Cockpit drawings coincide with what we know about the characteristics of the Blackfriars playhouse. To be sure, the theatre in Drury Lane was smaller than its cousin in the city, but both appear to have had room for audience members on all four sides of the stage. At the Cockpit the all-roundness of the performance arrangements was reinforced by the actual roundness of the auditorium end of the house, a shape that shows in plan a fairly close kinship to the Roman theatre. Hitherto it has been assumed that the Blackfriars differed from the Cockpit in this most important respect, and resembled instead the rectangular temporary theatres at Court. But if Wright's Truman was correct to convey the idea that the two playhouses were 'almost exactly alike' in those internal fittings that we have been able to check, could it be that he was accurate in this matter too, and that the Blackfriars had a U-shaped auditorium built around a similar-shaped pit?

The pit at the Cockpit playhouse was located on the very spot where the birds had originally fought out their mains in a flurry of blood and feather. We therefore owe the theatrical use of the word to Drury Lane, but it soon spread elsewhere, even to the Blackfriars. Leonard Digges, in his prefatory verses to the 1640 edition of Shakespeare's *Poems*, alludes to what he calls the 'Cockpit' of the Blackfriars at a typical performance of *Much Ado*:

> let but *Beatrice*
> And *Benedicke* be seene, loe in a trice
> The Cockpit Galleries, Boxes, all are full . . .[27]

The Blackfriars pit antedated that at the Cockpit, but was similar enough to go by the same new name once it was established in common speech. But the circularity of this feature is an important, even perhaps a distinguishing, characteristic: seldom do we come across square or rectangular cockpits. Shakespeare places the word 'cockpit' parallel with 'this wooden O' in the Prologue to *Henry V*, and its circular connotation is confirmed by examples given in the *Oxford English Dictionary*: 'In roundnesse such as it a Cock pit were' (1587), 'A Circle dug in the earth, like a Cockpit' (1719). The theatrical pit at the house in Drury Lane was certainly rounded in shape; both Wright and Digges imply that it was the same shape at the Blackfriars.

At Drury Lane the pit was defined by the forward faces of the surrounding galleries, and these too were rounded in plan. Lacking specific evidence on this point for both the Blackfriars and the Salisbury Court, we must turn for help to the internal evidence of the plays written for these private houses. Occasionally the prologues and epilogues will take notice of the design of the auditorium as they make their direct address to the audiences, and although explicit descriptions of the auditoria are rare, and sometimes even then difficult to ascribe with any certainty to a particular theatre, a few useful allusions do survive.[28] Most refer to the place where the audience is seated as an orb, a sphere or a round. Such words may be taken too literally to mean that the theatre itself was circular, but we know that this was not so at the Cockpit and it is very unlikely to have been so at the Blackfriars and the Salisbury Court. In fact it is common parlance to describe a rounded, U-planned range of theatrical seating as a 'circle', as in our modern term 'dress circle': Serlio calls the semicircular orchestra in his theatre scheme 'La parte circolare'.[29] With this necessary caveat in mind we may usefully turn to a few such allusions, beginning with those that can be associated with the Cockpit, an auditorium that was certainly rounded. In this theatre *The Sun's Darling*, a masque-like play by Ford and Dekker, was licensed for performance by 'the Cockpit Company' by Sir Henry Herbert on 3 March 1624. It was also presented at Court, but the dialogue appears to have been composed with the Drury Lane house in mind rather than Whitehall. At the end of Act I the sun speaks from an upper level:

> We must descend, and leave a while our sphere
> To greet the world – ha, there does now appear
> A circle in this round, of beams that shine,
> As if their friendly lights would darken mine.[30]

The compliment to an audience as a circle of shining beams is conventional enough, but in this case the circle is located 'in this round', a phrase that must refer to the architectural form of the auditorium. A similar conceit occurs in Heywood's *Love's Mistress*, '*Publikely Acted*', according to its title page in 1636, '*by the* QUEENS *comœdians, At the* Phœnix *in* Drury-lane [i.e. the Cockpit]', and also presented at Court. Here Apuleius speaks to Midas, alluding to the audience:

> See'st thou this spheare spangled, with all these starres,
> All these Love-arts; nor shall they part from hence
> With unfeasted eares.[31]

Much as in *The Sun's Darling* at the same playhouse, the audience is characterized as a cluster of lights – this time stars rather than beams – spangled about a sphere. The galleried auditorium of the Cockpit, with its ranks of degrees rising towards the perimeter wall, would indeed have resembled the interior of a sphere as seen from the stage. The same term is used by Shirley in the 'Female Prologue' addressed to the gentlewomen at the theatre during a performance of *The Coronation* in 1635:

> You are the bright intelligencies move,
> And make a harmony this sphere of Love.[32]

If such casual allusions serve to confirm the rounded shape of the Cockpit as we know it from Jones's drawings, a similar collection made from plays performed at the Salisbury Court playhouse indicates that it too had a 'circular' or rounded auditorium. Two plays by Thomas Randolph make such references in their epilogues. At the end of *The Muses Looking-Glass*, performed in 1630, the 'Epilogus' addresses the audience:

> Y'Have seen *The Muses Looking-glasse*, Ladyes fair,
> And Gentle youths; And other too who ere
> Have fill'd this Orbe . . .[33]

The youths and ladies have filled the orb of the theatre; the allusion is not merely a conventional courtesy to a brilliant social circle. The phrase is used again by Pilumnus when he epiloguizes at the end of *Amyntas*, also performed in 1630:

> Would every Lady in this orbe might see
> Their Loves as happy as we say they be![34]

In *A Fine Companion* (1632–3) the author – Shakerley Marmion – speaks the prologue:

> you wrong th'approved judgments of
> This noble Auditory, who like a Spheare
> Mooved by a strong Intelligence, sit round
> To crowne our Infant Muse, whose cælestiall
> Applause, shee heard at her first entrance.[35]

The epilogue to *The Careless Shepherdess* (performed *c.* 1638) was probably written by Richard Brome, who was contracted to provide such items at the Salisbury Court,[36] and both the *praeludium* and the prologue refer specifically to the playhouse. In it the *Grand Satyre* refers to the audience:

> For when he sees a Constellation rise
> Shot from the glorious light of severall eyes
> That gild the Orbe, he knowes these are not Bowers
> For Silvian dames . . .[37]

Lewis Sharpe repeated the formal compliment in the prologue to his play *The Noble Stranger*, published in 1640 '*As it was Acted at the Private House in Salisbury Court*':

> Blest Fate protect me! what a lustre's here?
> How many Starres deck this our little spheare?[38]

And a phrase in some prefatory verses contributed to this edition by Richard Woolfall make the matter of the rounded auditorium quite explicit:

> Friend, from me thou canst not expect a praise . . .
> No, 'tis thy owne smooth numbers must preferre
> Thy Stranger to the Globe-like Theatre.[39]

It seems clear, on the combined evidence of Jones's drawings and the allusions in the plays, that both the Cockpit and the Salisbury Court possessed rounded auditoria. The references in prologues and epilogues are particularly significant in view of the fact that there seem to be no counter-vailing allusions to a square or rectangular arrangement at these two houses. Yet such acknowledgments of a squared-off auditorium were sometimes made in plays written for the square Fortune playhouse. The prologue to Dekker's *Whore of Babylon*, acted there in about 1605, conjures the audience's attention:

> The Charmes of silence through this Square be throwne,
> That an vn-vsed Attention (like a Iewell)
> May hang at euery eare . . .[40]

And Sir Alexander Wengrave, in Dekker and Middleton's comedy *The Roaring Girl* (acted at the Fortune about 1610) describes his house in terms that actually refer to the physical characteristics of the theatre:

> Within this square a thousand heads are laid,
> So close, that all of heads, the roome seemes made.[41]

If the square Fortune could be so clearly characterized in casual allusions, one would have expected the private theatres, had they been square or rectangular, to have left a similar mark instead of the 'round' descriptions we have discovered.

If both the Cockpit and the Salisbury Court boasted round or segmental auditoria, what, then, of the Blackfriars, the third private playhouse mentioned by Wright's Truman as sharing the same form as the others? One piece of information suggests that on this occasion Truman was mistaken, for in John Day's *The Isle of Gulls* – 'As it hath been often playd in the blacke Fryars, by the Children of the Reuels' – there is a reference to the 'corners' of the galleries. Dametas is cursing poetasters and playwrights generally:

> Insted of plaudites, their chiefest blisses
> Let their desarts be crownd with mewes and hisses:
> Behinde each post and at the gallery corners,
> Sit empty guls, slight fooles and false informers . . .[42]

At first reading we should probably take these gallery corners as an indication that the Blackfriars was a rectangular house, but of course the word could as well be used of the angles of a polygon. That this is the correct interpretation is suggested by an exchange in the Induction to Ben Jonson's comedy *The Magnetic Lady*, performed at the Blackfriars in 1632. A couple of wits, Probee and Damplay, meet a boy of the house on the stage and discuss theatrical matters with him, claiming to speak for the more informed elements within the audience:

Pro.   Not the *Faeces*, or grounds of your people, that sit in the oblique caves and wedges of your house, your sinfull six-penny Mechanicks –
Dam.   But the better, and braver sort of your people! Plush and Velvet-outsides! that stick your house round like so many eminences . . .[43]

The phrase 'caves and wedges' is a literal translation of the Latin terms *cavea* and *cunei*, used to describe the segmental seating (*cavea*) and sectors of seating (*cunei*) in the Roman theatre. The terms are employed rather loosely here, and one suspects Jonson of snobbishly making Probee reveal the inaccuracy of his scholarship, for the word 'caves', in the plural, is certainly misapplied. Probee appears to confuse it with the further removes of the auditorium, at the back of the galleries perhaps, assuredly beyond the more expensive pit seating. But the adjective 'oblique' and the noun 'wedges' conspire to evoke an arrangement of seating somewhat along the lines of the polygonal structure set up by Simon Basil at Christ Church in 1605. Jonson had used the former word in the 'Dedication to the Reader' prefaced to his play *The New Inn*, published in 1631. Its meaning there is a little obscure, but he seems to have been making a punning allusion to the appearance of the spectators at the theatre and the woolly indirectness of their speech:

a hundred fastidious *impertinents* . . . [came to the play] To see, and to bee seene. To make a generall muster of themselues in their clothes of credit: and possesse the Stage, against the Play. To dislike all, but marke nothing. And by their confidence of rising between the Actes, in oblique lines, make *affidauit* to the whole house, of their not vnderstanding one Scene.[44]

Perhaps these dandies took their places on the stage itself on its ill-starred first performance, but if there were anything like a hundred of them they must have been seated in the pit, in oblique lines following the polygonal structure of the auditorium. Such a layout, though not identical with that shown by Jones at the Drury Lane Cockpit, was close enough to it to have suggested that the central parterre might properly be called a 'cockpit', and of course the surrounding galleries will have constituted something of the spherical shape noted so often at both the other private theatres. One further allusion makes the kinship of all of these playhouses quite clear. Davenant's play *The Wits* was 'Presented at the Private House in Blacke Fryers' and published in 1636. The prologue recalls past triumphs at the theatre:

> Conceave now too, how much, how oft each Eare
> Hath surfeited in this our Hemispheare,
> With various, pure, eternall Wit . . .[45]

'Hemispheare' is in fact a more appropriate word than the repeated 'orbe' or 'sphere' which we found at the Salisbury Court, and it indicates that the Blackfriars auditorium was semicircular in plan, even though polygonal rather than actually rounded in detail. There is no record of any extensive reconstruction at the playhouse between James Burbage's refitting of 1596 and the time of Davenant's observation, and we must conclude that it was Burbage himself who settled on the design.

Burbage constructed the Blackfriars theatre at a time when the lease on the property in Shoreditch on which the Theater stood was due to run out. The project was evidently his way of preparing for the future: the Lord Chamberlain's Men would move, not to a public playhouse such as the Globe eventually turned out to be, but to a more exclusive, smaller enterprise closer in to the city and the Inns of Court.[46] The deed of sale for the Blackfriars buildings[47] is dated 4 February 1596, but there are indications that the bargain had been made a month or so earlier.[48] The price was not small: at £600 it was almost as much as the Theater itself had cost to build. The project was therefore a major undertaking, and there was something over a year to go before the Shoreditch lease ran out. Burbage set about the conversion with dispatch, putting himself to what later legal testimony would describe as 'great charge and troble', quite beyond the 'extreame rates' of the purchase price.[49] As it happened the charge and trouble were, for the time being, in vain. The neighbours objected to the idea of a noisy and busy theatre on their doorsteps, and successfully petitioned the Privy Council to have it stopped. The petition, itself undated, is referred to in a later document as having been presented in November 1596, and it mentions that 'Burbage is now altering and meaneth very shortly to convert and turne the same [building] into a comon playhouse . . .'[50] It is not clear how immediate was the effect of the Privy Council's decision – its original minute no longer survives – but by his death the following February Burbage had completed the alterations, for his sons later testified that he had 'made it into a playhouse' during his lifetime.[51] The later history of the playhouse – it stood empty until 1600, then housed boys' companies for some years before reverting once more to the adult players – need not concern us here. For our present purpose what matters is that James Burbage built a playhouse with a segmental or U-shaped auditorium when he turned his attention away from the Theater. The only local precedent for such a design was the Banqueting House in Whitehall, which had been fitted with its 'iij Rounde Skaffoldes' in 1584–5.[52] As we saw in chapter 7 this building may have been converted into a substantial theatrical form by the introduction of the scaffolds and their associated seating, but the evidence is not clear enough to make the matter quite certain. Without the Whitehall model Burbage's enterprise appears to have been unprecedented in England, and indeed rare in the rest of Europe.

There was however the plan in Serlio's *Architettura*, which, though it described a scenic theatre, made very clear the possible compromise by which the round of an ancient *cavea* might be inserted into the narrow confines of a rectangular hall. Burbage's other familiar model for an indoor theatre lay in the rectangular arrangements set up in the Great Hall at Whitehall, where the Lord Chamberlain's Men often performed their Christmas plays at about this time. Evidently its form did not satisfy Burbage's larger ambitions, and he turned instead to the more complex structure that resulted in Davenant's 'Hemispheare'. The precedent nearest to hand was rejected in favour of something at once more thoroughgoing and more cosmopolitan, yet it may be that the polygonal form was also influenced by the structure of the Theater, whose galleried polygonal frame the Blackfriars was intended to replace.

That Serlio's plan lay behind the decision to insert a segmental auditorium into the Upper Frater is not certain. But the Serlian arrangements made at Christ Church nine years later, at a time when the Blackfriars was itself in busy use by the Children of the Revels, tend to confirm the idea. Here we find a fully developed auditorium made to a polygonal plan much like that which Burbage designed but without its superimposed galleries and their supporting posts. To be sure, the Christ Church theatre follows Serlio in providing a scenic stage, where the Blackfriars was equipped with something more like the doors of entrance and stage gallery that had presumably been features of the Theater. Indeed Basil's faithful rendering of the Serlian scheme is so close to its source as to repeat some of its major dimensions. Nevertheless it is also a very practical piece of auditorium design, with proper attention paid to such details as the entrances and their lighting, matters on which Serlio was almost silent. It may be, then, that the Works design, which was drawn up in London rather than on site in Oxford, reflected something of the one built precedent to which Basil could readily turn, the currently busy and successful playhouse at the Blackfriars. The Children of the Queen's Revels performed at Whitehall at least twice in January 1605,[53] and the Works that year were responsible for 'makeinge readie the hall and greate Chamber for plaies and showes at diverse tymes'.[54] Basil will have been responsible for the negotiations with these and other players, and will have seen them perform. Indeed some of the costumes for the Oxford performances later in the year were hired from Edward Kirkham and Thomas Kendall at the Blackfriars, and sent down to Christ Church by the Revels Office.[55] The playhouse was far from *terra incognita* to officers of the Works.

The single most practical lesson which Basil might have learnt from the professional theatre was the arrangement of the entrance stairs and gang-ways. In particular he may have derived his two staircases, which he marks B on his plan (plate 28), from similar structures at the Blackfriars. The room in which Burbage made his playhouse was reached by a great winding stair which is mentioned in the deed of 1596 as abutting the northern end of the Upper Frater.[56] We meet this stair in the epilogue to Davenant's *Love and Honour*, performed 'at the Black-Fryers' in 1634, where the playwright is touchingly imagined as waiting outside to listen to the comments of the audience as they emerge:

> Our Poet waits below to heare his destiny;
> Just in the Entry as you passe, the place
> Where first you mention your dislike or grace:
> Pray whisper softly that he may not heare,
> Or else such words as shall not blast his eare.[57]

The entrance to the chamber being established at its northern end, the stage must have been to the south. But we know that there were galleries in the auditorium, and the great stair will not have led to these. Some secondary staircases must have been introduced, doubtless inside the chamber, at the time when the galleries were built.[58] In a rectangular plan such stairs are something of a nuisance, for they take up a good deal of the gallery space, as may be seen in Webb's plan of the *Florimène* theatre. At the Cockpit Inigo Jones avoided this awkwardness by setting the stairs in exterior attached stair turrets, in much the same fashion as had already been established at the Globe. No such solution was available to Burbage, faced as he was with the strong fabric of the old priory, and all its complications of neighbouring and adjoining tenements. But his segmental or U-shaped plan permitted him to insert the gallery stairs in the dead corners of the chamber behind the oblique angles formed by the polygonal galleries. A similar solution was adopted by Basil for the Christ Church design.

The adoption of the polygonal pit and galleries at the Blackfriars, and their refinement in the rounded auditoria of the Cockpit and presumably the 'Globe-like' Salisbury Court, demonstrate that the main line of private theatre construction looked beyond the halls of Whitehall for its inspiration. The Christ Church drawing provides our best indication that the source of the design lay in the pages of the *Architettura*, though the completed buildings took little more than their fundamental shape from Serlio's woodcuts, modifying the Italian with great freedom. Such indeed was the custom among English surveyors. Basil himself was probably responsible for a plan of a huge lodge proposed by the Earl of Dorset at Ampthill in September 1605, the month after the Christ Church commission. The drawing is extant at Hatfield,[59] and shows a vigorous mixture of Italian and English plan-forms, in which corner pavilions are shaped as a Greek cross, each with a circular rotunda at its centre and smaller circles tucked into the angles between its arms. This Italianate form is developed with very English canted and semicircular bay windows in what Mark Girouard has called a witty rather than an illiterate fashion. Similarly sophisticated play with Italian sources is sometimes characteristic of John Thorpe's drawings, as in his development of Palladian house plans.[60] It was not until the return of Inigo Jones from his European tour in 1614 that a more purely 'Italian' style began to return to London – it had made something of an appearance there in the reign of Henry VIII, only to be outbid by Northern European influences – and even Jones's work before the journey is much like that of Basil or Stickells in its free and delighted treatment of foreign authority. His scheme for the New Exchange, intended to be built between the Strand and the river, contains elements derived from Serlio and Palladio, including a notable 'Venetian' window at the centre of the Strand front. But above the Serlian winged pediments there rise romantic flagged towers, and two great scrolls in the centrepiece remind one more of his masque designs than his later architecture.[61] In the event the scheme was not used, and the Exchange was erected in a great hurry by Simon Basil for the Earl of Salisbury. Possibly Basil made the final designs, taking the concept of a large centrepiece and two smaller pavilions from the rejected drawing by Jones. What is remarkable, then, about Basil's Christ Church scheme is the closeness of its adherence to the Serlian model. The Blackfriars was more characteristic of its time in the freedom with which it treated the main theme of the segmental auditorium, reinterpreting it in the English idiom that was doubtless most immediately derived from the Shoreditch playhouses. At the stage end little or nothing came from the *Architettura*, and in the auditorium the polygonal galleries modified the original scheme almost out of recognition. All but the main idea was subject to the contingent realities of the London building and theatre worlds. But the main idea did survive: the Blackfriars possessed an auditorium whose deepest origins lay in the half-round of the Roman theatre.

It had been Serlio's aim to include as much of the Roman auditorium as might be squeezed into the confines of a modern hall or courtyard. In the process he made his compromise by adopting an *ad quadratum* scheme that related the round of the orchestra to the width of the hall, as we saw in chapter 9. We have no plans of the Blackfriars to indicate that any such procedure was used there, and the Christ Church drawing follows Serlio so directly that it hardly needs to replicate his system of proportioning. But we have seen that when Inigo Jones laid out the plan of the Cockpit in Drury Lane he related the width of the pit to the depth of the stage in an *ad quadratum* construction evidently related to Serlio's (plate 39). Whatever the actual state of affairs at Blackfriars, Jones saw that its type of design – a type that he adopted wholesale at the Cockpit – readily lent itself to a Serlian geometric ordering.

James Burbage, faced in 1596 with the certain termination of his lease at the Theater in Shoreditch, constructed a playhouse in the Upper Frater at Blackfriars in which he deliberately – and at some considerable expense – created a rounded auditorium although the simpler design solution would have been to follow the custom of the Court arrangements and build his galleries straight along the walls. His decision may have been influenced by the structure of the public playhouses for which he had himself been responsible in earlier years, but equally it resulted in a plan reminiscent of the Roman theatres of antiquity. A theatre was, according to Thomas Cooper in his *Thesaurus* (1565), 'a place made halfe rounde, where people assembled to beholde playes'.[62] This definition, or something very like it, was repeated in numerous dictionaries, but Randle Cotgrave in 1611 gave it a remarkable change of tense: where Cooper made it clear that he had the ancient world in mind, Cotgrave rephrased the entry to apply it also to contemporary London: 'Theatre: m. A Theater; a publike Playhouse; an halfe-round house wherein people sit to behold publike Playes, or Games.'[63] Cotgrave's vision is double: he sees the modern playhouse and the ancient theatre as interpenetrating one another, two versions of the same thing. But that is what we have found in Burbage's Blackfriars too, as well as at Jones's Cockpit. At Drury Lane the pit seats stepped upwards towards the galleries, and viewed from the centre of the house they would have made a single scarcely interrupted range all the way from the centre gangway to the perimeter walls. They constituted, that is, a miniature Roman *cavea*, and Jones added structurally redundant posts above his upper gallery perhaps in imitation of the colonnaded porticos of the ancient theatre. The whole structure, though made of wood within the brick shell of the building, will have been painted stone colour, and the turned posts were treated as classical columns. On the *frons scenae* the terms and pediment may well have been gilded, and parts of the structure veined like marble. We do not know whether a similar decorative scheme was to be found at the Blackfriars, but it too is likely to have been fitted with a tiered pit, giving it the same *cavea* effect as at the Cockpit, or indeed at Basil's Christ Church auditorium. The latter was described, we recall, by Isaac Wake in terms borrowed from the language of Vitruvius:

Ab infimis Aulae tabulatis vsq[ue] ad summa laquearium fastigia cunei parietibus ingenti circuitu affinguntur; media cavea thronus Augustalis cancellis cinctus Principibus eregitur . . .[64]

(From the floorboards of the hall right up to the lofty trusses of the roof, great wedges (of degrees) were fixed to the walls in an arc. In the middle of the *cavea* the royal throne was set up for the princes, surrounded by a balustrade.) Ben Jonson found 'oblique caves and wedges' at Blackfriars, but it was left to Davenant to describe the house most tellingly as a 'Hemisphaere'. Even more than at Christ Church, where the scheme was compromised by the need to introduce the royal platform, the Blackfriars expressed the idea of the 'halfe-round' Roman theatre.

Christopher Wren was a young man in London at the time when the Cockpit still stood in Drury Lane. That he knew it at first hand seems certain, for when he was commissioned to design an auditorium at Oxford to house the annual ceremonies of the Act, he turned to it for inspiration almost as much as he considered its ultimate source, the ancient Theatre of Marcellus in Rome. The Sheldonian is a U-planned house with two galleries of raked seating. The upper one continues around the flat end of the house, and originally there appears to have been a pedimented aedicule at its centre, much like the music room window over the stage at the Cockpit, and intended for an organ case.[65] Wren did not have to provide a platform beneath this straight gallery, and his treatment of the design here becomes uncomfortably diffuse, as if the whole building lacked a feature that would have given it a firmer identity. But in the 'round' end he provided a set of raked degrees in the pit, rising to the elevated lower gallery in just the same manner as in Jones's playhouse. There are no upper columns to provide the effect of an ancient *porticus*, but in the ceiling there is a magnificent baroque painting contrived to resemble a Roman *velarium*, or canvas cover supported on a network of ropes, here represented in gilt plaster. On every side the woodwork is treated as if it were stone, the columns supporting the galleries being veined and mottled like marble. This treatment is of course now modern, but it continues the style of the original interior.[66] The building is much larger than the Cockpit – its span is 70 ft, against the Cockpit's 40 ft –

but in its general conception it is remarkably similar. One can still buy a ticket and take a few steps into the centre of the theatre, there to stand surrounded by a 'Roman' *cavea*, with its columns and *cunei* and its imitation marble, and feel almost palpably the living influence of Jones's Cockpit and beyond that of the Blackfriars that Burbage designed while Shakespeare was writing *The Merchant of Venice*.

III SERLIAN SCENES

13
Serlio's measurable scene designs

The private theatres were seldom required to house scenery, though the Cockpit in Drury Lane became a regular scenic playhouse after the Restoration.[1] There is some sign that it had been used for such purposes even as early as 1639, when Inigo Jones prepared a drawing endorsed 'for ye cokpitt for my lord Chamberalin 1639' and showing a full set of wings, backscene, clouds and backcloth arranged on a small railed stage.[2] Nevertheless no London playhouse, public or private, regularly exercised what John Webb later came to call 'the Scenicall Art'[3] before the Commonwealth; various proposals, such as that for Davenant's Fleet Street theatre,[4] were made to extend the courtly entertainment of painted scenery to a wider public, but little or nothing came of them.

At Court, however, the story was very different. After its beginnings in *The Masque of Blackness* and the plays performed before King James at Christ Church in 1605, the unified perspective setting soon became the norm for the more lavish dramatic spectacles. The budgets were generous, and there was much talent to hand. Not surprisingly, therefore, Inigo Jones rapidly developed a mastery of the subject of scene design so complete that his achievements were hardly to be superseded until the innovations codified by de Loutherbourg in the eighteenth century. Some of Jones's techniques were entirely original, his own unique inventions, but most were variants of those practised in many of the courts of Europe, and particularly those of Italy. In content his designs were indebted to a host of richly rewarding sources, ranging from Vredeman de Vries to Bartolomeo Neroni, whence came a thousand details of architecture, decoration, even complete settings.[5] But in technique the prime source seems once more to have been the Second Book of Serlio's *Architettura*, in which there appeared the three famous woodcuts of the Comic, Tragic and Satyric Scenes. It was here that Jones learned how to compose a three-dimensional foreshortened setting, and how to go about representing it as a two-dimensional image on a sheet of paper.

The earliest perspective scene designers were architects, and their drawings owed much to the conventions of architectural rendering as it was practised in Italy during the quattrocento. Wolfgang Lotz has written brilliantly on this subject, distinguishing between the types of representation of architectural interiors used by mediaeval builders, theoreticians such as Alberti, and practitioners like Bramante and Peruzzi.[6] As the principles of architectural design and the practices of the building trade changed over the centuries, so did the systems used by designers for putting down on paper the visual information required by those who had to put it to concrete use. Builders in different ages needed different prompting, and the designers themselves came to think of their work in different ways. Yet although the changes in the techniques of rendering a built interior arose in parallel with the changes in thought about architectural design, each of the various types of drawing went on coexisting with the others, at least until the seventeenth century.

The system used in the Middle Ages was generally limited to the plan. A plan, like a map, usually confines itself to a single plane and can therefore be drawn all to a single scale. Elevations were not necessary in practice because the builders would use a series of geometrical constructions to raise the structure from the dimensions given in the drawing. Sometimes in the early designs a skeletal section might be incorporated in the plan, indicating the geometry that the interpreter was expected to follow, but usually it was omitted, the procedures – whether *ad quadratum* or *ad triangulum* – being well enough understood to call for no further instruction. Some such procedure seems to have been followed at the Fortune by Peter Street, for there the contract originally provided a 'Plott' showing the relative positions of the stage, tiring house, stairs and frame. Street was expected to work out the details of the elevation for himself, though its major dimensions were given in the terms of the agreement. A second method of rendering an architectural interior was to provide a section through a single plane of the structure containing a perspective view of everything that could be seen beyond it. Here the section itself might be scaled, but the foreshortening of the perspective part made accurate measurement impossible, and the technique was used only when it was important to convey a sense of the character of the building rather than immediately useful technical information. Some Elizabethan drawings fall into this category, including several by John Thorpe, and the decorative amphitheatre illustrated in plate 8. A third type, developed when the demands of architecture itself called for an accurate commensurate sense of all parts of the space depicted, is the 'orthogonal projection', in which the interior was represented in depth, but not in perspective. Here the planes beyond the initial section were drawn to its scale and distinguished by shading rather than foreshortening. This was the method often used by Inigo Jones, as for example in his drawings for the Cockpit in Drury Lane (plates 37 and 38), where neither the exterior elevation nor the two sections show any sign of perspective foreshortening and much use is made instead of washes indicating a left light. We are thus made aware, in the elevation, that the form represented is rounded, and there is a satisfactory sense, in both the sections, of a spatial depth beyond the picture plane, yet at the same time all the details of the structure can be measured against a common scale.

A typical scene design of the sixteenth or seventeenth century is rather like an architectural rendering, and indeed many scenes did depict architectural forms, whether interior or exterior. But where an architect has simply to draw a perspective or 'orthogonal projection' of a structure that can be imagined as having real dimensions, the scene designer depicts a complicated system of foreshortened wings, raked stage and backcloth, all of which must be imagined as a perspective composition within the composition of the drawing itself. A scene design is – at least potentially – a sort of metascene, or perspective of a perspective. Its analysis poses special difficulties, made still more complicated in some drawings by the apparently incongruous presence of elements set down according to the principles of orthogonal projection. It will be useful, therefore, to begin our discussion by returning to a few of the main characteristics of linear perspective construction.

A helpful diagram of the ordinary so-called 'single-point' perspective can be found in the familiar picture of a pair of railway lines disappearing towards the horizon of a flat prairie landscape. Here the horizon is obvious enough, as is the vanishing point where the rails converge on one another. The sheet of paper on which the drawing is made constitutes the 'picture plane', which we can imagine as a notional window through which the artist looked when he saw the scene in his drawing. If the railway lines run at right angles to this plane they can be called 'orthogonals', and in a single-point perspective all the orthogonals will converge on one another at the vanishing point, just as our ribbons of steel do. Let us complicate the drawing a little by adding a line of telephone poles to the right of the track, and perhaps a dead straight prairie highway to the left, all running parallel with the railway. All will converge to a single vanishing point at the horizon, which will of course be elevated above the foreground for the simple reason that our eyes are in our heads, not our feet, and ordinary human perception requires that things should normally be seen – and depicted – from head height. We look downwards at the ground close by, but take a level gaze at the horizon.

An orthogonal projection is a vastly different scheme, with no horizon and no vanishing point. The scene before us would be reduced to a single line representing the flat ground, the tiny sections of each of the two rails, seen as if cut through at right angles, together with the section of one of the sleepers and an elevation of one of the telephone poles. There would be no convergence of the orthogonals, each of which would now be represented as a mere point on the paper. We should see only one sleeper, one pole, because all the others would be masked by the first, and the highway would appear in cross-section. Of course this scene is a very artificial one. No real landscape is altogether flat, and in fact the prairies of North America often roll spectacularly. The orthogonal projection would register each rise in the highway that was not masked by a nearer one, but the road would never appear to narrow. Let us suppose that the artist wished to convey the sense that some way down the track the highway made a jog of several metres to the left, and then resumed its parallel course. The perspective picture could show this divergence very clearly, but it would not be possible to scale it without going to a great deal of trouble. The orthogonal projection, however, would register the shift exactly as a scaled displacement of the section of the road to the left. Any incident in the scene that brought its further elements into view beyond the nearer ones, whether above them or to either side, would be represented in the same scale as the immediate 'foreground', and the whole drawing could be used for purposes of measurement, just like a plan. It would not, of course, show distances in depth, just as a plan will not show them in height. The perspective picture, on the other hand, would give a strong sense of depth, but could not conveniently be used for measurement.

Now let us complicate the matter further by adding a great billboard between the highway and the track, at right angles to both and therefore parallel to the picture plane. It is located some way down the line, so that the perspective will show it as a small rectangle fairly close to the vanishing point. The orthogonal projection will present it in exactly the same scale as the rest of the drawing, and it will seem enormous by comparison with its presence in the perspective. On the board is an advertisement for a building society, an image of a house seen cornerwise-on, in perspective. Because the billboard is parallel to the picture plane both the perspective picture and the orthogonal projection will manage a depiction of this advertisement with comparative, though it will appear much smaller in the one than in the other. Had the billboard been set at an angle to the highway and railway line it would have presented rather difficult problems to the perspective artist as he tried to foreshorten his view of the already foreshortened house. The orthogonal projection would likewise run into some difficulty, and for similar reasons, though the problem would not be quite so intractable.

Mercifully we shall not have to pursue our artist as he wrestles with this poser. Our subject is not perspective in itself, but the practice of early scene designers in Italy and England, and that practice is exclusively based on (though not, as we shall see, quite limited to) the single-point system in which the major elements of the scene are aligned either on orthogonals or on planes parallel with the picture plane, here represented by the line of the front of the stage. Later designers came to confront the complications of setting structures cornerwise-on to the stage front, and developed elaborate strategies for dealing with the matter, but they need not concern us here.

In nature there is no such thing as a horizon and a vanishing point. The perspective artist uses such concepts because they coincide with some of the facts of human perception, though not by any means with all, and can be demonstrated by a variety of geometrical proofs. If he is a mural painter he will establish his horizon at a convenient height, ideally perhaps at the height of an observer's eye, and then develop his orthogonal system to suit his intentions. A point has no dimension, but in practice his painted vanishing point will be something that we can actually touch, a specific if tiny piece of the wall. A theatrical scene is like a vast mural, but constructed in three dimensions where the mural aims to restrict itself to two. As in the mural the vanishing point will be a tangible object, and the orthogonals running towards it will be like their counterparts in the mural, deliberately drawn straight lines realized in paint and solid material. Here we must suppose that our prairie train has arrived at its destination, and we are in a city of noble buildings like those in a Serlian theatrical scene. Each is built securely on the level – we shall not complicate our study by imagining a picture of Clovelly or San Francisco – and we are standing in the middle of a straight street looking along it towards a triumphal arch. To the mural painter the task of representing the street on a single plane is fairly simple: he establishes his vanishing point, and then runs the bottom orthogonals of the buildings towards it just as if they were the railway lines of our first example. But our task is rather to understand the work of the theatrical designer, and the three-dimensional construction of a stage scene involves a new and special limitation. If these buildings are to seem to be level in the finished scene their orthogonals must follow the line of the stage floor, which will have to be made sloping, or 'raked', sufficiently steeply to permit the necessary convergence on the vanishing point. If the artist wishes to follow the simple painterly criterion of pitching the horizon and vanishing point at the level of a man's eye he will have to tilt the stage up quite alarmingly or else make it far deeper than most theatres can accommodate. In practice most stage wings were painted with a low vanishing point so that the rake of the stage could be fairly gradual, and the orthogonals in the upper part of the composition were angled down towards the horizon more acutely.

Now let us suppose that we have the whole three-dimensional foreshortened scene of a handsome street before us. The stage, which represents the surface of the road, rises gently upwards towards the back. To either side there are wings – we might make them 'angled' wings of the sort illustrated by Serlio – whose forward faces are all parallel to the front of the stage. The angled parts, representing the street façades of the buildings, are arranged as orthogonals where they meet the stage floor and lead towards a low vanishing point. But at the back the scene is closed off with the triumphal arch, so that we do not actually see the point where all the orthogonals converge, the arch itself being almost all in one plane and painted like a straightforward elevation. The upper orthogonals in the wings slant sharply

Scēna Comica.

44   Sebastiano Serlio, *Il secondo libro di perspettiva*, the Comic Scene.

down to the low vanishing point implied by the rake of the stage. Our task is now to render this elaborate construction as a drawing on a sheet of paper. We may adopt the perspectivist's stance, and aim to draw a perspective of a perspective, rather as our artist did when he drew his picture of the billboard showing a foreshortened house. Every regular single-point perspective implies a fixed place from which it is meant to be viewed, and from which all its foreshortenings will make perfect sense. This is true of mural paintings, and just as true of stage scenes; indeed in the latter, as we move away from the correct station point, all the wings and other parts of the construction will appear to slip out of alignment. If we imagine, therefore, that we make our drawing from the exact and correct station point, we shall record a simple single-point scheme, no different from a drawing of a mural painting. If, on the other hand, we choose to make an orthogonal projection of the scene we shall still record a single-point scene, but there will be a slight though

212

significant difference. The further wings will be rendered in the same scale as the closer ones, where our perspective drawing will have foreshortened them doubly, once because they are actually foreshortened as they stand there on the stage, and again because these diminished wings are further away from the observer than the nearer ones, and look smaller still. In the orthogonal projection the distances between the pairs of wings to either side of the stage will remain in scale, where the perspective will show them as more narrowly spaced towards the back. The result, when we compare the two drawings, will be that although both are evidently single-point compositions, with all the orthogonals running to a vanishing point, the 'perspective of a perspective' will seem to indicate a deeper space than the orthogonal projection does, its rear wings diminishing more sharply and so approaching more closely to the vanishing point.

Occasionally scene designers of the sixteenth and seventeenth centuries would imagine their work as quite simple single-point schemes, with no regard whatever for the complexities of the actual built wings. More often, however, they tried to give some notion of the placing of the wings, the backscene and other elements of the stage, by adopting a point of view that was higher than the intended station point. Such drawings show rather a lot of the stage floor, where in the built scene the audience might expect to see a surface rising only a little from front to back. The most practical type of scene design would be an orthogonal projection, for here every part of the design that represented a plane parallel to the front of the stage might be scaled up by the scene painters directly from the drawing. To the modern eye, often untutored in such matters, most scene designs look like ordinary perspectives, to be dealt with on much the same terms as a landscape by Corot or – at best – a street scene by Piero della Francesca. A glance at one of Serlio's scenes (plate 44) may suggest that there is really nothing very remarkable about their obvious single-point composition, but a moment's thought will be enough to set us asking questions. Why do their stage floors seem to rear up so abruptly? Could such scenes as these actually be built in the type of theatre that Serlio himself illustrates in the Second Book? Do these famous scenes really look like what we imagine methodical Renaissance perspective stages to have been? When we have answered these questions we shall have discovered that the scenes are not ordinary perspectives at all, nor even 'perspectives of perspective', but ingenious diagrams that combine the most useful qualities of an orthogonal projection with the similar characteristics of a plan.

This is a problem which Serlio addressed with all of his customary thoroughness, providing lessons that were learned by Jones and Webb as well as by Italian followers such as Lorenzo Sirigatti and Pietro Accolti. In confronting the question of how to present in two dimensions the difficult foreshortening of a constructed three-dimensional perspective scene, Serlio opened the way also for an exploration of its measurability, and with it, as we shall see, its capacity to relate to the scale of the human form. We have already found, in chapter 9, that Serlio's theatre auditorium was proportioned according to the scale and proportionality of the human body, taking as its repeated module the depth of a seating degree and shaping its *cavea* according to the ratios of the *homo ad quadratum*. Now we must extend the enquiry to the proportions of the scene itself, but in order to do so we must first learn how to read the three scene designs published in the Second Book of the *Architettura*.

The woodcuts in Serlio's books of perspective offer us more information than strikes the eye at first, and indeed more than even the letterpress text allows. Often, as we saw in chapter 9, the illustrations carry the argument where the words do not, offering greater precision and more theoretical coherence. It follows that the thesis is not properly to be understood without careful analysis of the illustrations, pressing them further than would at first seem warranted by the words alone. Our first task, in a methodical exploration of the scene designs, must therefore be to decide which of the work's many editions we should rely on as adequately conveying Serlio's original intention. Hitherto he has not been well served by scholars who indiscriminately print illustrations from late editions, some from the seventeenth century, as if these differed not at all, or only insignificantly, from the earliest period. Yet the case of the theatre scheme in the Second Book shows that the later editions sometimes altogether fail to reproduce the techniques presented by Serlio himself while others present only a part of what the designer originally wished to convey.

The Second Book was first published, in a parallel text Italian and French version, in Paris in 1545, with woodcuts presumably close to the author's intentions, for he was in France to supervise their preparation. Fairly accurate copies were made for the first Venetian edition of 1551, reprinted with some minor alterations in 1560. A Flemish translation by Peeter Coecke appeared in Antwerp in 1553 with new woodcuts rather more faithful to the Parisian originals than the Venetian ones. These Antwerp blocks were reused for the Dutch editions of 1606 and 1616, published in Amsterdam, and for the English translation which appeared in London in 1611. Meanwhile Venetian editions after 1560 came out in a quarto format with new woodcuts which – so far as the theatre scheme goes – marked a radical degeneration in which the intellectual justification of Serlio's design was almost completely lost. These were published in Italian-language editions of 1566, 1584, 1600, 1618 and 1619, and in a Latin/Italian folio of 1569. It follows that the most reliable text is the Parisian one of 1545, where the fineness of the theatre plan in particular probably reflects the quality of Serlio's original drawings more adequately than any of the Venetian copies. These, together with the Antwerp cuts, are nevertheless useful as early commentaries on and perhaps clarifications of the scheme; the Venetian cuts of 1566 and later should be ignored as debased and unreliable.[7]

The authoritative 1545 edition consists of an Italian text with a French translation by Jean Martin, the two languages appearing in alternation, the Italian first in italic and the French following in upright roman type. The presentation of the theatre scheme is spacious, with text and diagrams arranged elegantly into sections fitted to the page or opening and each cut commanding a full page to itself. Words and illustrations therefore come satisfactorily together.[8] Each folio is printed on both sides, with the exception of the one bearing the Comic Scene, which is perhaps the most influential of all of Serlio's theatre illustrations. In fact the sheet on which it is printed forms no part of the signature of the book, but is tipped in here or there in various exemplars of the volume, unfoliated and with its verso blank. Sometimes it is bound up to face the plan, sometimes to face the Satyric Scene, sometimes it appears among the text after the section.[9] Evidently the sheet was originally a loose leaf which has been set in the volume in various places at the whim of the individual binder. Its omission from the layout of the original signatures can hardly have been an error, so careful is the planning of the text; it appears rather that the cut of the Comic Scene was intended to be a detached illustration capable of being transferred by the reader from opening to opening for purposes of comparison with the other scenes as well as the section and the plan.

Something of the spacious method of the Parisian volume is found also in the Venetian edition of 1551. Here again each part of the account of the theatre design is given at least a page, and usually both sides of a folio, to itself. Indeed the early editions of most of the books of the *Architettura* show a similar distinction in the placing of the text and illustrations, and Serlio's careful manuscript of the Sixth Book, now in the Avery Library at Columbia,[10] embodies the working methods by which he achieved it, each folio of drawings having a corresponding but separate folio of commentary to match it. Similarly methodical, though not of course identical, arrangements are found in the Venetian edition of 1560 and the Antwerp of 1553, the blocks from the latter appearing with much the same text layout in the Amsterdam edition of 1606 and the English translation published in 1611. But the Venetian editions of 1566 and later years compress the text and illustrations into an economical continuity, and the original relation of words to woodcuts is quite lost.

One result of the layout of the earlier editions is that the plan of the theatre may readily be compared with the Comic Scene. The loose leaf of the 1545 edition could easily be carried across to the plan for detailed comparison, at least until the binder tipped it in. Later editions printed the Scene as a regular part of the volume, but in the Venetian editions of 1551 and 1560 the use of an exceptionally light paper enables the reader to see the plan shining through the cut of the Scene, which is printed on the succeeding folio. The overlay effect is doubtless no more than an accident, but it makes obvious what the freely portable Comic Scene of the original edition also conveyed, that both plan and scene are drawn in such a way that they can be fitted together. The Scene (plate 44) is of course a kind of perspective, so that the squaring of the forestage yields larger units at the front than those at the back, but measured along the front of the raked stage proper the scale of the cut exactly matches that of the plan. Here the interval between the inner corners of the front wings is 24 squares wide in both cases, and measures – in the edition of 1545 – 137 mm in both. We have seen that each square is one Venetian 'minute' wide, and the whole plan is consistently drawn to the scale of the Venetian foot. But where the plan is 34 squares wide the scene is 36, so that its overall width on the page is two minutes greater. The reasons for this disparity will be made clear shortly; for the moment we may observe that the identity of scale between the plan, the section and the Comic Scene extends also to the Tragic Scene, where each floor division is twice as large and there are half as many, and in a general way at least to the Satyric, though here the main lines are obscured by stage foliage and so are difficult to measure. This internal consistency holds true in the original edition, the Venetian ones of 1551 and 1560, and the Northern European ones of 1553, 1606 and 1611. But the Venetian editions of 1566 and later destroy it. Not only is the layout of the text and illustrations now confused, but the Comic Scene, still 36 squares wide at the front of the raked stage, is drawn exactly the same width overall as the 34-square plan, so that the identity of scale is lost in favour of a more superficial match, and none of the designs is scaled by the parts of a Venetian foot. The detailed disposition of the stage in plan and perspective scene varies a little even among the more reliable earlier editions, and it will be necessary for simplicity's sake to confine our present discussion to the Parisian text of 1545.

The careful integration of text and illustrations in the early editions, and especially in that of 1545, suggests that the plan, the section and the scenes should all be considered together as coherent parts of a single scheme. So close is the general compatibility that it seems worth asking why Serlio did not make the Comic or the Tragic Scene altogether consistent with the stage shown in the plan. One reason is to be found in the identity of scale between them, an identity that applies, in the case of the Comic Scene, only to the plane that cuts through the front edge of its raked stage. All other parts of the design are foreshortened in perspective, so that the forestage squarings are larger than those shown in the plan, and of course those in the raked area are violently reduced as they diminish towards the vanishing point. Examining the forestage area with some care, we notice that Serlio has contrived to show both its front and its rear edges in whole numbers of squares, 36 at the back and 28 at the front. Given that the depth between front and rear is 6 squares,

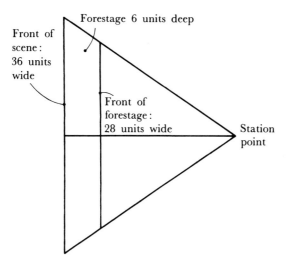

Distance of station point from front of scene $= 36 \times \frac{6}{8} = 27$ units

Figure 9   Serlio's theatre plan: calculation of station point.

we may calculate that the station point from which this Scene is viewed is 27 units from the front of the raked stage (fig. 9).

The need to represent the forestage in terms of integers that would permit such a calculation to be made explains its difference from the plan, where the dimensions are 34 squares wide by 5 deep. The diagram we have just used illustrates the way the lateral span of the foreshortening implies the station point, but a similar calculation from the vertical dimensions can also be made. These are also in whole numbers, for the 6 squares of the depth of the forestage are actually seen in a vertical interval of 2, as measured according to the scale of the units along its front edge. We can locate the vanishing point of this scene by projecting the orthogonals of the forestage squaring upwards until they meet at a point just 9 units above the front edge of the stage. This enables us to use another simple diagram (a section this time, rather than a plan) to calculate that the station point is $6 \times \frac{9}{2} = 27$ units from the raked stage (fig. 10). Thus the vertical dimensions of the foreshortened forestage confirm the lateral ones in their indication of the position of the station point. Serlio's depiction of both sets of dimensions as integers makes the calculation easy, and it is just the kind of quite elementary deduction he expected an attentive reader to make from his designs, one certainly no more demanding than the feats of calculation called for in the First Book and in the discussion of perspective earlier in the Second.

We find a further confirmation of our conclusion when we turn to the plan

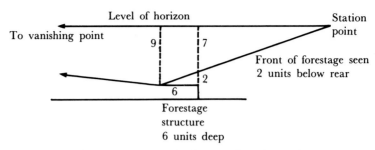

Figure 10   Serlio's theatre section: calculation of station point.

and section of the theatre (plates 29 and 30). The station point from which to view a single point perspective scene must be located somewhere along a line projected from the vanishing point at 90° to the picture plane (here represented by the forward faces of the front wings). Both the station point and the vanishing point will be on the level of the horizon, and a line establishing that level is indicated in Serlio's section projecting backwards from the scene; extended forwards into the auditorium it strikes the riser at the back of the fourth row of degrees. If there is a station point physically accessible within the auditorium, it must be here. Measured on the plan, this spot is just 27 units from the front of the raked stage, at the very place where our calculations from the information given by the Comic Scene suggested that it would be. Thus the plan, the section and the Comic Scene combine to indicate the whereabouts of a theoretically ideal point of view, which however leaves no mark on the structure of Serlio's auditorium. In the plan there is no seat in this position, only the steps of a central entrance gangway.

It has become a commonplace of theatre history of recent years that the prime seat in a Renaissance court auditorium was located at the ideal point of view from which to observe the foreshortened scene. Such a notion is not supported by Serlio's woodcuts. His early and best editions locate the prime seat well forward of the station point and substantially below the horizon. Later editions do nothing to bring the prime seat and the ideal point of view together. Yet it would appear that Serlio did give attention to the matter, for he took care to indicate in both the Comic Scene and the section and plan just where the station point was located; that he devoted that spot to an audience gangway and not to a seat suggests that he thought of his scene's ideality as an abstraction, somewhat like that of Leonardo's *Last Supper*, where the station point is far above the head of any observer standing on the refectory floor at S. Maria delle Grazie. In distinguishing the middle of the orchestra seats with the catch letter F Serlio perhaps indicates that it is the chief among them, the place fit for a duke or a king. Its position appears to be fixed in relation, not to the perspective scene, but to the semicircle of the orchestra, as in the ancient theatre. The prime seat occupies the mid-point of the orchestra's perimeter. But Serlio has so arranged his plan that the centre of the seat F is just 17 units distant from the forestage, so that it is also the point where the angle subtended by the whole extent of the forestage left and right is precisely 90°. In the seventeenth century Niccolo Sabbatini advised that the prime seat should be placed in an identical relation to the scene itself, and described how the location might be made by sighting along the arms of a carpenter's square.[11] It seems likely that the tradition of what might be called the '90° rule' had its origins in interpretations of the Roman plan, for of course the diameter of a semicircle, such as the ancient orchestra usually was, subtends 90° at any point along its circumference. In Serlio this pattern is ingeniously extended to include also the angle subtended by the forestage; by Sabbatini's time the 90° rule had come to apply to the angle subtended by the extent of the scene left and right and was probably thought to correspond to the normal span of human vision.[12]

In all of its books the *Architettura* is a practical guide, whether to building design or historical enquiry. The section on the theatre has the intending architect so far in mind as to give workmanlike hints not only on such important but subsidiary matters as lighting techniques but also on how to establish the necessary proportions of the scenic foreshortening in practice as well as in theory. Serlio would like to stretch a line from the vanishing point through the area of the scene to help with making the correct single-point foreshortenings, but because such a line in his scheme would have to pass through the solid wall of the hall or loggia behind the backscene he recommends making a model of the theatre instead:

and for that men should breake the wall, if they would vse all this Horison in grosse, which may not bee done, therefore I haue alwayes made a small modell of wood and Paper iust of the same bignes, and by the same modell set it downe in grosse, from piece to piece.[13]

In his plan and section Serlio gives scaled information of just the right kind to make possible the construction of such a model, indicating the presence and site of the back wall in the section, but omitting it from the plan in favour of a clearer representation of the kind of lines he has described, fixed at the vanishing point (O), diverging through the area of the scene to mark its limits to either side, and including for good measure an indication of the central ray. Manipulation of these lines might establish not only the orthogonals marked on the stage floor but also those trickier angles to which the inner faces of the wings will have to be cut and painted.

In the original editions the plan and section match each other very well, and it would be no trouble to follow Serlio's advice and make a model of the theatre. Only when we try to set up one of his three generic scenes on the stage so constructed do we encounter much difficulty, for then we are brought up short by an apparent inconsistency in the design. In each of the three scenes the horizon is much too high to fit into the scheme given in the plan and section. This disparity is the more remarkable for the general agreement of scale between all the scenes and the plan, and the detailed agreement between it and the Comic Scene in particular. Despite its exact congruity the scene will not fit into the stage shown in the plan and section until we have learned how to interpret its specialized type of composition.

The section gives the level of the horizon at 2 squares above the forestage, yet the Comic Scene expresses the same interval (measured from its vanishing point) as precisely 9 squares. The Tragic Scene shows an identical elevation (the horizon is $4\frac{1}{2}$ squares above the stage front, but the squares are double those of the Comic Scene), and the general lines of the Satyric Scene, so far as they may be judged, follow the others in this respect. When we try to imagine what the floor plan of the stage shown in the Comic Scene might look like we find that it could not possibly be accommodated in a theatre of the proportions given in Serlio's section. Either it would have to be extremely deep (54 squares to the backscene) or its rake would have to be impossibly steep in order to reach the 9-square horizon height. Just how impossible may be judged from the fact that while the raked stage in the plan is nearly $5\frac{1}{2}$ squares deep, it is shown in the Comic Scene as just 6 squares high to the foot of the backscene. Even if the stage shown in the plan were stood on end and propped up at 90° it would not be deep (or high) enough to yield the sort of view contained in the cut of the scene.

There is, indeed, a curious blatancy about all three of the scenes. They have, in John Peacock's admirable phrase, a 'despotic effect':

In both the *Tragic* and *Comic Scenes* we find great freedom in the variety of forms depicted but at the same time a marked constraint in the organization of space. Two disadvantages result from this: the buildings look preposterously miscellaneous, and they also look huddled together and hence not completely solid, unreal.[14]

The scenes tilt themselves at the observer in a manner that reminds one of some of Cezanne's table edges or the up-ended furniture in a Matisse, and not at all of the careful perspective demonstrations of the remainder of the Second Book of the *Architettura*. Indeed if one mentally recasts the designs into the direct, fine medium of Serlio's drawings as we know them from the Avery MS. of the Sixth Book, their fundamental incongruity is all the more apparent. To be sure, the steps in all of the designs and the level forestage of the Comic Scene seem unexceptionally foreshortened as if viewed from a determined point, but beyond them all becomes ambiguous as the space represented enters the three-dimensional but contracted world of the theatrical designer. Indeed it would seem that these famous and influential woodcuts are not consistent perspectives at all, but practical diagrams of use to the workmen in the theatre.

The decisive clue to their interpretation is to be found in the Comic Scene's representation of the raked stage floor. If we isolate this part of the design for a moment, ignoring the forestage and the architectural wings, we see an arrangement of diminishing trapezoids exactly comparable in scale and kind to the depiction of the stage given in the theatre plan. If this ziggurat-like shape is treated as a plan indeed, and set in the relation to the auditorium that is defined by the remainder of Serlio's text, it will prove the basis of a new visual interpretation of the scene. Because the wing feet are all marked on this plan to the same scale (as in any regular plan), their vertical dimensions must follow suit, and we may treat each of their front faces and also the backscene as true elevations all to the same scale as the plan, though of course the objects depicted on them diminish according to the perspective foreshortening. One notices that the two forward buildings at stage right and the central tall building stage left are all of similar height to the eaves measured actually on the paper: about 21 units high on the scale of the front of the scene. In accord with the practice described in his text, Serlio places a lower building at front stage left in order that the rear parts of the scene should not be obscured. But when all the wings are set up on the stage indicated here and treated as a plan raked at one part in nine as Serlio specifies, the character of the whole scene is radically altered. Its blatancy is replaced by restraint, its fussy crowding by an order that is far more dignified, as may be seen in the schematic model shown in plate 45. The proportions of the angled faces of the wings may be measured from the design in the same way as the elevations themselves, the back part of each wing being just as high to scale as it is represented in the woodcut, though of course the angle of the foreshortening will differ. The geometry of similar triangles ensures that the regular convergence of the orthogonals onto the vanishing point will still be retained. The vanishing point itself will be registered at a point on the backscene lower than appears from the woodcut, but here one notices that Serlio has contrived this part of his composition as a straightforward elevation, without painted orthogonals, and therefore without a vanishing point defined at some fixed location upon it. The new level of the horizon will be one-third of a unit above the foot of the backscene (or, in terms of the scale proposed in the text, eight inches). Thus the open-faced nature of Serlio's woodcut permits his reader to measure, directly from the page, the plan of the raked stage, the elevations of the backscene and the forward wing faces, and the dimensions of the angled surfaces of the wings.

The stage in the Comic Scene, considered as a plan, is not quite identical with that shown in the theatre plan proper, for while it is 24 squares wide between the front wings its altitude – or, if we take it as a plan, its depth – to the vanishing point is only 9 squares, or $\frac{2}{3}$ the depth of the theatre plan. In the Comic Scene this depth – or altitude – is divided by the foot of the backscene in the ratio of 4 : 9, where the full plan's ratio is 3 : 2. Thus the Scene offers an alternative scheme rather than a repetition of the one already illustrated, but it is an alternative conceived within consistent limits, capable of being set up within the structure shown in the large plan, and of course identical to it in scale.[15]

The curious combination of regular elevation with regular perspective in the scenes represents a remarkable sophistication of the specialized technique of preparing drawings of practical use to the designer and the painters. A theatrical scene design is, in one aspect, a perspective like any other, a sketch for a vast mural; but it is also – or it ought to be, if it is to be of direct practical value to the workmen – a consistent architectural elevation of a complex structure, capable of being squared up and transferred full-scale to the board and canvas of the painters' bench. Serlio's achievement in the *Architettura* is to contain his perspective scenes in the medium of an orthogonal projection, so that while each represents an object that contains foreshortening (the constructed scene itself), its own rules are exactly similar to those of a plan, and detailed scaled measurements may readily be made. Of course so radical an invention had its effect on Serlio's followers, as he intended that it should.

45   Schematic model of the Comic Scene mounted on a stage designed according to Serlio's plan and section.

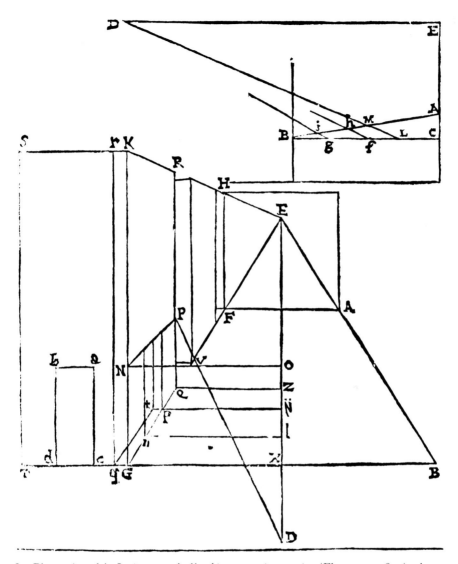

46   Pietro Accolti, *Lo inganno degl'occhi, prospettiva pratica* (Florence, 1625), theatre scheme.

After the *Architettura* constructive diagrams whose rationale derives from the woodcuts of the scenes became quite common; such, for example, is the illustration in Pietro Accolti's *Lo inganno degl'occhi, prospettiva pratica* (Florence, 1625), chapter XVIII, in which the plan of a perspective stage is drawn with elevations of its wings, all to the same scale (plate 46). The impact of such practical thinking was felt in England too, where both Inigo Jones and John Webb came to value the utility of the orthogonal projection

223

in their professional theatre work. But Jones in particular was not content to follow the master's habit of designing within the constraints of single-point perspective, and in London some of the achievements of the Second Book were carried to a new level of refinement.

14
Inigo Jones's scene designs

Serlio's famous theatrical scenes are neither straightforward single-point perspectives, nor even 'perspectives of perspective', but diagrams organized to convey scaled information about the structure of the stage, wings and backscene. A proof that the convention was understood in England lies in a drawing made by John Webb to illustrate some of the principles that lay behind the designs for *Florimène* (plate 47).[1] Here the angled wings appear in plan to the left, while to the right the vertical elevations of their faces are shown, complete with an indication of their foreshortening, all to the same marked scale. A section, or 'Profyle', indicates the very shallow rake of the stage, and includes some key letters that are difficult to interpret, for they seem not to match those on the plan diagram above. Nevertheless the combination of plan and elevation in the upper diagram is clear, and represents exactly the convention established by Serlio in his scene designs. From Inigo Jones we have nothing quite so explicit, though in his earliest designs he readily accepted the high-horizoned look of Serlio's diagrams. Whether he did so for strictly Serlian reasons, or whether he had preoccupations of his own are questions well worth asking, for Jones was the father of the scenic stage in England, and the techniques he developed for its management had a profound influence on later generations of theatre people.

A modern observer of Jones's scene designs will be struck first by their astonishing assurance. They are the first truly 'Italian' drawings in England, the first to catch the graceful vigour of Renaissance and Mannerist *disegno*. Leafing through the two great volumes of Stephen Orgel and Roy Strong's definitive edition or, even better, studying the drawings at first hand in the butler's pantry at Chatsworth, it is easy to be so taken with their fluent strength that one overlooks the fact that a great many were intended for use on the floor by craftsmen who would square them up to scale. The signs of this activity are everywhere: in the ubiquitous patterns of squaring that appear over so many of the drawings, in scale bars and in written dimensions. Of a total of 134 scenic designs by Jones and John Webb published by Orgel and Strong (hereafter O&S) exactly half – 67 – possess some marks of being intended for scaled-up enlargement; 53 are simply squared, whether in lead or with the pointer, and 10 have some sort of scale bar (O&S 122, 123, 141, 148, 246, 250, 328, 340, 409, 412). Rather more – 17 in all, for these categories overlap – are drawn within carefully ruled outlines evidently intended to define the proportions of the scene in order that it should fit a particular building or frontispiece opening (O&S 123, 135, 141, 163, 190, 191, 216, 245, 246, 267, 268, 269, 279, 326, 409, 447, 462). Five have inscribed dimensions (O&S 39, 64, 109, 277, 445), and a few others have some sort of numbering that appears to have a scale function (O&S 101, 279, 280, 329). In addition to all these, two further drawings have incised lines which may indicate scalability (O&S 61 and 74), and one (O&S 162) has numbers that may be dimensions or may not. That so many of the designs are intended to be copied out full-size in the theatre by some simple process of scaling-up suggests that Jones thought of his stage drawing in almost architectural terms. Few of the earliest sheets are scaled, but after 1619 the habit of covering a sketch with incised or lead squares became quite fixed, the practice tailing off rather by the late 1630s. That many of the drawings – both squared and unsquared – were actually used by the painters is shown by the splashes of distemper with which so many of them are marked. However spritely and flowing Jones's hand – one would, alas, never call Webb's hand that – it commonly worked within the tight limits of detailed practicality. The art is free but deliberate, and the deliberation permits us now to analyse the drawings with a view to understanding the ordering of their painted world of illusion.

Jones's earliest stage scenes appear to have mixed elements of the old Tudor method of constructing stage 'mansions' with the newer criterion of foreshortening in perspective. Serlio's angled wings are indeed little more than mansions of the old type, compressed into the rapidly diminishing space of his shallow stage. But by about 1620 Jones had developed a rather different way of handling perspective in the main part of the scene. Behind a front curtain stood a gently raked stage on which were mounted sets of side wings painted in foreshortening to direct the eye to an area at the back which was closed off by a pair of great sliding shutters. On these the continuation of the scene was painted, though as we shall see this part of the whole was often discontinuous with the perspective system of the wings. The shutters could be slid apart in grooves to reveal a 'scene of relieve' beyond. This was usually a series of profiled flats set up in front of a backcloth, giving further depth to the whole stage picture. Many of the designs are detailed and sometimes scaled drawings of the backscene, from which we can discover a good deal about their perspective ordering. Once this method of representing spatial recession was fully established, Jones appears to have turned his attention more to the mechanics and visual display of the upper parts of the scene, where increasingly the sky was enlivened with opening Heavens, mobile

47   John Webb, interpretive diagram of the *Florimène* stage.

clouds and descending deities. Here, however, the ordinary laws of perspective were suspended along with the more adventurous masquers, and in the present chapter we shall be concerned rather with the system of raked stage, foreshortened wings and backscene that went to make up the earthlier elements of the moving picture.

The wings might be angled like those in the Serlian stage, with their inner faces foreshortened according to the perspective system, or they might be constructed as simple flats whose single face lay parallel to the front of the stage. It is not always easy to tell from Jones's drawings which of these types he intended to use. Many – perhaps most – of the designs after 1620 indicate a series of flat wings placed at more or less regular intervals behind one another, but angled wings were certainly used for *Florimène*, for which Webb has left us his detailed stage plans (plates 41 and 47). The perspective sketches for this production are unambiguous in representing the angled wings, but there are other drawings among the Jones canon where the matter cannot be so easily settled. We know, for example, that the scenes in *Britannia Triumphans*, staged in the Masquing House in 1638, were constantly changed, and two of the full stage designs for this production quite clearly show that flats were used, with three wings to each side. Yet several other drawings for the remaining scenes in the masque show wings apparently with angled inner faces of the Serlian type. It is extremely unlikely that the two types could coexist on the same stage, and it is in any case very difficult to arrange for a satisfactory way of changing angled wings. We have Webb's detailed plan and section of the Masquing House stage as it was prepared for *Salmacida Spolia* two years later, and these show that the flat wings were arranged in clusters or 'bunches' of four, so that four complete settings could be accommodated.[2] As one scene changed to another each of the wings was withdrawn along its grooves and replaced by another thrust out from the bunch. Simultaneously the backshutter might be opened, or itself changed in the same way as the wings. Angled wings cannot be thrust on and off stage along grooves, and although Niccolo Sabbatini recorded a method of changing them by covering them with cloths there is no evidence that Jones resorted to any such desperate expedient. It seems clear that the four drawings of scenes for *Britannia Triumphans* that show the wings as angled must in fact have been constructed as flats, and the same is likely to be true of most of the other designs of a similar type.[3]

The perspective system which Jones used on his wings, whether angled or flat, seems always to have been based on the regular single-point scheme, in which all the elements of the scene are so arranged that they present their faces parallel to the stage front, and are diminished in proportion as they recede from the viewer towards a single vanishing point. In the straightforward method this point lies on a level with the prime observer's eye, and all the orthogonals converge upon it. These represent lines that are objectively perpendicular to the plane of the stage front, such as the faces of square-planned buildings which present one wall parallel to that plane. All of Jones's 'architectural' scenes are ostensibly of this type, and many of them are so indeed, projecting their orthogonal lines to a single point located on the horizon. A drawing made in this fashion is useful as an indication of what a constructed scene might look like, but it has little practical value to the workmen whose task is to realize its quality in the theatre. If the design were to adopt the correct station point it would show very little of the raked stage floor, and give only a confused account of how the wings were separated. Serlio's method of combining plan and elevation, on the other hand, gives only a poor impression of how the scene will look when it is built, and in most cases Jones seems to have reached a compromise by composing his drawings – as distinct, of course, from the scenes themselves – with a horizon pitched lower than it is in the Serlian scheme, yet higher than it would appear in a regular orthogonal projection. As perspective views of foreshortened sets they should not show the orthogonals as continuous straight lines, as they are, for example, in the single-point perspective engravings recording the designs of Giulio Parigi (plate 48), but as bent to a new direction at the backshutters. Looking somewhat downwards into a perspective set we should see the backshutters higher in relation to the front wings than they would be in an elevation. Any orthogonals marked on them will no longer be continuous with those marked on the wing flats, which themselves will appear staggered. The altitude of the horizon on the shutters is fixed because it is painted there all on a single plane, and because this plane appears in true elevation even in a perspective it should in theory retain its original ortho-gonals, as should the wings, each independently. But all this is mere theory, suitable for a textbook perhaps, though hardly for the press of ordinary practice. In fact Jones drew his scenes with the wing orthogonals in simple alignment. Nevertheless the majority of his drawings do mark the difference between the front and rear parts of the scenes by changing the direction of the orthogonals on the backscene, but they do so in what is – at least in theory – the wrong direction. A true perspective of a three-dimensional scenic vista viewed under the conditions we have just described should pitch the vanishing point marked on the backshutters lower than that reached by projecting the orthogonals of the wing corners (fig. 11). But in Jones's drawings the back vanishing point and horizon are frequently pitched higher than those of the front scene, so that the orthogonals bend upwards towards it (fig. 12). This habit of composition readily conveys a sense of the structure of the scene, but if it is no more than a convention for that purpose it seems an oddly perverse one, the very opposite of what experience teaches. It appears, therefore, that Jones did actually intend to show a high horizon marked on the backshutters, and when we turn from the composite stage designs to the separate ones for the backshutters alone we often find direct confirmation

229

TENPIO DELLA PACE INTERMEDIO SESTO

Come: rapp: nelle notte di
Ser: Principe di Toscan
(an 1606. Giulio Parigi
. et F.

48   Giulio Parigi, 'Tempio della pace', engraved by Remigio Canta-Gallina.

that he did so. Many of the drawings are meticulously organized over a carefully scored-in framework of incised lines run along a straight-edge, and it is evident that Jones quite deliberately constructed his scenes with two horizons, a high one for the shutters and relieves, and a lower one for the wings.

We shall return a little later to this question of the double horizon, but first we must take note of a quite separate visual convention which entered Jones's representation of scenes, and probably the scenes themselves, at about the time when he worked on *Chloridia* in 1631. This is the first of a series of masques whose designs are based, often remarkably closely, on the engravings illustrating the scenic work of Giulio Parigi. In *Chloridia* the landscape set of wings and shutters is adapted from Parigi's scene of Mount Ida in *Il giudizio di Paride* (Florence, 1608), with the chief difference that Jones's backscene area is much narrower than his source's, so that the whole composition is compressed, as it were, inwards from the sides. Parigi's scene

230

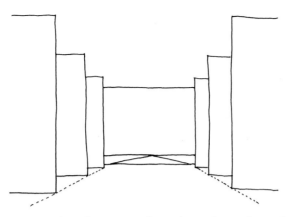

Figure 11   True perspective of stage seen from above the station point. Note the low horizon.

is much wider than it is tall, while in Jones's the scenic opening is almost square. In comparing the design with its source one has the impression that Jones has merely transferred the shape of Parigi's tree wings to his own sheet without substantially altering their rate of diminishment to suit his own narrower stage, with the result that they converge, not on a single vanishing point but rather on two. The orthogonals of the wings to the left seem to converge towards the right of centre, and those on the right seem to do the reverse. Because these wings are all tree and rock forms they do not lend themselves to confident orthogonal analysis, but in *Albion's Triumph*, produced the next year, there is a substantial and wholly architectural scene, again developed from *Il giudizio di Paride*, in which the compression effect may be much more clearly assessed. In the print after Parigi (plate 48) all the orthogonals of the perspective project to a single low vanishing point (the figures represented in the sky always excepted); no attempt is made to

Figure 12   Jones's perspective scheme: note the high horizon.

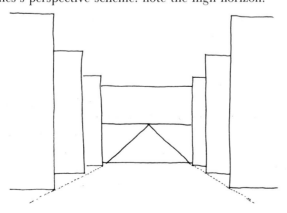

231

distinguish perspectively between the parts of the scene, which is therefore represented as if viewed from its station point. In *Albion's Triumph* Jones takes Parigi's view of the Tempio della Pace and recasts it as what the text calls 'a *Romane Atrium*', again narrowing the backshutter area and so compressing the whole view into a squarer shape (plate 49). As in his source, the wings are certainly representations of four-square classical architecture, and each building has one side placed parallel to the front of the stage. Accordingly, as in the Parigi print, the orthogonals should converge to a single point, but they do not. At first glance it seems that those to one side project too far to the opposite, and vice versa, so that the two sets of wings, when projected to their horizon, appear to overlap. It is important to distinguish this form of composition from the more usual two-point perspective, in which right-angled buildings are set cornerwise to the stage front and do not align on orthogonals at all. The *Romane Atrium* in *Albion's Triumph* is not such a perspective: its buildings are clearly set parallel to the stage front, and just as clearly their inner faces do not converge to a single point. Yet the overlap is no mistake, for the 'orthogonals' of the wings are set on lines deliberately scored along a straight-edge. Nor is it simply a matter of Jones naively or carelessly taking Parigi's wings and copying them literally down onto his sheet, for in fact their foreshortening is subtly altered in the English design, so that the entablatures align with one another rather differently, and the bases rise more steeply to a higher vanishing point.

Here, then, is a further type of scenic design, not found in Jones's sources. Happily the deliberation of the underdrawing gives us a clue to the meaning of its strange overlapping technique. The 'orthogonals' of the wing tops are established on lightly scored lines which are continued un-inked until they meet each other at a point on the central axis of the drawing somewhat above the apparent horizon of the backshutters. Similar scored lines run from the podium steps at either side to converge at another point on the central axis a corresponding distance below the backshutters' horizon. Once they have converged on each other at these two points the lines are discontinued: they do not run to vanishing points to the left and right of centre. A further set of 'orthogonals' is established by scored lines on the backshutter area, with an apparent vanishing point located midway between the other points of convergence of the wings. We therefore have three pricked points, all deliberately established on the axis of the drawing, and all somehow involved in its orthogonal perspective system. In addition the drawing possesses a scale bar, inked along the very bottom of the sheet, where it has been largely cropped away. It is nevertheless recognizable as marking 15 divisions in groups of five. By this scale the overall dimensions of the design are 34 units by 31, figures which correspond exactly to the thorough squaring-up of the frontispiece design for *Albion's Triumph* (O&S 190; plate 50), where the opening measures 34 squares wide by 31 squares high. Almost certainly each

49   Inigo Jones, 'a *Romane Atrium*' from *Albion's Triumph* (1632).

square in this design represents one foot, and it follows that the *Atrium* drawing's scale bar represents feet too, at the ratio of 2 ft 3 ins to the inch. The frontispiece drawing shows an architectural assembly of entablature, frieze and pilasters which are to be realized in the theatre in cardboard and wood. The construction is all in one plane, and the whole design can readily be squared up from the sheet, the painters merely transferring the small squares on the paper to 1 ft squares in their full-sized work. But we know that a perspective scene is not so easily to be transferred by such methods. If the drawing from which the craftsmen are taking their cues is a regular single-point perspective they will be able to take the dimensions of the front wings from it readily enough, but the deeper ones will cause them problems. The single-point system diminishes these wings as if they were all to be viewed in the same plane as the front of the scene, but in fact the further wings will be placed several feet beyond the nearest ones, and when viewed from a fixed

233

50   Inigo Jones, frontispiece for *Albion's Triumph*.

station point in the auditorium will diminish even more than appears on the designer's sheets. The result, in the constructed scene, will be a vista that appears to surge more deeply towards the horizon than is shown in the original sketch. Of course this effect can be countered if the workmen increase the size and lateral separation of the further wings, but in that case they will be unable to scale them up directly from the drawing. The artist therefore has the choice either of drawing what the scene will look like when it is finished, or of making a scaled diagram useful to the production team.

It seems that Jones and John Webb sometimes chose the one course, and sometimes the other. Webb's design (plate 51) for the standing scene of Davenant's 'opera', *The Siege of Rhodes*, performed at Rutland House and the Cockpit in Drury Lane in the 1650s, may happily be compared with a detailed plan of the stage. The separation of the wings, to the left and right of the scene, almost exactly coincides with that given in the plan. The drawing

234

51 John Webb, frontispiece for *The Siege of Rhodes* (*c.* 1656).

is developed over a meticulously scored underdrawing, with an intermediary stage in lead before the final ink version was set down. Although the wing forms are shown as irregular rocky cliffs, they are drawn on neatly ruled rectangles indicating the shapes of the flats on which they were painted, and these are proportioned exactly as in the section of the stage which survives alongside the plan. Here the rake of the stage is shown as rising to a level 4 ins above its front by the time it reaches the foot of the backshutters, and again the scene design agrees, markng the same interval as 4 ins. This drawing, which is squared up extensively, is therefore an orthogonal projection of a perspective scene. Each part of it may be directly scaled by the workmen for transfer to the full-sized frontispiece and wings. Once it has been built, the scene will appear to diminish more rapidly towards the horizon than it does in the drawing, though because the stage is comparatively shallow this effect will not be very marked.

The standing scene design for *Florimène*, on the other hand, is presented in perspective form (plate 52). The main interest of this drawing lies in the border, with its vigorous decoration and unusual stage steps, and here the outlines are ruled in lead beneath the ink, at a scale of 3 ft to the inch. There is no sign of squaring for the transfer to the full-size work, but clearly the design

235

could be used as a working drawing in the preparation of the frontispiece. In the scene itself, however, the 3 ft scale breaks down. If, for instance, one measures the opening between the furthest wings, through which the back-shutters may be seen, and scales it at the ratio that serves for the frontispiece, it appears to be about 9 ft 6 ins wide. According to the plan, however, this rear opening was 13 ft across, and several associated backscene designs are ruled up 13 squares wide. Evidently then the parts of the *Florimène* scene beyond the frontispiece are shown as what I have called a perspective of a perspective, and they cannot be used for scaling up. It is not surprising that this drawing is not squared for enlargement: its presentation of the scene shows how the finished work would look, but does not indicate its measurements to the painters.

Yet an apparently similar drawing, for *The Shepherd's Paradise*, is squared

52   Inigo Jones, standing scene for *Florimène* (1635).

up all over with a pointer, each square representing 1 ft 6 ins (plate 53). Here the backshutter opening, measured across the feet of the furthest wings, is approximately 7 ft, judged against the squaring. The plan of the stage (plate 40) also shows this interval as 7 ft, and the design is evidently an orthogonal projection, each part like those of *The Siege of Rhodes* standing scene capable of being scaled up to the full size.

Having distinguished these two classes of Jones's perspective scene design we may now return to the interesting case of the Roman *Atrium* drawing for *Albion's Triumph* (plate 49). We have established that this is a scaled drawing, made at 2 ft 3 ins to the inch. In this case we have no plan for comparison, but the opening between the rear wings scales at about 12 ft, and because the associated backshutter design for an amphitheatre is ruled off into a width of 14 squares it seems likely that the whole scene is an adaptation of the orthogonal projection type (the backscene often being made a little wider than the opening to it, so that it safely filled the gap as seen from all parts of the auditorium). Of course it is not a regular or thoroughgoing orthogonal

53   Inigo Jones, standing scene for *The Shepherd's Paradise* (1633).

projection, for if it were the stage floor would hardly be visible. Jones has adopted a bastard convention which presents the wings in pure elevation while still retaining something of the quality of a perspective of perspective. We appear to look downwards into the raked stage area, but all the vertical planes presented to us in the design are drawn to a common scale, and can be enlarged in the theatre according to a single system of measurement or squaring up. The angles of the orthogonals on the foreshortened parts of the flat wings cannot be copied directly from the drawing, because the shallow rake of the actual stage floor will be quite different from what Jones has drawn. But the geometry of similar triangles ensures that the wings, even in the foreshortened parts, will remain in common scale at full size. In this respect Jones's drawing is precisely like Serlio's woodcuts of the generic scenes; it differs from them in not offering a plan of the stage floor along with the scaled elevation of the wings.

But the *Atrium* scene is also of the type that does not diminish to a single vanishing point; the orthogonals at the top converge high up, while those at the bottom come together lower down. The result of this configuration is that the rear wings are drawn taller than they would be in a regular single-point perspective. Yet the orthogonals defining the cornices of the buildings in the wings are clearly ruled in ink, and are the result of much deliberation. The design is contained within a ruled, scaled frame; several scored vertical lines establish the location of the wings; and at the bottom a number of scored orthogonals define the placing of the podium steps to either side. Nothing in the preparation of the design on the sheet suggests the least informality of approach. The general technique is in fact similar to that of a carefully developed architectural drawing.

The strange orthogonal system, with its three pricked vanishing points and scored underdrawing, is evidently a considered and methodical approach to the problem of perspective design for the stage. A further proof of this conclusion lies in a scored line which runs on the left side of the sheet from the architrave of the front wing to converge on the lowest of the three vanishing points, the point, that is, where the podium orthogonals meet. The line forms part of the initial preparation of the sheet, for it was scored in before the wash was applied and one can see where the colour has gathered in its channel. For this reason its direction can now be seen even in photographs: it cuts across the furthest column on the left side of the design, just a little below the capital, and appears again running through the wash that shades the coffering behind it. Connected as it is with the orthogonal system of the podium steps, this line represents a further orthogonal of a single-point perspective, established presumably at the beginning of Jones's design work and later superseded by the less steeply foreshortened orthogonals that actually serve for the upper part of the composition. Not only is the drawing a considered piece of work, but part of its very deliberation consists in the establishment and subsequent rejection of a simple single-point scheme. The *Romane Atrium* design shows Jones moving well beyond the straightforward perspective of Serlio and also of his specific source on this occasion, the engraving of Parigi's 'Temple of Peace' for *Il giudizio di Paride*.

The effect of the system is to increase the height of the further wings, thus avoiding the uncomfortably steep foreshortening that seems sometimes to have characterized single-point perspectives on the stage. But there is also a general loosening of the orthogonal bonds in the drawing, caused by the separation of the two vanishing points, upper and lower. All the podium steps project to the lower point, and all the entablatures project to the upper, with the result that the architecture opens itself upwards like a hinge as it recedes from the viewer. The spatial ambiguity which is created by this device is sufficiently subtle to have gone unnoticed hitherto – Orgel and Strong, for example, mistakenly observe that the drawing 'is scored with lines of perspective to a single vanishing point'[4] – and yet it is both deliberate and all encompassing. The upper vanishing point is used for all the elements of the scene down to the sill of the window visible beyond the first column to the right, where the disparity with the lower elements is acutely felt. Because this technique became so common in Jones's work, especially in the scenes which he based on Parigi, we need a word to describe it. Perhaps 'stretched' will do: the orthogonals in the upper part of the drawing are raised so that the buildings seem to be stretched upwards as they stand deeper in the scene. In thus departing from the strict and simple rules of the conventional sort of perspective Jones was working in what we have come to think of as a baroque fashion, flouting the scientific orderliness of the method in order to achieve something more humane and expressive, and at the same time liberating the scene from the implacable march of regular foreshortening.

The *Romane Atrium* drawing is splashed with scene painter's distemper and was evidently used as a scaled working design in the preparation of the masque. The rather similar drawing, again based on a Parigi engraving, for the vale of Tempe in *Tempe Restored* (1632; plate 54) again takes all the orthogonals in the upper part from a high vanishing point, and all the lower ones from a separate low one. The design is contained within an outline frame 358 mm wide and 327 mm tall, precisely in the 34 : 31 proportion customary in the Banqueting House masques, but there is no further scale or sign of squaring. The narrowness of the opening between the rear wings to the backscene suggests that the design is not actually capable of being scaled, but is itself a perspective of the foreshortened scene. Yet here too the vanishing points are pricked into the paper and the independent systems of orthogonals are scored as well as inked where they are incorporated into the wings. Occasionally the scored lines are also traced in lead. The deliberation of the method can hardly be doubted, though there is no evidence here of a tentative or canonical single-point system from which the finished design

54   Inigo Jones, 'the vale of TEMPE' from *Tempe Restored* (1632).

departs. An altogether freer design made for *Britannia Triumphans* (1638, in the Masquing House) shows a prospect of London on the backshutters, with wings representing houses in the foreground (O&S 334; plate 19). The forms are rendered freehand, but there is a system of orthogonals ruled in lead beneath the ink of the finished work. All converge on a point close to the river bank below St Paul's, and therefore represent a single-point perspective organization. The wing feet follow these orthogonals fairly closely, but their heads do not. Again the upper part of the scene projects to a higher vanishing point than the lower, and the presence of the ruled single-point orthogonals shows that the departure from the regular system was a considered strategy. John Webb's version of the same design (O&S 335) also includes the orthogonals converging to the same spot beneath St Paul's, but here the whole drawing follows the single-point method. Whatever Jones's purposes in developing his unusual system, they had not as yet been learned by his assistant.

240

55   Inigo Jones, 'the ruines of some great Citie' from *Coelum Britannicum* (1634).

Nevertheless Jones's method seems to have spread from the wings to the backscene designs, and before long a great proportion of his drawings came to embody it. Even in the backshutter represented in the *Romane Atrium* design for *Albion's Triumph* the 'peeces of Architecture of a Pallace royall', though converging to a single vanishing point located between those of the wings, project above the orthogonals in the middle part. The earliest scene of the 'stretched' type seems to have been the woodland setting for *Chloridia* (1631, in the Banqueting House), in which the outline of the frontispiece is carefully ruled and the whole drawing is squared up with a pointer for transfer to full scale (O&S 163). An alternative study for the same scene (O&S 164) follows the same pattern. Many of the drawings associated with *The Shepherd's Paradise* (1633) are of this type, including one for an architectural interior constructed as a relieve (O&S 249). Another Parigi-based design, that of the ruined city for *Coelum Britannicum* (1634, in the Banqueting House), is scaled and drawn within ruled limits to the 'stretched' pattern, though the decayed

241

56 John Webb, 'the suburbs of a great City' from *Salmacida Spolia* (1640).

state of the buildings shown makes strict analysis impossible (plate 55). The scored squaring is taken over the whole design, even across the void at its centre, and it seems likely that Jones intended it to be used by the painters for scaling up. It is splashed with their distemper. A grove scene for *The Temple of Love* (1635, in the Banqueting House) has larger rear wings than a single-point system would require, and is evidently of the 'stretched' type even though there are no ruled elements to make the matter certain. Other scenes of the type include an Indian shore for *The Temple of Love* (O&S 295), 'the difficult way . . . to the Throne of Honour' (O&S 404, by Jones; the Webb version, O&S 405, is drawn as a straightforward single-point perspective), 'the suburbs of a great City' (O&S 409, by Webb, and very confused), both for *Salmacida Spolia*, and various shutter, relieve and minor scene designs by both Jones and Webb (O&S 445, 446, 448 and 454).

One of these drawings, Webb's carefully inked perspective of 'the suburbs of a great City' for *Salmacida Spolia*, seems to be a riot of confusion (plate 56). Yet it is composed within a scored and inked ruled frame and is accompanied by a scale bar indicating 2 ft 6 ins to the inch. A scored orthogonal establishes the line of the wing feet to the right, and a further scored line runs down the centre of the scene. The backshutter of a bridge is precisely drawn in ink over lead, and in the wings a lead underdrawing sometimes makes rather more orthogonal sense in the upper parts, where the balconies, attics and cornices go astray in the final inked version. This architecture is derived from a totally assured engraving after Veronese,[5] and it would not have been beyond Webb's competence to render the source in an equally correct single-point system. The general proportions of the design appear to show that it belongs to the 'stretched' type, but there is little of the exact system of the *Albion's Triumph* drawing. Webb appears to have been seeking to find a way of achieving Jones's transcendence over the mere geometry of the traditional perspective techniques, but without much success on this occasion. The drawing is, however, not a practical working one but a document of record, to be associated with Webb's plan and section of the same stage.[6] Like them it includes a great quantity of past-tense description of the scene down the margin, none of it unfortunately devoted to the method of its perspective construction. Webb had previously recast Jones's 'stretched' scene of London for *Britannia Triumphans* into a straightforward single-point mould; a drawing for *Luminalia* (O&S 386) had no perspective to trouble him, and only now, after the last of the great Stuart masques, did he attempt to master something of Jones's subtlety and expressive freedom.

The question of the multiple vanishing points is further complicated by the technical need to align the wing feet on orthogonals, which must coincide with the actual rake of the stage. This point is perhaps most readily to be understood in the case of angled wings of the Serlian type. In Serlio's stage plan (plate 29) the inner faces of the angled wings are set on orthogonals to converge at the vanishing point, whose location in his foreshortened scheme is fixed at 13.5 squares from the front of the scene (the square-units being measured from the reticulation of the forestage). Likewise, in the section of the theatre (plate 30), the stage is raked upwards to meet its horizon at just this distance from the front. Both plan and section agree, so that the rake of the stage is incorporated into the whole orthogonal system, but only at the cost of building the stage to the very steep rake of about 1 : 8 (in the text Serlio describes the rake as 1 : 9, but the section marks it a little steeper). The most fully documented case of the use of angled wings by Jones is that of *Florimène*, for which Webb prepared two sectional drawings, both of which give a much shallower rake than this (1 : 23 in one, and 1 : 27 in the other).[7] Yet the associated plans show the inner faces of the angled wings converging to a point either at or just in front of the backcloth, only some 8 ft or 9 ft beyond the backshutters (plate 41). If the floor of the stage were treated as truly orthogonal – as it is in Serlio – it would intercept the horizon in line with this vanishing point, only about four inches above the backshutter opening. Yet all the backshutter designs for *Florimène* show the horizon very much higher than that. Either the drawings are irrational judged as perspective structures, or the wing feet are not orthogonal.

The wings in *Florimène* are not rigidly architectural in character, but intersperse rustic cottages with trees. These irregular forms might have obscured the orthogonal tyranny of the wing feet, but such evasions could not succeed in a more strictly architectural setting. That the tops of the wing structures need not necessarily be orthogonal is proved by the design made for the Lord Chamberlain's play at the Cockpit in 1639 (O&S 443; plate 57). Here the orthogonals of a single-point system are sketched in, with the tents on the main stage rendered continuously with those painted on the backshutters. But the tops of the wings are also apparently marked with lines which slope downwards less steeply than the orthogonals. In this case the upper parts of the wings were treated as structures not in themselves proportioned by the single-point scheme, but rather as surfaces onto which the scheme might be projected. It might be possible to do the same thing with the bases, painting them to represent the ground and pitching the ground-lines of buildings and trees part way up them so as to establish a higher horizon, but on the whole such a trick seems unlikely because the surface of the stage would assert itself all too evidently against the line of the ground thus depicted. Either the rake of the stage must be steep enough to be incorporated into the single-point orthogonal system, or that system must be modified in the execution.

Earlier in this chapter we saw that Jones often made the horizon of his designs higher than it should be in a regular foreshortening. In such drawings the wings project to a lower vanishing point than is shown on the backshutters. The first hint of such a double-horizon system comes in a set of rough sketches on the verso of a drawing for an unknown masque of 1621 (O&S 111; plate 58). Here a plan of a very shallow stage with flat wings, backshutters and relieves includes some lines struck across the right-hand wings. One, which appears to have been answered by a corresponding line through the left wings before the drawing was cropped, runs roughly parallel to the wing edges and appears to represent an orthogonal. Just such lines are scored across the wings in Webb's diagrammatic plan of the *Florimène* stage (O&S 324) to converge at the vanishing point, and others are scored similarly into the plan for the Paved Court theatre at Somerset House (plate 40). But if in Jones's design of 1621 these lines are indeed orthogonal, they do not match a second set drawn cutting across the relieves. Evidently the plan shows at least two orthogonal systems, one for the front of the scene and the other for the back, and the two are not consistent with each other. That such a double system might include double horizons is first made clear among Jones's drawings by a series of designs made for plays rather than masques.[8] The standing scene for *Artenice* (1626) gives a set of wings of the Serlian

244

57   Inigo Jones, scene design for the Cockpit in Drury Lane (1639).

58   Inigo Jones, plan of a masque stage (*c.* 1621).

angled type drawn in single-point perspective and converging to a vanishing point substantially lower than the horizon marked on the backshutters. The same construction is seen even more clearly in the 'Tragic Scene' (1633 or after),[9] where the wing orthogonals are carefully ruled in a lead under-drawing to converge well below the vanishing point required for the back-shutters. At this period most of Jones's masque designs conform to the single-point Serlian type (O&S 113, 115, 129 and 147); the double-horizon scheme seems to have been developed especially to suit the demands of the

246

scenic dramas performed at Court, of which the extensive drawings for *Florimène* provide us with the fullest record.

In the standing scene designs for *Florimène* (plate 52) the wings of trees and cottages lead to a backshutter painted with a sea coast, the horizon clearly marked at a level well above that to which the orthogonals of the forepart of the scene converge. One of the associated drawings (O&S 327) shows the shutters in detail, marking the horizon almost exactly half way up their overall height. The importance of the horizon to a perspective scheme is of course fundamental: without it the system has no line of reference. A correct linear perspective locates the orthogonal vanishing point on the horizon, and this in turn is established at the same height as the station point from which the prospect is to be viewed. In a masque or scenic drama the most obvious and exact way of indicating the horizon is as the furthest part of a plain, or even better as the furthest part of the ocean. Scenes which establish the horizon in this forthright fashion are accordingly common, and it is not perhaps very remarkable that they are often mentioned in the *libretti* in terms that stress their function in a perspective rationale. In *The Argvment of the Pastorall of 'Florimène'*, for instance, the backscene of the sea is described as taking the view to its ultimate limit: 'and a farr off, to terminate the sight, was the mayne *Sea*, expressing this place to be the *Isle of Delos*'.[10] The text of Jonson's *Masque of Blackness* gives this theme an early and complete expression:

the *Scene* behind, seemed a vast Sea (and vnited with this that flowed forth) from the termination, or *horizon* of which (being the leuell of the *State*, which was placed in the vpper end of the Hall) was drawne, by the lines of *Prospectiue*, the whole worke shooting downewards, from the eye; which *decorum* made it more conspicuous, and caught the eye a far of with a wandring beauty.[11]

Here the language of many later masques is fully anticipated. In *Tethys' Festival*, for example, Daniel set the first scene at a 'Port or Hauen', where 'beyond all appeared the Horison or termination of the Sea'.[12] Jonson included many sea scenes in his masques, and for one of them there survives a Jones design that shows the horizon very clearly marked (O&S 147). But his descriptions of them are – like most of his references to Jones's work – regrettably scanty. With Townshend's *Tempe Restored* in 1632 the technical terminology returns, indicating perhaps that it had originated with Jones rather than Jonson:

a farre off [was seen] a Landscipt and a calme sea which did terminate the Horizon . . .[13]

For this masque too there is a shutter design (O&S 217) with the horizon marked half way up. Similar language is found in the text of Davenant's *Temple of Love* (1635):

the Sceane is all changed into a Sea somewhat calme . . . In the Sea were severall Islands, and a farre off a Continent terminating with the Horrizon.[14]

Jones's drawing (O&S 295) shows a high horizon on the backshutters, and four pairs of rocky wings apparently converging to a lower vanishing point. A marine scene in *Britannia Triumphans* (1638, in the new Masquing House) is again described in the familiar way: 'the Scene changed, and in the farthest part the sea was seene, terminating the sight with the horizon'.[15] For this masque we have two versions of a backshutter design showing the nautical horizon, and both mark it half way up the overall height. In *Salmacida Spolia* there was a tempestuous sea, but it is only briefly described in Jones's text: 'a farre off was a darke wrought sea'.[16] A full-setting drawing (O&S 401) shows the turbulent waves, with the horizon placed well up the backshutters.

Every independent backscene design that possesses a clearly marked horizon establishes it at a level well above the vanishing point of the wing-feet orthogonals, and even above the pseudo vanishing point projected from the tops of the wings where those are proportioned according to the 'stretched' system. Where the wings are represented as a single-point perspective the disparity is the more remarkable. The uncanonically high horizon seems to have entered Jones's practice early in the 1620s, and it was not until a decade later that he began making drawings with 'stretched' foreshortening in the wings. Yet both techniques resisted the merely mechanical aspects of a Serlian perspective system, and it is not surprising to find that they are often brought together on a single stage. Sometimes the result is merely incoherent, as in the various backscene designs for *The Shepherd's Paradise*, where the horizon level shifts from drawing to drawing without apparent justification. But the well-documented case of *Florimène* shows that the system could on occasion be tightly disciplined. Here we have a methodical section of the stage, and can tell that a horizon located half way up the shutters would be 5 ft 6 ins above the stage front, at the level, that is to say, of the head of an actor standing on the stage. But the orthogonals of the angled wings projected to a vanishing point only $4\frac{1}{2}$ ins above the base of the shutters, well below their horizon. The stage was raked upwards from 4 ft 6 ins at the front to 5 ft 6 ins at the shutters, so that the orthogonal vanishing point of the wing feet will have been 5 ft $10\frac{1}{2}$ ins above the floor of the hall, at a height, that is, closely approximate to the level of the king's eye as he sat on his halpace beneath the state. Thus two criteria of perspective were met at once: on the stage the high horizon of the backscene corresponded to the scale of the actors who played in front of it, while the main station point was located in the auditorium according to the orthogonals of the wings.

The habit of placing the horizon of a picture at the level of the head of a human figure shown standing on a level floor was first given a coherent theoretical justification by Alberti in the *De pictura*. Chiefly concerned with the development of perspective compositions, Alberti observed that the size of objects shown in foreshortening is ambiguous, for a small object close to the observer will subtend an angle at his eye equal to that subtended by something much larger but further away. His solution to this problem is to appeal to the principle of comparison:

Comparison is made with things most immediately known. As man is the best known of all things to man, perhaps Protagoras, in saying that man is the scale and the measure of all things, meant that accidents in all things are duly compared to and known by the accidents in man. All of which should persuade us that, however small you paint the objects in a painting, they will seem large or small according to the size of any man in the picture.[17]

Having given this reason for taking the figure of a man as the basis for proportioning a painting, Alberti proceeds to describe his method of preparing the *quadro* for a perspective underdrawing:

First of all, on the surface on which I am going to paint, I draw a rectangle of whatever size I want, which I regard as an open window through which the subject to be painted is seen; and I decide how large I wish the human figures in the painting to be. I divide the height of this man into three parts, which will be proportional to the measure commonly called a *braccio*; for, as may be seen from the relationship of his limbs, three *braccia* is just about the average height of a man's body. With this measure I divide the bottom line of my rectangle into as many parts as it will hold; and this bottom line of the rectangle is for me proportional to the next transverse equidistant quantity seen on the pavement. Then I establish a point in the rectangle wherever I wish; and as it occupies the place where the central ray strikes, I shall call this the centric point. The suitable position for this centric point is no higher from the base line than the height of the man to be represented in the painting, for in this way both the viewers and the objects in the painting will seem to be on the same plane.[18]

He then goes on to describe the system which we have in modern times come to call *costruzione legittima*, tracing orthogonals from the baseline divisions to converge on the centric point, which is thus established as the level of the horizon. It is of great significance to Alberti that the constructions he is describing are not to be thought of as abstract geometry; they employ some of the language and many of the methods of geometry, but they take their origins in the characteristics of human perception and especially in the proportions of the human frame. Even the squares of the geometrical floor are to be scaled according to the human *braccio* dimension, the length of an arm, or the third part of a body's height. Every part of the composition will be influenced by this fundamental choice: the horizon set as high as a man's frame, the objects placed on the squared floor, the very dimensions of the *quadro* itself.

In setting the horizon for *Florimène* 5 ft 6 ins above the raked forestage of his

Court theatre, Jones appears to have followed the painterly advice of Alberti, though to be sure at 5 ft 6 ins he must have been allowing for the headdresses of the ladies who performed the play to bring them up to the required height. John Webb seems to have adopted the same method for his drama scenes. We have a full set of wing and backscene designs for *The Siege of Rhodes*,[19] and in them the horizon is located five feet or so above the floor, although the wing feet project to a much lower vanishing point. The stage which Webb designed for the Hall Theatre at Whitehall in 1665 was intended for use 'for the Queens Ballett' in that year, and was subsequently adapted for plays, including a performance of Orrery's *Mustapha* in the following year. For this we have a series of backscene designs,[20] although the drawings for the wings have not survived. From the detailed plan and section of the stage[21] we find that the backshutters were drawn 11 ft 6 ins high to scale, but marked variously in lead and ink, '11fo', '11fo 8[yns]' (this cancelled), and '12fo 6'. Both plan and section are liberally supplied with noted dimensions, most of which represent departures from the scale, and it is clear that the drawings are working documents which record several revisions of the proportions of the stage. The backscene designs for *Mustapha* are all ruled up 15 squares wide by $11\frac{1}{4}$ or $11\frac{1}{3}$ high, and it seems likely that they were intended to fit a shutter assembly scaled much as it is drawn in the section, though rather wider than it appears in the plan. Once again the horizon marked on the exterior scene of 'Buda beleaguered' is established about half way up the design, five feet or so above the stage. Webb left several other backscene designs for this theatre, one of them a marine prospect showing the sun rising out of a stormy sky beyond a harbour.[22] Here the horizon exactly bisects the drawing.

In the Court drama, therefore, and even in one of Davenant's operas, both Jones and Webb appear to have taken care to set the horizon of the backscene at the level of the height of a man on the stage, just as Alberti would have advised. For the masques the matter is complicated by the great, sometimes monumental, scale of the visual effects. Here much of the scenic entertainment took place at the upper level, in the skies, and the masquers descended to the main stage not as merely human agents but as deities and personifications of great moment. Thence they would pass down to the dancing floor and the human scale of the auditorium; but as long as they stayed within the confines of the vast scenes which Jones erected on his lofty stages they retained a more than human quality. The drama stages tended to be comparatively low, ranging from 1 ft 6 ins at the Paved Court to 4 ft 6 ins for *Florimène*. At the Hall Theatre Webb drew the stage 4 ft high at its front, then had second thoughts and labelled it as '5 fo.', the dimension that was, according to the Works accounts, actually built: 'Stage for the Sceens . . . 39 foot long 33 foot wide and v foot high.'[23] Masque stages were usually higher: Webb records one of 7 ft for *Salmacida Spolia*, and others of a like height are mentioned in the Works accounts.[24] Mounted on such a stage the frontispiece border often towered 40 ft above the hall floor, and the front wings would frequently exceed 30 ft in height. Descending clouds and ranks of masquers would have a spectacularly long way to go before they touched the boards, and there was little about the scenes that related directly to the human scale of the participants. The section of the stage prepared for *Salmacida Spolia* shows shutters 14 ft tall, and one might estimate the horizon of the stormy sea in the first scene (O&S 401) to have been drawn about half way up them, or over 7 ft above the front of the stage. Below this looming and windracked scene the figure of Fury emerged from a fiery globe:

> *Blow winds! untill you raise the Seas so high*
> *That waves may hang like Teares in the Sunnes eye,*
> *That we (when in vast Cataracts they fall)*
> *May thinke he weeps at Natures Funerall.*[25]

On this occasion the high horizon had an obvious justification, for the sea will have appeared ready to flood the auditorium. But the much more peaceful backscene of a sea at the end of *Britannia Triumphans*, performed in the same room and perhaps on a similarly scaled stage, also pitched the horizon half way up the shutter opening (see O&S 341 and 342). Here the waves were a setting for Galatea riding a dolphin and for a mechanical representation of ships tacking towards a harbour. It seems that the human scale of the drama scenes was sometimes abandoned in the masques, where the convenience of spectacular display and the desire for monumental impressiveness led to a general enlargement of the stage picture.

By the decade of Jones's most ambitious Stuart masques the technical lessons taught by Serlio had long been learnt, and some perhaps forgotten or superseded. Nevertheless the wide dissemination of the *Architettura*, and the clear authority of its tone, had made it the most influential of the perspective handbooks in theatrical use. Jones's earlier designs had echoed its iconic content as well as its technical methods, and Webb's theoretical studies – especially those concerned with *Florimène* – owed it considerable debts. Yet Jones often constructed his scenes according to systems quite different from those espoused by the master. His employment of flat, changeable wings and backshutters, and the provision of movable scenes of relieve, often made for much more complicated carpentry. Yet Jones never – and Webb seldom – used the type of squared stage floor that permitted a systematic exploitation of perspective foreshortening to make a full contribution to the visual effect. The use of the irrationally high horizon and the introduction of 'stretched' foreshortening in the wings and shutters involved a progressive loosening of the strict mathematical ties that held the Serlian stage world in thrall.

Most of these departures from the Serlian canon appear to have been the result of deliberate artistic choice, not of indifference. The 'stretched' system, with its multiple vanishing points, presupposed a mastery of single-point stage foreshortening for its development, and the high horizon made its presence felt in Jones's work only after he had explored a wide range of Serlian methods. At first, indeed, with *The Masque of Blackness*, he outdid Serlio in perspective organization by setting the horizon of the scene on a level with the king's eye in the auditorium, a criterion of painterly practice that he was later to reject in the theatre. But as time went on Jones appears to have left the mathematical theorizing more and more to Webb, while his creative eye rose quite literally to higher things. His comment at the close of the text of *Luminalia* (1638, in the Masquing House) aptly sums up the combination of breathtaking wonder and technical ingenuity that seems so much to have fascinated him in the later productions:

After this song the upper part of the heaven opened, and a bright and transparent cloud came forth farre into the scene, upon which were many *Zephyri* and gentle breasts with rich but light garments tuck'd about their wasts, and falling downe about their knees, and on their heads girlands of flowers: These to the Violins began a sprightly dance, first with single passages, and then joyning hands in rounds severall wayes. Which Apparition for the newnesse of the Invention, greatnesse of the Machine, and difficulty of Engining, was much admir'd, being a thing not before attempted in the Aire.[26]

These are the confident words of a master, for whom the technical hand-books of the age had doubtless faded in the long daylight of familiarity.

Appendix
Serlio's virtual field of vision

Every perspective handbook of the sixteenth and seventeenth centuries begins its presentation of the subject with a demonstration of how a squared pavement may be foreshortened in accordance with some regular system or other. This is the basis of the so-called *costruzione legittima* as described by Alberti in the *De pictura*.[1] It has its roots, as Alberti himself makes clear, in less rigorously geometrical habits of composition well known in the Middle Ages; Alberti, prompted perhaps by his friend Brunelleschi, published for the first time a system by which the foreshortening of a squared floor could be exactly related to a specific station point. To Serlio such matters were a basic, even an elementary, part of the learning of a painter and an architect. He illustrates Alberti's method in the opening pages of the Second Book, using as his example a squared floor that is variously three or four times deeper than it is wide. In the ensuing demonstrations of how to render more complex shapes in perspective he generally bases his diagrams on a square plan, just as deep as it is wide, to which the more demanding forms of the polygons and circles may be referred. It is hardly surprising, therefore, that two of the theatrical scenes make much use of familiar squared floors whose units, as we saw in chapter 9, coincide even with the modular units employed in the design of the auditorium.

One of the virtues of the squared floor is that the observer may count his way into it, judging its foreshortened depth against its width and so establishing for himself the ambience of its space and the relative positions of the objects placed upon it. The reticulation of any squared floor in a Serlian demonstration is therefore a matter for exploration, but we shall need a magnifying glass to discover that the scene shown in the theatre plan is marked off into 48 divisions in depth. Since they are represented as continuous with the squares of the forestage they are clearly to be interpreted as squares also. The stage is thus painted to represent 48 squares of depth to the backscene, with a forestage of 5 squares giving a total of 53 overall. In the 1545 original of the Comic Scene we find that the forestage is 6 squares deep and the scene is marked with 47 intervals, for a total again of 53. The plan in the Antwerp edition of 1553 repeats the numbers of its original, but the Comic Scene now gives only 44 divisions on the raked stage. This is, however, fronted by a forestage 9 squares deep, so that the total is again 53. While these constituent figures vary somewhat, the repeated total of 53 seems to indicate some sort of method, and in particular the plan of the original text again demands analysis.

We have established that the station point in the plan is located 27 units from the front of the scene. An observer positioned here would look into a foreshortened space between the front wings just 24 squares wide and marked off as 48 squares deep. The angle wings crowding in from either side limit the range of this view, but if we were to wish them away we might think of the observer looking into a space much wider than the 24 squares visible at its front, wider indeed by a precise amount which we may now calculate. In order to do so we shall make practical use of the proportion we have observed in the division of the distance between the vanishing point and the front of the raked stage by the line of the backscene's foot, in the case of the large plan a ratio of exactly 3 : 2. (The overall distance between the scene front and the vanishing point is 13.5 squares, so that the scene is 5.4 squares deep in actuality and the distance from the backscene to the vanishing point is 8.1 squares.) The station point is located 27 squares from the front of the scene, and is therefore just twice as far from the front of the scene as that is from the vanishing point. Taking, for the sake of convenience, the right side of the scene alone, we may calculate the field of vision thus (fig. 13):

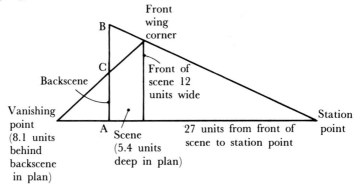

Figure 13   Serlio's theatre plan, right side. Calculation of breadth of field of vision.

Here the distance AB represents the extent of half of the field of vision seen between the inner corners of the front wings. AC represents 12 squares at the foreshortened scale of the backscene, and AB may be calculated to represent 24 units similarly scaled.[2] The whole field of vision, that is to say, is 48 squares wide. Since it is marked off as 48 squares deep it represents a larger square 48 by 48 in size.

In the Comic Scene the stage is depicted, as we have now established, as a plan analogous to that contained in the overall theatre plan, sharing its same 24-unit width, but differing in respect of its depth to the vanishing point. This is located, as we may discover by projecting the orthogonals on the floor to their common point of convergence, just 9 units above the front of the scene. The interval is divided by the foot of the backscene in the proportion 4 : 9, where the large plan has the simpler ratio of 3 : 2. One would expect such variant conditions to produce quite different results in the matter of the virtual field of view, and indeed they do so. But the width of the field, which we may calculate using the same diagram as before, is far from unharmonious with the remainder of the proportions of the design: AC, representing 12 units at the reduced scale of the backscene, is in this case just one-quarter of

254

A B.[3] Our diagrammatic plan is restricted to one side of the scene, and the whole width of the field is therefore 96 units, exactly twice the figure yielded by the large plan. One could hardly ask for a stronger confirmation of the deliberation that informs Serlio's method, for this demonstration produces a virtual field apparently intended to be in the shape of a double square. The symmetry is not quite perfect, however, for in this case the forestage is given an extra unit of depth, and the scenic stage proper is marked off in only 47 divisions. Only the large plan, it seems, fully realizes the goal of providing a square virtual field.

The matter cannot however be left in this satisfactorily tidy state. For while Serlio is careful to mark 48 squares of depth in his large plan, the relative space actually perceived from the station point would be considerably less than that, as may be judged from the following diagrammatic section (fig. 14):

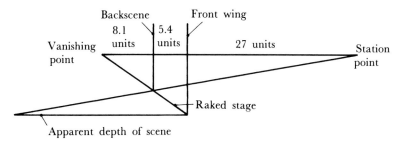

Figure 14　Serlio's theatre section: calculation of depth of field of vision.

Here the line running from the vanishing point to the front edge of the scene (the forward part of which marks the slope of the rake) is divided by the backscene in the ratio 3 : 2. For the sake of clarity I have raised the horizon and so steepened the rake of the stage, but this expedient has no effect on the particular calculation we must now make. The distance from the station point to the vanishing point is 40.5 units (27 + 13.5), and it follows that the distance from the edge of the scene to the foot of the backscene as projected on a level ground (that is, as shown by the horizontal line at the bottom left of the diagram) is 27 units.[4] This is the depth which Serlio marks with 48 intervals, so that while he seeks to give the illusion of a square field of vision the actual geometry of his theatre plan and section constrains him to do so within an apparent depth of only 27 units. His 48 by 48 field of vision, with its elegant rapport with the *ad quadratum* logic of the theatre plan, is no more than an act of the designer's will in the face of the actual mathematics of his scheme.

We recall Serlio's predilection for the square plan in matters of room design: 'Among the quadrangular forms I find the rectangle the most perfect. And the more the rectangle moves away from the perfect square the more it loses its perfection . . .'[5] This is, of course, more than a matter of mere taste. In Serlio's case it is a simplified, pragmatic Pythagoreanism, to be considered in the same light as the individual soul's perfection as it approaches or removes itself from God. The theatre illustrated in the Second Book is no temple, but it is – at least potentially – a place where all the glories of human civilization can be seen compressed by art to a wonderful concentration:

Among all the things that may bee made by mens hands, thereby to yeeld admiration, pleasure to sight, and to content the fantasies of men; I thinke it is placing of a Scene, as it is shewed to your sight, where a man in a small place may see built by Carpenters or Masons, skilfull in Perspectiue worke, great Palaces, large Temples, and diuers Houses, both neere and farre off; broad places filled with Houses, long streets crost with other wayes: tryumphant Arches, high Pillars or Columnes, Piramides, Obeliscens, and a thousand fayre things and buildings, adorned with innumerable lights, great, middle sort, and small, as you may see it placed in the Figure, which are so cunningly set out, that they shew foorth and represent a number of the brightest stones; as Diamonds, Rubins, Saphirs, Smaragdes, Iacinthes, and such like.[6]

These are the works of humanity rather than those of God, and if there is a mystery in Serlio's imagining a theatre whose plan derives from a geometrical union of the square and the circle, and whose scene is erected in a virtual space bounded by the square, it is likely to concern the human rather than the divine. Our analysis of Serlio's theatre plan showed that the auditorium was designed according to the proportions contained in the well-known theory of the Vitruvian *homo ad quadratum*. Now we have found that the auditorium cannot be considered independently from the scenic stage. The plan of the theatre derives from a square 34 units each way, the round of the orchestra being defined by a concentric circle arrived at *ad quadratum* from the square. At 24 units across, the orchestra is just as wide as the *occhio*, or opening between the front wings through which the raked stage is visible. And this stage, 24 units wide at the front, is marked up 48 units deep and represents a virtual space 48 units wide. A square area 48 units across is harmonious with the *ad quadratum* proportioning of the auditorium, for it represents the next larger stage in the $\sqrt{2}$ sequence of dimensions after the 34-unit width of the plan $[34 \times \sqrt{2} \approx 48]$. An observer placed at the notional station point would look across an auditorium defined by the 34-unit square; the fully expressed semicircle of the first rank of degrees constitutes a *cavea* which occupies half of the square. But the space that such an observer might see between the front wings is a further square related to the first as $\sqrt{2} : 1$. In short, the geometry of the scene, as depicted in the plan, is related to that of the auditorium not only by means of the common module but also by the *ad quadratum* system of proportioning. Serlio's theatre scheme, as it is presented in the original edition of his work, is an astonishingly coherent piece of design.

In England neither Inigo Jones nor John Webb followed this part of Serlio's method to its conclusion. The 'virtual space' represented in the foreshortening of the scene in Serlio's theatre is square in plan, and proportioned to agree with the *ad quadratum* system used in the development of the auditorium layout. Although both Jones and Webb followed Serlio in their employment of *ad quadratum* methods of auditorium design, they did not carry them through to the proportioning of the virtual space represented by the scene. Jones left no methodical studies of his scenic stages, but in Webb's more exact drawings we do find a careful proportioning of the division of the depth to the vanishing point by the backscene – here generally represented by the backshutters – in terms of simple ratios. At the Paved Court the figures are 1 : 4, and in the *Florimène* scheme 1 : 6, but no adequate indication is given of the location of the station point, so that it is impossible to calculate the proportions of the virtual space bounded by the scene. At the Paved Court (plate 40) the royal halpace located the king just twice as far from the scene as the scene itself was deep to the vanishing point, but even if we take this pattern as signifying that the king's seat was identical with the station point, the virtual space of the scene as calculated according to our procedure in this Appendix would bear no clear relation to the dimensions of the auditorium itself. Similar measurements cannot easily be made for the *Florimène* scheme because the raked forestage extends the scene forwards and makes it hard to establish whether the virtual space of the scene begins at its front or seven feet or so further on at the frontispiece. In his diagrammatic section of the stage (plate 47), Webb appears to indicate a station point 27 ft from the frontispiece, a point well forward of the royal halpace in the auditorium, and not rationally proportioned to the scene itself. In these matters neither Jones nor Webb was prepared to accept the full mathematical integration of the Serlian scheme.

Notes

Note: Where a place of publication has not been given in a reference, the work was published in London.

1 GOODLY THEATRES

1. E. K. Chambers, *The Elizabethan Stage*, 4 vols. (Oxford, 1923), II, 527.
2. 'But see yonder, / One like the vnfrequented Theater / Walkes in darke silence, and vast solitude', Edward Guilpin, *Skialetheia* (1598), satire v, sig. D6ᵃ. After the dismantling the building was alluded to as 'the late greate howse called the Theatre'. Public Record Office (PRO) E134/44–5 Elizabeth, Interrogatory 9 and answers, cited by Herbert Berry, 'Aspects of the Design and Use of the First Public Playhouse', in *The First Public Playhouse: the Theatre in Shoreditch 1576–1598*, edited by Herbert Berry (Montreal, 1979), p. 31.
3. The stage at the Fortune, for example, was to be largely 'Contryved and fashioned like vnto the Stadge of the saide Plaiehowse Called the Globe', R. A. Foakes and R. T. Rickert, editors, *Henslowe's Diary* (Cambridge, 1961), p. 308. The Hope was to be built 'of such large compasse, fforme, widenes, and height as the Plaie house Called the Swan', Irwin Smith, *Shakespeare's Globe Playhouse* (New York, 1956), p. 220. Such allusions to built models were not uncommon in Elizabethan contracts.
4. Sig. G4ᵇ–5ᵃ.
5. See Chambers, *The Elizabethan Stage*, II, 380 and 383; and compare O. L. Brownstein, 'A Record of London Inn-playhouses from *c.*1565–1590', *Shakespeare Quarterly* 22 (1971), 17–24. Fencing 'prizes' were fought at several inns on many occasions before 1576, but they did not require a full theatrical setting.
6. William Lambarde, *A Perambulation of Kent* (1576), pp. 187–8. Compare the edition of 1596, p. 233.
7. In the prologue to *The Glasse of Government* (1575), sig. Aiijᵇ.
8. The earliest references to plays at inns of the London area date from 1557. In that year the Privy Council ordered the Mayor to stop 'a Lewde playe' at the Boar's Head '*without* Algate', possibly the same Boar's Head that became a permanent theatre at the turn of the century. See Herbert Berry, *The Boar's Head Playhouse* (Washington, 1986), p. 16. A play performance in the same year is

mentioned as having taken place at the Saracen's Head, Islington, by John Foxe in his *Monumentes*. See O. L. Brownstein, 'The Saracen's Head, Islington: a Pre-Elizabethan Inn Playhouse', *Theatre Notebook* 25 (1970–1), 68–72. Neither reference gives any indication that the performance took place in the innyard.

9. *Early English Stages 1300 to 1660*, 3 vols. (1959–81), II (part 1), 186–96.

10. Malone Society *Collections*, II (part 3), 292.

11. Ibid., II (part 3), 295.

12. Ibid., I (part 2), 175.

13. In 1580 John Brayne, the builder of the Theater in Shoreditch, took over the lease of the George Inn, Whitechapel, 'hoping that he might do some good upon it, intending to build a playhouse therein', PRO C24/314/85, cited by C. J. Sisson, *The Boar's Head Theatre: an Inn-yard Theatre of the Elizabethan Age*, edited by Stanley Wells (1972), p. 14. Sisson interprets this reference, made in a deposition of 1605, as proving that Brayne intended to build his theatre in the yard of the inn. But the word 'therein' might equally well apply to an enclosed auditorium in one of the inn's larger rooms. In any case, nothing seems to have become of the venture.

14. PRO KB29/219 m. 150, printed in *Records of Early English Drama: Norwich 1540–1642*, edited by David Galloway (Toronto, 1984), p. 71.

15. *The Boar's Head Playhouse*. See also Sisson, *The Boar's Head Theatre*.

16. PRO C24/278/71, cited by Berry, *The Boar's Head Playhouse*, p. 160. There was also, of course, a good deal of more formal measurement and setting out, undertaken by the carpenters.

17. Ibid.

18. See, for a necessarily cautious discussion, Wickham, *Early English Stages*, II (part 2), 97–8 and 108–9. A full 'Comparison with the Playhouses of London' is given by John J. Allen, *The Reconstruction of a Spanish Golden Age Playhouse: El Corral del Príncipe 1583–1744* (Gainesville, Florida, 1983), pp. 111–17. Leslie Hotson, *Shakespeare's Wooden O* (1959), pp. 70–8, draws parallels between the English public theatres and the pageant stages in Spain.

19. Allen, *The Reconstruction of a Spanish Golden Age Playhouse*, pp. 11–94, and N. D. Shergold, *A History of the Spanish Stage* (Oxford, 1967), pp. 197–208 and 383–414.

20. Archivo Municipal del Ayuntamiento de Madrid, Secretaría 3–135–5, cited and translated by Allen, *The Reconstruction of a Spanish Golden Age Playhouse*, p. 66.

21. Berry, 'Aspects of the Design and Use of the First Public Playhouse', pp. 36–7.

22. PRO C24/226/11 (part 1), transcribed by Charles William Wallace, *The First London Theatre: Materials for a History* (Nebraska, 1913; reprint New York, 1969), p. 142.

23. The 'copperplate' map and its derivatives are discussed by John Fisher, *A Collection of Early Maps of London, c. 1553–1667* (Lympne, 1981), sheet 2. See also James L. Howgego, *Printed Maps of London c. 1553–1850* (Folkestone, 1978).

24. Extant copies bear the Stuart arms and date from c. 1633. The woodcut itself may be the *Carde of London* entered by Gyles Godhed in the Stationers' Register for 1562–3. The spire of St Paul's, destroyed in 1561, is not shown, but the Royal Exchange, opened in 1570, is inserted as a wedge in one of the blocks and evidently represents a revision made to take account of the new development.

25. British Library (BL) Sloane MS. 2596, fol. 52. The map is associated with Smith's description of England, dated 1588. It differs from the printed maps in many respects, and may include independent topographical information. It appears to have been drafted *c.* 1575.

26. 'Why Didn't Burbage Lease the Beargarden? A Conjecture in Comparative Architecture', in *The First Public Playhouse*, edited by Berry, pp. 84–5.

27. In 1546 a licence was issued for baiting the king's bears 'at the accustomed place at London, called the Stewes', *Letters and Papers, Henry VIII*, XXI (part 2), 88. A Spanish visitor two years before had seen baiting 'In another part of the city' (than the Tower) – presumably Bankside. The place was characterized as an 'enclosure', and there were both bearbaiting and the baiting of an ape on the back of a pony. Frederic Madden, 'Narrative of the Visit of the Duke of Nájera to England, in the Year 1543–4', *Archaeologia* 23 (1830), 354–5.

28. 'Un loco rittondo circondato de palchi co*n* li suoi coperti per la poggia, e per il sole . . . che e richiuso attorno, e non se ui puo uscire se non aprono alcune porte . . .'. The Italian text is printed, from Folger Library MS. v. a. 259, fol. 169, by Giles Dawson, 'London's Bull-baiting and Bear-baiting Arena in 1562', *Shakespeare Quarterly* 15 (1964), 98. The translation is mine.

29. Ibid.

30. C. L. Kingsford, 'Paris Garden and the Bear-baiting', *Archaeologia* 2nd series 20 (1920), 176.

31. John Stowe, *Annales*, continued by Edmund Howes (1631), p. 696.

32. John Field, *A Godly Exhortation* . . . (1583), sig. B8ᵃ.

33. Ibid., sig. cij^b.

34. Ibid., sig. cij^a.

35. Printed by Chambers, *The Elizabethan Stage*, II, 455.

36. Smith, *Shakespeare's Globe Playhouse*, p. 219.

37. Ibid., p. 220.

38. Chambers, *The Elizabethan Stage*, II, 379–80.

39. Ibid., p. 380.

40. Pp. 4–6.

41. 'An Elizabethan Lawsuit: John Brayne, his Carpenter, and the Building of the Red Lion Theatre', *Shakespeare Quarterly* 34 (1982), 298–310.

42. PRO KB27/1229 m. 30, cited by Loengard, ibid., pp. 309–10.

43. *OED* Court *sb.* 1, 1: 'formerly . . . a farm-yard, a poultry-yard'.

44. Loengard, 'An Elizabethan Lawsuit', p. 310.

45. The procedure was one of long standing, and for centuries was an inseparable part of the technique of timber framing. Timbers for Westminster Hall were prepared at 'a place called the Frame by Farnham' before being delivered to the site in 1395. See L. F. Salzman, *Building in England down to 1540* (Oxford, 1952), pp. 199–200. In our period, Sir Thomas Tresham had a 'framinge place, lodgement table, or by whatt name soever ytt ys prope*r*ly to be termed' on his estate: BL Add. MS. 39831, fol. 68^b. A carpentry account for an addition to the Red Lion at Ospringe, Kent, as late as 1748 gives a detailed sequential outline of the procedure. The builder and his man or men spent two days in March 'a hewing' the timber; on 4 April they prepared 'a sill of oakes', then returned to hewing and 'cuting of the tops' for two days. Then eight days were spent 'a

framing'; that is, the posts and other timbers were cut and jointed to suit the sills that had been prepared first, the whole structure being developed from its plan on the ground. When this process was complete, on 21 April, the day was spent 'a geting it to the Lyon'. Only now did they turn to 'a puling down the old hous' which was to be replaced by the new structure. Extra men were hired on the following day for 'a raising the house'. Then several more days of work were spent on the rafters, the weatherboarding, making doors and thatching the roof. See Elizabeth Melling, *Kentish Sources V: Some Kentish Houses* (Maidstone, 1965), p. 46. Condensed accounts of the procedure may be found in Trudy West, *The Timber-frame House in England* (Newton Abbot, n.d. [1970]), pp. 60–1, and in R.J. Brown, *Timber-framed Buildings of England* (1986), pp. 27–41. The deed of partnership drawn up between Philip Henslowe and John Cholmley on 10 January 1587 for the site of the Rose records that on that date the new playhouse was 'now in framinge and shortly to be ereckted and sett vppe vpone the same grounde', Carol Chillington Rutter, editor, *Documents of the Rose Playhouse* (Manchester, 1984), p. 37. The deed makes the customary distinction between the processes of framing and setting up.

46. Kent T. van den Berg, *Playhouse and Cosmos: Shakespearean Theater as Metaphor* (Newark, NJ, 1985), p. 47.

47. 'A Note on the Swan Theatre Drawing', *Shakespeare Survey 1* (Cambridge, 1948), p. 24.

48. Wallace, *The First London Theatre*; and Herbert Berry, 'A Handlist of Documents about the Theatre in Shoreditch', in *The First Public Playhouse*, edited by Berry, pp. 97–133.

49. PRO Req. 2/184/45, cited by Wallace, *The First London Theatre*, p. 241.

50. Ibid., p. 231.

51. Berry, 'Aspects of the Design and Use of the First Public Playhouse', p. 30.

52. PRO C24/228/10, in Wallace, *The First London Theatre*, pp. 126 and 127.

53. Ibid., p. 114.

54. PRO KB27/1362 m. 587, in ibid., p. 178.

55. Chambers, *The Elizabethan Stage*, II, 358.

56. In 1595. See *Henslowe's Diary*, edited by Foakes and Rickert, p. 7.

2 THE FESTIVE TRADITION

1. The angular playhouse to the left of the view was identified as the Curtain by Leslie Hotson, 'This Wooden O', *The Times*, 26 March 1954, pp. 7 and 14, and in *Shakespeare's Wooden O*, pp. 304–9. The identification was challenged by Sidney Fisher, *The Theatre, the Curtain, and the Globe* (Montreal, 1964), pp. 2–4, who pointed out that a square flag shown flying somewhat to the south of the visible playhouse probably belonged to the Curtain, which was sited on lower ground and obscured by intervening houses. Careful plotting on a modern map shows that the visible playhouse is located on a site consistent with that of the Theater.

2. Hotson, *Shakespeare's Wooden O*, pp. 310–11.

3. The Abbey is correctly located in the panorama, but the angle of view to it is not consistent with that taken up for the more easterly part of the composition. The

artist must have filled out the detail of the building by referring to another sketch taken from a point further west.

4. Richard Hosley, 'The Theatre and the Tradition of Playhouse Design', in *The First Public Playhouse*, edited by Berry, pp. 47–79. My allusion is to p. 74 of this important essay.

5. Richard Turpyn, 'The Chronicle of Calais', in *The Chronicle of Calais in the Reigns of Henry VII and Henry VIII*, edited by John Gough Nichols, Camden Society 35 (1846), p. 29, from BL Harleian MS. 542.

6. *I diarii di Marino Sanuto*, edited by F. Stephani (Venice, 1879–1902), XXIX, col. 251.

7. Turpyn, 'The Chronicle of Calais', p. 29.

8. *I diarii di Marino Sanuto*, XXIX, col. 252.

9. *Le triumphe festifz . . . faict . . . en la ville de Calais* (Arras, 1520), cited by Sydney Anglo, *Spectacle, Pageantry and Early Tudor Policy* (Oxford, 1969), p. 160.

10. Anglo, *Spectacle, Pageantry and Early Tudor Policy*, p. 160.

11. Turpyn, 'The Chronicle of Calais', p. 29.

12. Anglo, *Spectacle, Pageantry and Early Tudor Policy*, p. 162.

13. *The Chronicle of Calais*, edited by Nichols, p. 83.

14. Anglo, *Spectacle, Pageantry and Early Tudor Policy*, p. 164n, citing W. Jerdan, *The Rutland Papers*, Camden Society (1842), p. 55.

15. Ibid., p. 166.

16. PRO E36/197, fol. 76, cited by Anglo, ibid., p. 167.

17. Turpyn, 'The Chronicle of Calais', p. 30.

18. *I diarii di Marino Sanuto*, XXIX, col. 254.

19. Turpyn, 'The Chronicle of Calais', pp. 29–30.

20. Robert de la Marck, seigneur de Fleurange, 'Mémoires', in *Nouvelle collections des mémoires pour servir à l'histoire de France*, edited by Joseph François Michaud and Jean Joseph François Poujoulet, 1st series, vol. V (Paris, 1838), p. 69. My translation.

21. *The Chronicle of Calais*, edited by Nichols, pp. 83 and 85.

22. The banqueting house at the Bastille had lined a courtyard with three storeys of galleries, but the décor of the canvas ceiling had included themes based on the zodiac. There had also been a semicircular stage. See *I diarii di Marino Sanuto*, XXVI, col. 349, dated 22 December 1518, and *Calendar of State Papers (Venetian), 1509–19*, pp. 481–2.

23. *The Chronicle of Calais*, edited by Nichols, pp. 79–80.

24. Martin du Bellay, 'Mémoires', in *Nouvelle collection des mémoires . . .*, edited by Michaud and Poujoulet, 1st series, vol. V, pp. 131–2. My translation.

25. Vaux complained that even if the timber arrived at Calais, he would have 'to carry it to Guysnes, whiche is ix. Englisshe myles by lande . . . [letter burned away] to be hewed, sawed, framed, arered, with the garnisshing of the rofes, [&c. must a]ske a great tyme', *Chronicle of Calais*, edited by Nichols, p. 81. He therefore asked for sawyers to be sent as well as carpenters and bricklayers.

26. BL Harleian MS. 293, fol. 217.

27. A. de Wicquefort, *L'ambassadeur et ses fonctions* (Cologne, 1689), I, 210, cited by Per Palme, *Triumph of Peace* (1957), p. 115.

28. PRO E351/3216 (1581–2), payment to 'Johne Atfeild and others Carpenters'.

29. PRO E351/3216, summary account.
30. H. M. Colvin, general editor, *The History of the King's Works: Volume IV, 1485–1660 (Part II)* (1982), p. 319.
31. The Revels account for 1604–5 includes the entry: 'Hallamas Day being the first of Nouembar A Play in the Banketinge house att Whitehall Called the Moor of Venis', PRO AO3/908/13.
32. PRO E351/3216.
33. See *OED* Tuscan *a.* and *sb.*, A. (d.).
34. Illustrated from a contemporary MS. by George R. Kernodle, *From Art to Theatre* (Chicago, 1944), p. 96. The structure was erected for the visit of Philip II: see *Le siège et les fêtes de Binche*, edited by Charles Ruelens (Mons, 1878), pp. 116–19.
35. These figures are rough estimates, and probably err in being too low. A contract for woodwork in the chapel at Corpus Christi College, Cambridge, in 1578–9 gives exact scantlings for each of the timbers in the roof, and lists 435 individual pieces in addition to the wall plates. See Robert Willis and J. W. Clark, *The Architectural History of the University of Cambridge*, 3 vols (Cambridge, 1886), I, 310–12.
36. PRO Req. 2/87/74, in Wallace, *The First London Theatre*, p. 191.
37. Salzman, *Building in England down to 1540*, p. 199, documents several mediaeval instances of the removal of timber-framed buildings; later instances are recorded by West, *The Timber-frame House in England*, pp. 177–80.
38. PRO C24/226/11, in Wallace, *The First London Theatre*, p. 152.
39. PRO C24/228/10, in ibid., p. 115.
40. PRO C24/226/11, in ibid., pp. 141–2.
41. Ibid.
42. Ibid., p. 140.
43. *A Sermon Preached at Paules Crosse* (1578), pp. 134–5.
44. C. A. Mills, in *The Times*, 11 April 1914, p. 6, citing a Vatican MS. quoted during a lecture in Rome by J. A. F. Orbaan.
45. John B. Gleason, 'The Dutch Humanist Origins of the De Witt Drawing of the Swan Theatre', *Shakespeare Quarterly* 32 (1981), 324–8.
46. The bottom edge of the tiring house front, which is elevated above the yard presumably by the same distance as the height of the stage, stands well forward of the lower gallery of the frame. The topmost part of the turret is presented in multiple station point style which permits the draftsman to show its side as well as its front. The whole depth of the structure is drawn as standing forward of the eaves of the frame. For a discussion of the tiring house and its location see chapter 4.
47. 'Cuius quidem formam quod Romani operis vmbram videatur exprimere supra adpinxi.' 'A Note on the Swan Theatre Drawing', p. 24.
48. *Theatre of the World* (Chicago, 1969).
49. For a survey of library holdings see Lucy Gent, *Picture and Poetry 1560–1620* (Leamington Spa, 1981), pp. 78–86.
50. Dee's catalogue of 1583 is in BL Harleian MS. 1879, fols 20ᵃ–108ᵃ.
51. *Di Marco Vitruvio Pollione i dieci libri* (Venice, 1556).

3 GOODLY DEVICES: EMBLEMATIC DESIGN

1. The most useful general study of the subject remains Katharine A. Esdaile, *English Monumental Sculpture since the Renaissance* (1927).
2. Anglo, *Spectacle, Pageantry and Early Tudor Policy*, p. 163.
3. Raphael Holinshed, *The Third Volume of Chronicles . . .* (1587), p. 861.
4. Bodleian Library Ashmole MS. 1116.
5. *Le triumphe festifz*, cited by Anglo, *Spectacle, Pageantry and Early Tudor Policy*, p. 161.
6. Oliver Lawson Dick, editor, *Aubrey's Brief Lives* (Harmondsworth, 1962), pp. 220–1.
7. A. Feuillerat, editor, *The Prose Works of Sir Philip Sidney*, 4 vols. (Cambridge, 1912; reprint 1962), I, 91.
8. *The Renaissance Garden in England* (1979), pp. 45–71.
9. Cecil Papers, Hatfield, 140–94, printed by Marion Colthorpe, 'The Theobalds Entertainment for Queen Elizabeth I in 1591, with a Transcript of the Gardener's Speech', *Records of Early English Drama* 12, no 1 (1987), p. 7. Strong, *The Renaissance Garden in England*, p. 46, uncritically repeats Bullen's century-old attribution of the speech to George Peele, though this has long been disputed.
10. An account of the ceiling is given by Margaret Jourdain, *English Decorative Plasterwork of the Renaissance* (n.d. [1926]), p. 33. There are panels representing 'Spes, Fides, Charitas; War and Peace; Peace, again, and Plenty, the Senses, and the Four Elements, relieved against coloured backgrounds.' The panels illustrating the elements are based on engravings by Galle after Marc Gheeraerts; those of the senses follow engravings by Nicholas de Bruyn; and the overmantel panel of Abraham and Isaac adapts an engraving by Abraham de Bruyn published in 1581. See Geoffrey Beard, *Decorative Plasterwork in Great Britain* (1975), p. 30.
11. BL Add. MS. 39831, fols 48^a–61^b. On fol. 42^b a plan of the lodge is doodled out of the capital letters A and V.
12. The legends were transcribed by J. A. Gotch, *The Buildings of Sir Thomas Tresham* (1883), p. 25: APERIATVR TERRA & GERMINET SALVATOREM (Let the earth open and bring forth a Saviour); QVIS SEPARABIT NOS A CHARITATE CHRISTI (Who shall separate us from the love of Christ?); CONSIDERAVI OPERA TVA DOMINE ET EXPAVI (I have considered Thy works, O Lord, and was afraid).
13. The foundations were dug in early August 1594, and building progressed rapidly for the remainder of the season. The chimney was finished during the week of 11 July 1595. BL Add. MS. 39832, fols 20^b, 22^a–26^a, and 49^b.
14. RIBA Drawings Collection, Smythson I/24.
15. Clare Williams, *Thomas Platter in England* (1937), pp. 195–7.
16. *The Book of Architecture of John Thorpe in Sir John Soane's Museum*, edited by John Summerson, Walpole Society, vol. XL (1966), T 155, plate 72 and pp. 87–8. The drawing appears to be connected with a preliminary phase of the design, and records a larger project than the achieved building.
17. For Longford and its documentation see Christopher Hussey, 'Longford Castle,

Wilts: the Seat of the Earl of Radnor', *Country Life* 70 (1931), 648–55, 698–702 and 724–30. The *Longford Inventory* is cited on p. 701.

18. Dorset County Record Office, MW/M4, fol. 24, cited by Malcolm Airs, *The Making of the English Country House* (1975), p. 6.

19. Cited by Arthur Oswald, 'Chantmarle, Dorset', *Country Life* 107 (1950), 1968.

20. 'Chilham Castle', *Country Life* 50 (1924), 816.

21. Willis and Clark, *The Architectural History of the University of Cambridge*, I, 173–80.

22. See discussions in chapters 6 and 12 below.

23. Mrs Baldwyn-Childe, 'The Building of the Manor-House of Kyre Park, Worcestershire (1588–1618)', *The Antiquary* 21 (1890), 202–5 and 261–4; and 22 (1890), 24–6 and 50–2.

24. *Henslowe's Diary*, edited by Foakes and Rickert, p. 308.

25. Ibid., pp. 6–7.

26. Chambers, *The Elizabethan Stage*, II, 5.

27. The city authorities found the claim to ancient authority mockably pretentious. In 1594 the Lord Mayor, Sir John Spencer, wrote to Burleigh complaining that Francis Langley was preparing 'to erect a niew stage or Theater (as they call it)', Malone Society *Collections*, I, 74. But Spencer was partial to a bit of classicizing design himself, and five years later constructed a series of magnificent emblematic ceilings at his house in Canonbury. See chapter 6, pp. 98–9.

4 THE STAGE COVER

1. It is described, for example, as a 'round circumference' in the epilogue to *The Travailes of the Three English Brothers* (1607), sig. H4^b. See Eric Bentley, *The Jacobean and Caroline Stage*, 7 vols. (Oxford, 1941–68), VI, 216n. In *A Warning for Fair Women* (1599) it is possibly the Curtain that is described as 'all this fair circuit . . . this Round'.

2. PRO Req. 2/184/45, in Wallace, *The First London Theatre*, p. 127.

3. Leon Battista Alberti, *Ten Books on Architecture*, translated by James Leoni (1725; reprint 1955), pp. 178 and 179.

4. [Edward Halle,] *The Vnion of the Two Noble and Illustre Famelies of Lancastre & Yorke* (1548), fol. clvi^{a-b}.

5. Ibid., fol. clvi^a.

6. For the sky cloths see John Orrell, *The Theatres of Inigo Jones and John Webb* (Cambridge, 1985), pp. 109 (for the Cockpit-in-Court), 115 (Paved Court), 154–5 (Masquing House) and 172 (Hall Theatre). For Windsor see my article 'A New Witness of the Restoration Stage, 1670–1680', *Theatre Research International* n.s. 2 (1976–7), 93.

7. Eleanore Boswell, *The Restoration Court Stage (1660–1702)* (Cambridge, Mass, 1932), p. 249.

8. BL Harleian MS. 1653, fols. 35^a–36^a.

9. (1612), sig. D2^b.

10. *A Dictionarie of the French and English Tongves* (1611), sig. Mmmiij^a.

11. Smith, *Shakespeare's Globe Playhouse*, p. 220.

12. *Henslowe's Diary*, edited by Foakes and Rickert, p. 308.

13. Ibid., p. 7.

14. Ben Jonson, *Workes* (1616), sig. A3^a.

15. PRO C24/304/27, cited by Berry, *The Boar's Head Playhouse*, p. 111. See also Sisson, *The Boar's Head Theatre*, p. 46.
16. *Praeludium* to Richard Brome, *Five New Plays* (1653), sig. A2^b.
17. See especially Thomas Heywood, *The Silver Age* (1613), which includes several descents; and *The Bronze Age* (1613), which presents a spectacular hand in the Heavens.
18. Sicilius Leonatus prays Jupiter to appear: 'Thy Christall window ope; looke, looke out . . . Peepe through thy Marble Mansion.' Thereupon '*Iupiter descends in Thunder and Lightning*', speaks, and ascends again, leaving behind him a 'sulphurous' smell, presumably of fireworks. As he goes, Sicilius watches him: 'The Marble Pauement clozes, he is enter'd / His radiant Roofe', *Cymbeline* v, iv, 81–121. Glynne Wickham has argued that the earlier theatres possessed neither a stage cover nor a descent machine: '"Heavens", Machinery, and Pillars in the Theatre and Other Early Playhouses', in *The First Public Playhouse*, edited by Berry, 1–15. In a sensitive and informed discussion, John Astington separates the question of the machinery from that of the stage cover, asserting that early flying effects may well have been managed from a small projecting bay cantilevered over the stage: 'Descent Machinery in the Playhouses', *Medieval & Renaissance Drama in England II* (New York, 1985), pp. 119–33.
19. *Henslowe's Diary*, edited by Foakes and Rickert, p. 308.
20. PRO C33/103, fol. 43^{a–b}, cited by Berry, *The Boar's Head Playhouse*, p. 164.
21. PRO C24/304/27, cited in ibid., p. 209, n. 9.
22. Smith, *Shakespeare's Globe Playhouse*, p. 219.
23. Wallace, *The First London Theatre*, p. 127.
24. *Henslowe's Diary*, edited by Foakes and Rickert, pp. 13 and 319.
25. It may be significant that early references to a tiring *room* are rare. J.M., in the prefatory material to Shakespeare's First Folio, alludes to 'the Graues-Tyring-roome' (sig. A7^a), but Hugh Holland refers to the grave in the same place as 'Deaths publique tyring-house' (sig. A5^a). The earliest specific reference to a particular theatrical tiring room appears to be in Davenant's licence of 1639 for a proposed scenic theatre in Fleet Street (Bentley, *The Jacobean and Caroline Stage*, VI, 305). John Webb's Restoration drawing of the Cockpit-in-Court records something of the arrangements established there in 1629, and shows what might well be a tiring room behind the stage; indeed a Works account of 1662 mentions the introduction of 'the upper tyringe roome' in the Cockpit, evidently established above the original one (PRO LC5/60, p. 309). At Trinity College, Cambridge, there was a 'tyringe house' between the hall and the Master's lodging, evidently used for academic rather than theatrical purposes. Its exact nature and location are unknown, but it was also called 'the Attyring chamber' or 'the tyreing chamber' in the Junior Bursar's accounts of 1614–15 and 1619–20. See Willis and Clark, *The Architectural History of the University of Cambridge*, II, 624.

5 JOHN NORDEN'S PICTURE OF THE THEATRES

1. 'The Bankside Theatres: Early Engravings', *Shakespeare Survey 1* (Cambridge, 1948), plates IV and VIII, and pp. 28–31.

2. *Shakespearean Playhouses* (Cambridge, Mass., 1917), p. 328. But J.Q. Adams considered that Visscher 'represented the "Bear Garden" . . . and the Globe as they were before their reconstruction' in 1613 and 1614 (p. 328).

3. London County Council, *The Site of the Globe Playhouse, Southwark*, 2nd edition (1924), pp. 51–3.

4. Ida Darlington and James Howgego, *Printed Maps of London, circa 1553–1850* (1964), pp. 14–16.

5. *The Quest for Shakespeare's Globe* (Cambridge, 1983), pp. 59–62.

6. Differences between the views of Southwark contained in the panorama and the inset map suggested to R. A. Skelton that a hand other than Norden's may have contributed to the southern part of the former. There is, however, no necessary reason why inconsistent work should be the responsibility of more than one person. See J. Hurstfield and R.A. Skelton, 'John Norden's View of London, 1600', *London Topographical Record* (1965), 23.

7. D. F. Rowan, 'The "Swan" Revisited,' *Research Opportunities in Renaissance Drama* 10 (1965), 42–5. Alternatively the curious wavy line at most of the eaves may be taken to represent pantiles, but if so it is an indication that de Witt (or his copyist, van Buchell) saw through Low Country eyes. Pantiles were not manufactured in England before the seventeenth century, and only a few were imported. It is most unlikely that they would have been used in a large building such as a public playhouse. See Alec Clifton-Taylor, *The Pattern of English Building* (1972), pp. 275–6. Charles I issued a patent 'for the making of Pantiles or Flanders Tyles' in 1636; they were used on the Masquing House at Whitehall in 1638. See Wickham, *Early English Stages*, II (part 2), 225.

8. The map is reproduced in R. A. Foakes, *Illustrations of the English Stage 1580–1642* (1985), p. 24.

9. Chambers, *The Elizabethan Stage*, IV, 322–3, from the Privy Council minutes. The minuted letter is addressed to the magistrates of Middlesex and concerns the Theater and the Curtain, but the record also shows that a similar letter was sent to Surrey to cover the Bankside houses.

10. The story is told in full by Wickham, *Early English Stages*, II (part 2), 9–29. But the Privy Council's minute, dated 28 July 1597, must be seen as separate from the *Isle of Dogs* affair, which appears to have broken out in August. See Rutter, *Documents of the Rose Playhouse*, pp. 113–18.

11. Chambers, *The Elizabethan Stage*, IV, 325, from the Vestry records of St Saviour's, Southwark, dated 1 May 1598.

12. Berry, *The Boar's Head Playhouse*, p. 37.

13. There is notice on two subsequent occasions of some sort of theatrical activity in the upper parts of the Swan's stage. In 1602 Richard Vennar promised, in his waggish prospectus for *England's Joy* at the Swan, to have Elizabeth 'taken vp into Heauen, when presently appeares, a Throne of blessed Soules'. Such a scene, if intended to be performed by actors, would have taken place in the stage gallery without benefit of a Heavens and its trap. *A Covrtly Masque: the Device Called the World Tost at Tennis* (1620), by Thomas Middleton and William Rowley, was written for an entertainment at Somerset House in 1619–20. This Court production appears to have been cancelled, but the work was subsequently revised and played by the Prince's Men at 'the Princes Armes', which there is

NOTES TO PAGES 86–89

some reason to believe may have been an alternative name for the Swan (though the Prince's Men were currently installed at the Curtain). See Bentley, *The Jacobean and Caroline Stage*, IV. 910 and VI. 134–5. It is not clear how completely the revision took account of the change of location. The text as it stands requires an '*vpper Stage*' where 18 masquers can be '*discouer'd*' in a single tableau (sig. c4ᵃ); 'three seuerall' doors of entry onto the main dancing stage (sig. c4ᵇ); and the capacity for a descent of Pallas. Jupiter also descends, from his 'Orbicular Chariot' (sig. c3ᵇ), and reascends (sig. f2ᵇ). In a paper distributed at the Shakespeare Globe Centre's London conference in April 1986 – 'The World Tossed at Tennis and the Swan Playhouse' – Richard Hosley concluded that in 1620 'Evidently the suspension gear of the Swan heavens was up to snuff' (p. 2). It is, however, by no means clear that the revised text had fully erased the original Court staging arrangements.

14. *Henslowe's Diary*, edited by Foakes and Rickert, p. 308.

6 THIS MAJESTICAL ROOF

1. *Early English Stages*, II (part 1), 302–3.
2. In 1599 Thomas Platter saw *Julius Caesar* performed 'in the house with the thatched roof' [*in dem streuwinen Dachhaus*] (*Julius Caesar*, edited by T. S. Dorsch, The Arden Shakespeare (1965), pp. vii and 166). This phrase should not be taken in an exclusive sense: Henslowe recorded payments to a thatcher 'a bowte my playe howsse' in 1592, along with sums for quarters, rafters and laths among other materials (*Henslowe's Diary*, edited by Foakes and Rickert, pp. 9–12).
3. Clifton-Taylor, *The Pattern of English Building*, p. 340.
4. *Shakespeare's Second Globe: the Missing Monument* (1973), pp. 68–72.
5. *The Tragicall History of the Life and Death of Doctor Faustus* (1616), sig. H2ᵃ. It is generally agreed that the text of 1616 largely represents what Marlowe wrote before 1593, but if the throne that Henslowe fitted into the Heavens at the Rose in 1595 was an innovation rather than a replacement it is likely that the stage direction 'Musicke while the Throne descends' is an insertion made after that date to take advantage of the new machine. In that case it would be one of the 'new Additions' referred to on the title pages of the editions of 1619 and later. The Good Angel's reference to 'yonder throne' may originally have been a purely poetic device.
6. 'For the Globe [from 1599 to 1609], at least so far as the plays demonstrate, no machinery for flying existed', Bernard Beckerman, *Shakespeare at the Globe, 1599–1609* (New York, 1962), p. 94. Of course many of the plays performed at the Globe in those years have been lost. Richard Hosley, 'The Playhouses', in *The Revels History of Drama in English: Volume III 1576–1613*, general editors Clifford Leech and T. W. Craik (1975), pp. 192–3, argues that of the surviving works 'Two plays require suspension gear': *A Larum for London* (1602) and *Antony and Cleopatra* (1623; produced *c.* 1606–7). The former includes a stage action involving a 'strippado': 'Hoise him vp and let him downe againe' (sig. d4ᵇ). Some sort of gear was certainly needed here, but it is unlikely to have been worked from the Heavens. The episode that Hosley cites from *Antony and Cleopatra* is that in which Antony is heaved aloft to Cleopatra on the monument.

Suspension gear may possibly have helped here, but any precise interpretation of the staging requirements must be speculative. Certainly the passage cannot be taken as proving that the Globe possessed a hoist located in the Heavens.

7. *The Malcontent . . . With the Additions . . . by Iohn Webster* (1604), sig. A3[a].

8 *Epigrammes and Elegies* (Middleborough, n.d. [1596]), sigs. C2[a] and A4[a].

9. *The Gvls Horne-booke* (1609), pp. 28-9.

10. Sig. Lll 1[b].

11. *Rvle a Wife and Have a Wife* (1640), sig. D2[a].

12. pp. 153-4.

13. Berry, *The Boar's Head Playhouse*, p. 132 and map 4.

14. 'Shakespeare's Outdoor Stage Lighting', *Shakespeare Studies 13* (1980), p. 239.

15. Ian Liddell of Buro Happold Consulting Engineers, and Martin Wilkinson, University of Bath. The photographs were taken by John Stone, Pentagram Design, London.

16. 'Nicholas Hilliard's Treatise concerning "The Arte of Limning"', edited by Philip Norman, *Walpole Society I* (1911-12), p. 29.

17. 'Shakespeare's Outdoor Stage Lighting', pp. 242-4.

18. *Henslowe's Diary*, edited by Foakes and Rickert, p. 21, entry for 23 January 1594. Despite the designation, the play had probably originated with Lord Strange's Men at the Rose *c.* 1592. See *Titus Andronicus*, edited by Eugene M. Waith, The Oxford Shakespeare (Oxford, 1984), pp. 2-10.

19. BL Harleian MS. 293, fol. 217[a].

20. PRO E351/3219, 1584-5.

21. PRO E351/3239.

22. Henry Vaughan, *Poems* (1646), p. 27.

23. From the account of the Duke of Wirtemberg in 1592, translated by William Brenchley Rye, *England as Seen by Foreigners* (1865; reprint New York, 1967), p. 44.

24. Kent County Record Office, U269, A1/1, 'A Booke of Severall Accompts of Thomas Earle of Dorsett' (1607). For Dungan at Whitehall, see H. M. Colvin, general editor, *The History of the King's Works: Volume III 1485-1660 (Part I)* (1975), p. 410, and *Volume IV*, p. 322n.

25. Willis and Clark, *The Architectural History of the University of Cambridge*, II, 260.

26. Historical Manuscripts Commission, *Salisbury*, II, 200.

27. *The Elements of Architectvre* (1624), p. 108.

28. *The Bromley Room*, Victoria and Albert Museum, Department of Woodwork Monographs (1922).

29. Jourdain, *English Decorative Plasterwork of the Renaissance*, pp. 26-7.

30. Lawrence A. Turner, 'A Middlesex Jacobean Plasterer', *Country Life* 35 (1914), 919-22, studies the repetition of forms in Middlesex ceilings.

31. H. Avray-Tipping, 'Broughton Castle, Oxfordshire, III', *Country Life* 67 (1930), 128-9 and figs. 9 and 10. A similar modular unit of intersecting ribs appears in the gate-house of Oriel College, Oxford, illustrated in Jourdain, *English Decorative Plasterwork of the Renaissance*, p. 41.

32. PRO E351/3239, cited by Eric Mercer, 'The Decorations of the Royal Palaces from 1553-1625', *Archaeological Journal* 110 (1953), 153. Mercer remarks: 'Throughout the greater part of the period the only reason for leaving anything

unpainted seems to have been the physical impossibility of reaching it with a brush' (p. 152).

33. *The Whore of Babylon* (1607), sig. A4[b].

34. John Abbott (Plasterer's design book . . .,) 2 vols., photocopy at the national Art Library, Victoria and Albert Museum. See Kathleen and Cecil French, 'Devonshire Plasterwork', *Transactions of the Devonshire Association* 89 (1957), 124–44.

35. Esdaile, *English Monumental Sculpture*, pp. 117–24.

36. BL Add. MS. 54332, fol. 163[b]. The lines were written apparently *c.* 1668, but the round house was built in 1631: '1631 made the walk in Oxinden Carust And then builded the round house' (fol. 25[b]).

7 THE ELIZABETHAN BANQUETING HOUSE, WHITEHALL

1. 'To the Reader' in *The White Divel* (1612), sig. A2[a].

2. See pp. 113–15.

3. *Specvlvm Britanniae . . . Middlesex* (1593), unpaginated map.

4. There is a copy at the Huntington Library, California.

5. 'Leonard ffrier Sergeant Painter for laying upon Canvas in the Ceeling of the great Banquetting house v[c]xxxij yardes square of worke called the Cloudes in distemper, at x[d] the yard square – xxij[li] iij[s] iiij[d], PRO E351/3239.

6. RIBA Drawings Collection, Smythson I/10, reproduced in Stephen Orgel and Roy Strong, *Inigo Jones: the Theatre of the Stuart Court*, 2 vols. (1973), I, 81.

7. PRO E351/3217.

8. Ibid.

9. PRO E351/3239, Whitehall taskwork.

10. PRO E351/3231.

11. PRO E351/3216.

12. Holinshed, *The Third Volume of Chronicles*, p. 1315.

13. Albert Feuillerat, 'Documents Relating to the Office of Revels in the Time of Queen Elizabeth', in *Materialen zur kunde des älteren Englischen dramas*, edited by W. Bang, XXI (Louvain, 1908), 340–2.

14. PRO AO3/2045/7.

15. Feuillerat, 'Documents Relating to the Office of Revels', p. 345.

16. PRO E351/3217, for 1582–3.

17. Ibid.

18. PRO E351/3216, for 1581–2.

19. See chapter 2 above, p. 39 and n. 27.

20. [Halle,] *The Vnion of the Two . . . Famelies*, fol. clvi[a].

21. *I diarii di Marino Sanuto*, XLV, col. 266–7.

22. Holinshed, *The Third Volume of Chronicles*, p. 850.

23. [Halle,] *The Vnion of the Two . . . Famelies*, fol. clvi[b].

24. PRO E351/3218.

25. PRO E351/3248.

26. PRO E351/3219.

27. PRO E351/3228.

28. PRO E351/3233.

29. PRO E351/3239.
30. PRO E351/3240, for 1604–5.
31. *Ben Jonson*, edited by C. H. Herford and Percy and Evelyn Simpson, 11 vols. (Oxford, 1925–52), VII, 169–72.
32. Raphael Gualterotti, *Feste nelle nozze del serenissimo Don Francesco Medici* . . . (Florence, 1579), cited by Enid Welsford, *The Court Masque* (1923), pp. 176–8.
33. Dudley Carleton, writing to John Chamberlain on 7 January 1605, cited in *Ben Jonson*, edited by Herford and Simpson, X, 449. For the MS. of the masque (BL Royal MS. 17. B. XXXI) see ibid., VII, 195.
34. PRO E351/3240, Rewards.
35. PRO E351/3241.
36. Stowe, *Annales*, p. 891.

8 THE CHRIST CHURCH THEATRE

1. See J. Thomas Oosting, *Andrea Palladio's 'Teatro Olimpico'* (Ann Arbor, 1981), p. 120.
2. See Tomaso Buzzi, 'Il "Teatro all' Antica" di Vincenzo Scamozzi in Sabbioneta', *Dedalo* 8 (1927–8), 488–524. The theatre was inaugurated in 1590.
3. [Domenico Mellini,] *Descrizione dell' apparato della comedia* . . . (Florence, 1566).
4. For Lyons, see *La magnifica et triumphale entrata del Chistianissimo re di Francia Henrico secondo . . . colla particolare descrizione della comedia* . . . (Lyons, 1549).
5. Cambridge University Library Add. MS. 34, fol. 44^b.
6. Matthew Gwinne, *Vertumnus: sive annus recurrens* (1605).
7. *Rex Platonicus* (Oxford, 1607), p. 78.
8. Burton's letter, written to his brother William on 11 August 1605, in which he reports having written parts of one of the plays, 'especially those scenes of the Magus', is published from Staffordshire County Record Office D649/1/1 by Richard L. Nochimson, 'Robert Burton's Authorship of *Alba*: a Lost Letter Uncovered', *Review of English Studies* n.s. 21 (1970), 326–7.
9. See F. S. Boas, 'James I at Oxford in 1605', Malone Society *Collections*, I, 251–2.
10. See Orrell, *The Theatres of Inigo Jones and John Webb*, pp. 30–8.
11. BL Add. MS. 15505, fol. 21^a, top.
12. The analogous feature in Serlio's plan and section is called the 'piazza della scena' in *Tvtte l'opere d'architettvra* (Venice, 1566), fol. 43^b, and in subsequent editions. In earlier editions it had been called the 'proscenio'.
13. 'et ponian caso che vno quadro sia dua piedi', *Il secondo libro di perspettiva* (Paris, 1545), fol. 65^b; 'and suppose that each Quadran containeth two foote on eyther side', *The Second Booke of Architecture . . . Translated . . . into English* (1611), fol. 24^a.
14. The depth of the Vicenzan theatre was 80 ft (*Il secondo libro*, fol. 63^a), and the forestage was 60 ft wide (ibid., fol. 64^b). The English version of Serlio's text disconcertingly reports the depth as 28 ft (*The Second Booke of Architecture*, fol. 23^b).
15. See Samuel Marolois' treatise on perspective, in *Opera mathematica* (The Hague, 1614). Marolois linked the field of vision to the physical structure of the eye.
16. Cambridge University Library Add. MS. 34, fol. 30^a.
17. Ibid.

18. *Rex Platonicus*, pp. 46–7; my translation of the Latin text.

9 SERLIO'S THEATRE PLAN

1. *The Book of Architecture by Sebastiano Serlio, London, 1611*, introduction by A. E. Santanello (New York, 1980), II, fol. 24ᵃ. For the sake of convenience I quote where possible from this reprint of the first English edition of Serlio, dedicated by Robert Peake to Henry, Prince of Wales. Unfortunately the English text is sometimes inaccurate; in such passages I translate from Serlio's earliest edition.
2. Ibid.
3. Ibid., III, fol. 20ᵇ.
4. Vitruvius, *The Ten Books on Architecture*, translated by Morris Hicky Morgan (Cambridge, Mass., 1914), p. 146.
5. *Ten Books on Architecture*, translated by Leoni, p. 177.
6. Ibid., p. 180.
7. *Di Marco Vitruvio Pollione i dieci libri* (Venice, 1556). The theatre plan is on p. 154. Our plate is from the Latin edition of 1567, p. 188.
8. RIBA Drawings Collection.
9. *The Book of Architecture by Sebastiano Serlio*, II, fol. 26ᵃ.
10. *The Ten Books on Architecture*, translated by Morgan, p. 13.
11. Ibid., p. 14.
12. Ibid.
13. Ibid., p. 72.
14. See Rudolf Wittkower, *Architectural Principles in the Age of Humanism*, 3rd edition (1962), pp. 101–54; and G. L. Hersey, *Pythagorean Palaces* (Ithaca, 1976), *passim*.
15. *The Book of Architecture by Sebastiano Serlio*, II, fol. 24ᵃ.
16. Even in the best, original, edition of 1545 the profile, though generally matching the plan, fails to meet it in every particular. It introduces an extra seating degree between the two cross aisles, and it increases the depth of the orchestra a little. The wall behind the stage is likewise about 1 mm more than 17 units from the centre of the orchestra.
17. *The Book of Architecture by Sebastiano Serlio*, III, fol. 1ᵇ.
18. Ibid., III, fol. 9ᵇ.
19. Ibid., III, fols 22ᵇ and 23ᵃ.
20. *Tvtte l'opere d'architettvra* (Venice, 1566), fol. 56ᵇ.
21. *The Ten Books on Architecture*, translated by Morgan, p. 150.
22. *The Book of Architecture by Sebastiano Serlio*, II, fol. 24ᵃ.
23. *The Ten Books on Architecture*, translated by Morgan, p. 146.
24. Ibid., p. 148.
25. Cited and illustrated by Hersey, *Pythagorean Palaces*, p. 47.
26. Ibid., p. 51.
27. *The Book of Architecture by Sebastiano Serlio*, I, fol. 2ᵇ.
28. Ibid.
29. Ibid., fol. 3ᵃ.
30. Ibid., fol. 11ᵇ.
31. On the use of the quadrate technique in building design, see Paul Frankl, *The*

Gothic: Literary Sources and Interpretations during Eight Centuries (Princeton, 1960), pp. 50–2.

32. *The Book of Architecture by Sebastiano Serlio*, I, fol. 13ᵃ.
33. *Architectural Principles*, pp. 126–7.
34. *The Ten Books on Architecture*, translated by Morgan, p. 73.
35. Ibid.
36. See Wittkower, *Architectural Principles*, pp. 13, 16 and plates 2c and 3.
37. Laurentian Library, Florence, Ashburnham 361, fol. 5ᵃ, printed in Wittkower, *Architectural Principles*, plate 2a.
38. *M. Vitruvio Pollione de Architectura* (Como, 1521), III, fol. 50ᵃ.
39. Some of these illustrations are reprinted in Yates, *Theatre of the World*, plate 2.
40. *The Book of Architecture by Sebastiano Serlio,*, V, fol. 1ᵇ.

10 THIS GOODLY FRAME: THE PUBLIC THEATRES

1. *Henslowe's Diary*, edited by Foakes and Rickert, p. 308. Glynne Wickham (*Early English Stages*, II (part 2), 111–12), suggests that the shape of the Fortune was hardly a matter of deliberate choice at all, but strictly defined by the placing of neighbouring buildings. The auditorium described in the contract was not, in this view, an independent structure but a series of galleries set up against the walls of an existing courtyard, 80 ft square. If this were indeed the case any theory about the planning of the theatre would have to start with its external dimensions as a *donnée*; the square shape, similarly justified, might then have been no more than a happy accident. But the contract itself discounts the idea of an *ad hoc* design. If the frame of galleries was set up against existing walls it could not have been rendered on the outside, nor of course would it need to be. Street was specifically relieved of certain aspects of the internal decoration, including the job of 'Rendringe the walls within'; but he was equally specifically charged with covering the whole exterior of the frame with lath and plaster:

   And also all the saide fframe and the Staircases thereof to be sufficyently enclosed withoute with lathe lyme & haire . . .

   This clause makes it clear that the frame, with its attached stair turrets, was an independent free-standing structure. It was not an improvised conversion of an existing yard, like the Boar's Head or the later Red Bull, but a new and purpose-built playhouse, as the contract evidently implies when it describes the site

   in and vppon a certeine plot or parcell of grounde appoynted oute for that purpose Scytuate and beinge nere Goldinge lane . . ..

2. *Ten Books on Architecture*, translated by Leoni, p. 138.
3. *The Boar's Head Playhouse*, p. 107.
4. Historical Manuscripts Commission, *Salisbury*, XVII, 234, undated petition by Martin Slatiar, *c.* May 1605.
5. pp. 108–17.
6. The exact ratio is 1.41431 : 1, compared with the $\sqrt{2}$ ratio of 1.41421 : 1.
7. *Henslowe's Diary*, edited by Foakes and Rickert, pp. 307 and 308.
8. See A. W. Richeson, *English Land Measuring to 1800: Instruments and Practices*

(Cambridge, Mass., 1966), pp. 29–89. A representative text is Valentine Leigh, *The Moste Profitable and Commendable Science, of Surueiying of Landes, Tenementes, and Hereditamentes* (1578), which illustrates the lines used in squaring and triangulation.

9. The contract is printed by W. J. Lawrence and Walter H. Godfrey, 'The Bear Garden Contract of 1606 and What it Implies', *Architectural Review* 47 (1920), 153.

10. 'all the princypall and maine postes of the saide fframe and Stadge forwarde shalbe square and wroughte palasterwise with carved proporcions Called Satiers to be placed & sett on the Topp of every of the same postes', *Henslowe's Diary*, edited by Foakes and Rickert, p. 308.

11. See Orrell, *The Quest for Shakespeare's Globe*, pp. 84–107 and 120–6.

12. *A Discoverie of Sundrie Errours and Faults Daily Committed by Landemeaters* (1582), sig. G1^b.

13. *A Preparative to Platting of Landes and Tenementes* (1596), p. 14 (i.e. p. 10), sig. B3^b.

14. *The English Hvsbandman* (1613), pp. 120–4. Some of the patterns are based on an *ad quadratum* scheme, illustrated on p. 121: 'you shall begin to draw forth your knot in this manner: first, with lines you shall draw the forme of the figure next before set downe, and with a small instrument of yron make it upon the earth' (p. 122). On p. 123 is a design for 'Double Knots' which shows the method of 'pinning downe every line firme to the earth with a little pinne made of wood'.

15. Alberti, *Ten Books on Architecture*, translated by Leoni, p. 199. Henricus Cornelius Agrippa, *De occulta philosophia* ([Cologne], 1533), II, 23. 155. See Hersey, *Pythagorean Palaces*, p. 19.

16. *The Ten Books of Architecture*, translated by Morgan, p. 130.

17. *Tvtte l'opere d'architettvra* (1566), I, fol. 9^b, translated by Hersey, *Pythagorean Palaces*, p. 53. This is one of a number of neo-Platonic passages that have been omitted from the English version of 1611.

18. 1551 edition, I, fol. 8^b, my translation. This passage does not appear in the English version of 1611.

19. *The Book of Architecture by Sebastiano Serlio*, I, fol. 12^a.

20. *Il secondo libro di perspettiva*, fol. 65^b, my translation. This sentence does not appear in the English version of 1611.

21. BL Lansdowne MS. 84, no. 10, ii, printed by John Summerson, 'Three Elizabethan Architects', *Bulletin of the John Rylands Library* 40 (1957), 227–8.

22. BL Lansdowne MS. 84, no. 10, i, printed in ibid., pp. 226 and 227.

23. For Stickells' life see ibid., pp. 216–21.

24. 'George Weale in rewarde for drawinge of the ground plott of parte of Whitehall for the newe intended buildinge of the banquettinge house with the gatehouse and raunge of buildinges on the west side of the Courte *lx*^s Robte Stickles for drawinge of twoe uprightes on the same plott *lx*^s', PRO E351/3240, Rewards.

25. Archives of St Mark's, Venice, CLVII, Cod. MCXXII, fols. 72–5, cited and translated in Orgel and Strong, *Inigo Jones: the Theatre of the Stuart Court*, I, 279 and 282.

26. PRO E351/3243, Rewards.

27. My thanks are due to Lewis Cleverdon for pointing this out to me.

28. John Summerson, *Architecture in Britain 1530–1830*, 5th edition, Pelican History of Art (Harmondsworth, 1970), p. 59.

29. Ibid., pp. 67–8; compare *The Book of Architecture by Sebastiano Serlio*, III, fol. 71ᵇ (1566 edition, III, fol. 122ᵇ).

30. See Mark Girouard, 'Designs for a Lodge at Ampthill', in H. M. Colvin and John Harris, editors, *The Country Seat* (1970), pp. 16–17. The plan of Wothorpe is influenced by a church plan in Serlio, *Tvtte l'opere d'architettvra* (1566), V, fol. 213ᵇ (*The Book of Architecture by Sebastiano Serlio*, V, fol. 11ᵇ); the windows resemble ones printed in the *Architettura*, IV, fol. 178ᵇ (English version, IV, fol. 54ᵃ). For the Serlian influence at Kirby see Summerson, *Architecture in Britain*, p. 48.

31. E. Croft-Murray, *Decorative Painting in England, 1537–1837* (1962), pp. 120, 160 and plate 23, cited by Summerson, *The History of the King's Works*, edited by Colvin, IV (part 2), 242.

32. Mark Girouard, *Robert Smythson and the Architecture of the Elizabethan Era* (1966), pp. 81–3, 121, 179–80 and plates 81, 82 and 148–53.

33. [Cornelius Scribonius,] *La très admirable . . . entrée du . . . Prince Philipes . . . en la . . . ville d'Anvers* (Antwerp, 1550), the Spanish gate.

34. *Tvtte l'opere d'architettvra* (1566), IV, fol. 179ᵇ; *The Book of Architecture by Sebastiano Serlio*, IV, fol. 55ᵃ.

35. Girouard, *Robert Smythson*, p. 82.

36. BL Add. MS. 39831, fol. 3ᵃ. Compare *The Book of Architecture by Sebastiano Serlio*, I, fol. 12ᵃ. It seems likely that a similar technique was used at the first Jacobean Banqueting House at Whitehall. Before November 1607 one Acheson had provided 'the Module of a Geometricall roof for the banqueting howse': BL Lansdowne MS. 165, fol. 103ᵇ, cited by Summerson, *The History of the King's Works*, edited by Colvin, IV, 322.

37. Street's career is extensively documented in Susan Cerasano, 'Alleyn's Fortune: the Biography of a Playhouse 1600–1621', unpublished PhD thesis, University of Michigan (1981), pp. 17–42.

38. Chambers, *The Elizabethan Stage*, II, 384.

39. See above, chapter 2, n. 44.

11 THE COURT THEATRES

1. Buzzi, 'Il "Teatro all'Antica" di Vincenzo Scamozzi in Sabbioneta', pp. 488–524; and Franco Barbieri, *Vincenzo Scamozzi* (Verona and Vicenza, n.d. [1952]).

2. Now reconstructed after extensive war damage. See Vittorio Gandolfi, *Il Teatro Farnese di Parma* (Parma, 1980).

3. See Fabrizio Carini Motta, *Trattato sopra la struttura de' teatri e scene*, edited by Edward A. Craig (Milan, 1972), plate 11.

4. Adriano Cavicchi, 'Il teatro Farnese di Parma', *Bolletino del Centro Internazionale di Studi di Architettura Andrea Palladio* 16 (1974), 334 and plate 186. An anonymous plan for the tourney *Il tempio d'amore*, held on the same occasion, shows a similar U-shaped *cavea*, but *alfresco* and on a much larger scale: ibid., plate 191.

5. See ibid., plate 187.

6. In his copy of Palladio, on the fifth flyleaf, verso, transcribed by Bruce Allsopp, *Inigo Jones on Palladio*, 2 vols. (1968), I, 1.

7. 'New Sources for the Masque Designs of Inigo Jones', *Apollo* 107, no. 192

(February 1978), 98–111; 'Inigo Jones's Stage Architecture and its Sources', *Art Bulletin* 64 (1982), 196–216; and 'The French Element in Inigo Jones's Masque Designs', in *The Court Masque*, edited by David Lindley (Manchester, 1984), pp. 149–68 and plates 1–26.

8. *Inigo Jones: the Theatre of the Stuart Court.*

9. See John Orrell, 'Inigo Jones and Amerigo Salvetti', *Theatre Notebook* 30 (1976), 109–14.

10. Worcester College, Oxford, Jones/Webb 1/27. See John Harris and A. A. Tait, *Catalogue of the Drawings by Inigo Jones, John Webb and Isaac de Caus at Worcester College, Oxford* (Oxford, 1979), no. 4.

11. BL Lansdowne MS. 1171, fols 9^b–10^a (Paved Court theatre), 5^b–6^a (*Florimène* plan) and 7^b–8^a (*Florimène* stage section).

12. Worcester College, Oxford, Jones/Webb I/7B and 7C (Cockpit in Drury Lane) and II/84 (Webb's project); see Harris and Tait, *Catalogue of the Drawings by Inigo Jones . . .*, nos 10, 11 and 15.

13. Now in the RIBA Drawings Collection, BD xiii/5.

14. See the analysis of the scoring on the sheet in Richard C. Kohler, 'Vitruvian Proportions in Theater Design in the Sixteenth and Early Seventeenth Centuries in Italy and England', *Shakespeare Studies 16* (1983), pp. 295–8.

15. *The Book of Architecture by Sebastiano Serlio*, iii, fol. 25^b.

16. The structure is analysed in Orrell, *The Theatres of Inigo Jones and John Webb*, pp. 90–112.

17. PRO E351/3247, for 1612–13.

18. The reasons for believing that the Jones drawings, Worcester College Jones/Webb 7B and 7C, show the Cockpit in Drury Lane are given in *The Theatres of Inigo Jones and John Webb*, pp. 42–74. They are all circumstantial, though some involve matters of precise dimensions, and the identification can only be provisional. Indeed Wenceslaus Hollar, in his View of West London (*c.* 1657), shows the Cockpit site occupied by a square-planned three-bay building with a roof of three parallel ridges, quite unlike the Jones design. The roof type, perfectly familiar in London house building, requires load-bearing internal walls that would prevent the establishment of an auditorium. Leslie Hotson, when he first drew attention to this depiction of the Cockpit site (*The Commonwealth and Restoration Stage* [Cambridge, Mass., 1928], p. 91), concluded that it had little to tell us about the appearance of the theatre. Now Graham F. Barlow has returned to the question in 'Wenceslaus Hollar and Christopher Beeston's Phoenix Theatre in Drury Lane', forthcoming at the time of writing in *Theatre Research International*. Dr Barlow has very kindly let me see a draft of this article, in which he analyses the deeds, leases and other documents concerning the neighbourhood of the playhouse from 1609 to 1880. The site, a triangular piece of ground to the east of Drury Lane, was built up during the seventeenth century. At first there were houses along the greater part of its borders, with the Cockpit at the centre, over everyone's garden wall. Barlow concludes that the lots occupied by the perimeter buildings, together with the space later devoted to Cockpit Alley, left no room for a structure the size of that shown in the Jones drawings. He reprints Hollar's view of the area, maintaining that it accurately represents the disposition of the neighbourhood, including the design of the

Cockpit, with its triple-ridged roof. It should be observed, however, that the precise location of any alley leading to the playhouse in the seventeenth century is unknown; we first hear of a Cockpit Alley in the Morgan map of 1681–2, after the playhouse had passed out of use. Furthermore, a house which Barlow locates to the north of the theatre, apparently built at the same time as the original Cockpit and occupied by John Clegge at the time of a Chancery Bill of 1647, was a very minor tenement valued at only 22s. 4d. p.a., compared with £45 p.a. for the playhouse and from £25 to £50 p.a. for nearby houses. Neither the Chancery Bill nor any other document locates this building. It is forcing matters to identify it with a large three-bay house shown by Hollar to the north of the site roughly where 5 and 6 Pitt Place stood at the time of the clearances of the 1880s. Barlow holds that this house, together with its service alley, diminished the north–south extent of the Cockpit grounds to something like 60 ft, too small for the Jones building, though the available width at 65 ft left plenty of room for it. But the Clegge house is not located in the documents, and were it not situated where Barlow places it, but elsewhere in the block, there would have been adequate room for Jones's building. Clearly the matters raised by his study cannot be dealt with satisfactorily in this note; but unless the Clegge house can be definitely placed where Barlow rather speculatively locates it his evidence neither confirms nor denies the identification of the Jones drawings. William Morgan's *London . . . Actually Suruey'd* (1681–2) shows a disposition of buildings to the south of Cockpit Alley rather different from that indicated by Hollar, and may even include the remains of the theatre itself, a large rectangular structure orientated north and south, with its northern end by now incorporated into the cluster of buildings along the alley. Robert Morden and Philip Lea's *Actuall Survey of London, Westminster and Southwark* (1700) records a similar arrangement. Hollar's quite different depiction of the three-ridged block at the centre of the site is probably the result of guesswork. He surveyed the ground on foot, with the help of a chain, waywiser and no doubt a plane table. He was concerned primarily with the layout of major roads and landmarks; he did not record any alley leading to the Cockpit, nor is it likely that he surveyed the buildings that lay behind those that fronted on Drury Lane and the other streets.

19. The scene designs are at Chatsworth, and are printed by Orgel and Strong, *Inigo Jones: the Theatre of the Stuart Court*, nos. 245–51. O&S 136 should also be included in the set. The Works account entry is in PRO E351/3266; Webb's plan is in BL Lansdowne MS. 1171, fols. 9ᵇ–10ᵃ; and the notebook is at the Yale Center for British Art, Rare Books Collection. All are discussed in Orrell, *The Theatres of Inigo Jones and John Webb*, pp. 113–27.

20. PRO E351/3266.

21. The scene designs are at Chatsworth; the architectural drawings are in BL Lansdowne MS. 1171, fols. 5ᵇ–6ᵃ, 7ᵇ–8ᵃ, 13ᵇ–14ᵃ and 15ᵇ–16ᵃ. All are printed by Orgel and Strong, *Inigo Jones: the Theatre of the Stuart Court*, nos. 321–33, and are discussed in Orrell, *The Theatres of Inigo Jones and John Webb*, pp. 128–48.

22. O&S 323.

12 THE PRIVATE THEATRES

1. Michael Shapiro, *Children of the Revels* (New York, 1977), pp. 14–18.
2. The Prologue to Marston's *Antonios Reuenge* (1602), 'As it hath beene sundry times acted, by the children of Paules', alludes to the audience located 'within this round . . . within this ring' (sig. A2^{a-b}). Reavley Gair concludes that 'Paul's auditorium could have been semi-circular', John Marston, *Antonio's Revenge*, edited by W. Reavley Gair, The Revels Plays (Manchester, 1978), p. 54n. Gair discusses the Paul's theatre more fully in *The Children of Paul's: the Story of a Theatre Company, 1553–1608* (Cambridge, 1982), chapter 2, pp. 44–74.
3. The fullest treatment of the history of the Blackfriars is in Irwin Smith, *Shakespeare's Blackfriars Playhouse* (New York, 1964).
4. Bentley, *The Jacobean and Caroline Stage*, VI, 77–86. See also Susan P. Cerasano, 'Competition for the King's Men?: Alleyn's Blackfriars Venture', *Medieval and Renaissance Drama in England* (forthcoming).
5. Hotson, *The Commonwealth and Restoration Stage*, pp. 100–13.
6. *Volume III, 1576–1613*, Leech and Craik general editors, figs 50 and 51, pp. 216 and 217. In fig. 52, p. 219, Richard Southern gives a perspective rendering of the scheme.
7. The drawing was published in *The Times*, 21 November 1921, p. 5.
8. *Shakespeare's Blackfriars Playhouse*, p. 307.
9. Ibid., p. 291.
10. *The Revels History of Drama in English: Volume III*, pp. 211–12.
11. See Orrell, *The Quest for Shakespeare's Globe*, p. 19. Foakes, *Illustrations of the English Stage 1580–1642*, pp. 39–41, prints the drawing and also picks out the building among the myriad of rooftops shown in the etched *Long View* of 1647.
12. See Iain Mackintosh, 'Inigo Jones – Theatre Architect', *TABS* 31 (1973), 101–4; and Orrell, *The Theatres of Inigo Jones and John Webb*, pp. 39–49.
13. See Hotson, *The Commonwealth and Restoration Stage*, pp. 43 and 96.
14. *Historia Histrionica* (1699), p. 7.
15. *Dictionary of National Biography*, XXI, 1021.
16. Bentley, *The Jacobean and Caroline Stage*, VI, 87–92.
17. Smith, *Shakespeare's Blackfriars Playhouse*, p. 519.
18. 'And now my very fine *Heliconian* Gallants, and you my Worshipfull friends in the middle Region', Marston, *The Dvtch Covrtezan* (1633), sig. Dd5^{b}; compare 'See (*Captaine Martio*) he ith' *Renounce me* Band, / That in the middle Region doth stand'. H[enry] F[itzgeffrey], 'Notes from Black-Fryers', in *Satyres: and Satyricall Epigrams* (1617), sig. E7^{b}.
19. Smith, *Shakespeare's Blackfriars Playhouse*, p. 519.
20. Ibid., pp. 294–5.
21. PRO C115/M35/8391, cited by Herbert Berry, 'The Stage and Boxes at Blackfriars', *Studies in Philology* 63 (1966), 165.
22. 'The Playhouses', pp. 217–22.
23. George Chapman, Ben Jonson and John Marston, *Eastward Hoe* (1605), sig. A2^{a}.
24. 'The Playhouses', pp. 222–4.
25. See Foakes, *Illustrations of the English Stage 1580–1642*, pp. 72–3 and 159–61.

26. This particular quotation is from John Marston, *Sophonisba* (1606), sig. FI^b.
27. Sig. *4^a.
28. Not all plays may confidently be assigned to particular playhouses on the evidence of their title-pages alone, as T. J. King has pointed out in 'Staging of Plays at the Phoenix in Drury Lane, 1617–52', *Theatre Notebook* 19 (1964–5), 148–52. But since our present aim is to show that the private theatres were alike one another I have not felt the need to reject those texts whose title-page information is not confirmed from other sources, and have in general accepted the views of Bentley, *The Jacobean and Caroline Stage* and Chambers, *The Elizabethan Stage*. David Stevens, 'The Staging of Plays at the Salisbury Court Theatre, 1630–1642', *Theatre Journal* 31 (1979), 511–25, makes a similar point regarding the Salisbury Court; most of the examples I cite come from his Category A, of texts that may reliably be connected with that theatre.
29. *Il secondo libro di perspettiva*, fol. 65^b.
30. (1656), sig. B4^a.
31. (1636), sig. B2^a.
32. (1640), sig. A2^b.
33. Thomas Randolph, *Poems* (1638), sig. M4^a.
34. Ibid., sig. DD4^b.
35. (1633), sig. A3^a.
36. See G. E. Bentley, *The Profession of Dramatist in Shakespeare's Time 1590–1642* (Princeton, 1971), pp. 135–8.
37. T[homas] G[offe], *The Careles Shepherdess* (1656), sig. L2^b.
38. Sig. A4^b.
39. Sig. A4^a.
40. (1607), sig. A3^a.
41. (1611), sig. B3^a.
42. (1606), sig. G3^b.
43. (1640), sig. A3$^{a–b}$.
44. (1631), sig. (*)2$^{a–b}$.
45. Sig. A4^a.
46. My argument here is indebted to a brilliant paper by Andrew Gurr, 'The Discovery of the Globe', prepared for the Bear Gardens Museum, Bankside.
47. Printed by Smith, *Shakespeare's Blackfriars Playhouse*, pp. 471–5.
48. Ibid., p. 162; and Wallace, *The First London Theatre*, p. 23.
49. Chambers, *The Elizabethan Stage*, II, 508, note 3.
50. Ibid., IV, 320; the date of the petition is given by Chambers' item cvii.
51. Smith, *Shakespeare's Blackfriars Playhouse*, p. 558.
52. PRO E351/3219.
53. Chambers, *The Elizabethan Stage*, IV, 119 and 171.
54. PRO E351/3240.
55. See Boas, 'James I at Oxford', pp. 247–59. For the Revels involvement, see PRO AO1/2046/11.
56. Smith, *Shakespeare's Blackfriars Playhouse*, p. 471. Compare pp. 100–1.
57. (1649), p. 35.
58. There were stairs leading from the Upper Frater to the roof. They are mentioned in the deed of 1596 (Smith, *Shakespeare's Blackfriars Playhouse*, p. 471), but

they will have given only service access, and could not have served to carry the
audience to the galleries.

59. A facsimile is at the British Library, Facs. 372, ii, 8, 17. See Girouard, 'Designs
for a Lodge at Ampthill', pp. 13–17.

60. See Summerson, *The Book of Architecture of John Thorpe*, drawings T34 (i), T141,
T152 and T178.

61. John Summerson, *Inigo Jones* (Harmondsworth, 1966), p. 26; and Lawrence
Stone, 'Inigo Jones and the New Exchange', *Archaeological Journal* 114 (1957
[1959]), 106–21.

62. *Thesavrvs lingvae Romanae & Britannicae* (1565), sig. GGGggg6ᵇ. Compare John
Bulloker, *An English Expositor* (1616), sig. O5ᵇ: 'A place made halfe round where
people sate to behold solemne playes and games.'

63. *A Dictionarie of the French and English Tongves* (1611), sig. Ggggviᵇ.

64. *Rex Platonicus*, pp. 46–7.

65. For a general discussion of the Sheldonian, see Summerson, *Architecture in
Britain*, pp. 198–9. For the organ design see *Wren Society* 9 (1932), plate 41.

66. See *Country Life* 67 (1930), 753.

13 SERLIO'S MEASURABLE SCENE DESIGNS

1. See Colin Visser, '*The Descent of Orpheus* at the Cockpit, Drury Lane', *Theatre
Survey* 24 (1983), 35–53; and John Orrell, 'Scenes and Machines at the Cockpit,
Drury Lane', *Theatre Survey* 26 (1985), 103–19.

2. See Orrell, *The Theatres of Inigo Jones and John Webb*, pp. 60–4.

3. 'The Wren MS. "Court Orders"', *Wren Society* 18 (1941), App. part ii, 156
(Webb petition of 1668).

4. In 1639. See Bentley, *The Jacobean and Caroline Stage*, vi, 304–9.

5. See especially the articles by John Peacock listed above, chapter 11, note 7.

6. 'The Rendering of the Interior in Architectural Drawings of the Renaissance',
Studies in Italian Renaissance Architecture (Cambridge, Mass., 1981), pp. 1–65.

7. On the various editions of Serlio's work see William Bell Dinsmoor, 'The
Literary Remains of Sebastiano Serlio', *Art Bulletin* 24 (1942), 55–91 and
115–54.

8. Ibid., p. 65: 'The emphasis on illustrations . . . was the ideal which guided Serlio
in the preparation of his published works. It was a new conception in architectural writing, though it has since become so general that we tend to forget that it
was an innovation which we owe to him. Instead of composing a literary essay
accompanied by illustrations, he planned to make the illustrations the main
body of the work, each to be provided with a commentary more or less brief as
the nature of the case demanded, the ideal being one page of text opposite or
accompanying each drawing.'

9. In the copy of the Second Book at Chatsworth the Comic Scene is bound up to
face fol. 65ᵇ; at Harvard (in the Houghton Library) it follows the plan on fol.
66ᵇ; in the Fowler Collection at Johns Hopkins it is inserted between fols. 67ᵇ
and 68ᵃ; and at the Bodleian it follows the Satyric Scene on fol. 70ᵇ.

10. Published by Myra Nan Rosenfeld, *Sebastiano Serlio on Domestic Architecture* (Cambridge, Mass., 1978).

11. *Pratica di fabricar scene e machine ne' teatri* (Ravenna, 1638), pp. 9 and 55.
12. See above, chapter 8, note 15.
13. *The Book of Architecture by Sebastiano Serlio*, II, fol. 24ᵃ.
14. 'New Sources for the Masque Designs of Inigo Jones', p. 98.
15. The use of one diagram to convey information about two proportional schemes is not unusual in perspective handbooks. In Lorenzo Sirigatti's *La pratica di prospettiva* (Venice, 1596), for example, a plan and section are given (plate 43) of a theatre with a raked stage and foreshortened scene. One set of proportions is enshrined in the drawings, while another, quite different, is given in the text (chapter 43). Thus the distance between the vanishing point and the stage front is equally divided by the backscene in the plan and section (1 : 1), while in the text it is divided in the ratio of 3 : 2. Other figures, actually inscribed on the plate as well as in the text, refer to the latter scheme and are fully consistent with one another, while the plan and section are equally consistent in their depiction of the alternative scheme.

14 INIGO JONES'S SCENE DESIGNS

1. BL Lansdowne MS. 1171, fols. 13ᵇ–14ᵃ.
2. See Orrell, *The Theatres of Inigo Jones and John Webb*, plates 26 and 27.
3. Scenes for *The Vision of Delight* (1617), *The Masque of Augurs* (1622), *Neptune's Triumph* (1625), *Coelum Britannicum* (1634) and *Salmacida Spolia* (1640), many drawn as angled, were nevertheless changeable and doubtless constructed as flats. Those for *Albion's Triumph* (1631) and *Tempe Restored* (1632) were probably similar, but the matter is not certain: the necessary changes might have been made at the backshutters only. *Artenice* (1626) and *Florimène* (1635) both had angled wings with changeable backshutters, as did the stage set for the 'Tragic Scene' (O&S 141; after 1633 – see note 9 below).
4. *Inigo Jones: the Theatre of the Stuart Court*, II, 460.
5. See John Peacock, 'New Sources for the Masque Designs of Inigo Jones', pp. 104–10.
6. See Orrell, *The Theatres of Inigo Jones and John Webb*, plates 26 and 27.
7. Ibid., plates 22 and 24.
8. In fact the earliest double horizon design is that for an upper scene in *Time Vindicated* (1623; O&S 123), where the forepart has a low vanishing point located at the foot of the backshutter. The shutter is however very faintly drawn, and its evidence is therefore not reliable.
9. Orgel and Strong's dating of the drawing as 1629–30 (*Inigo Jones: the Theatre of the Stuart Court*, I, 397), which I followed in *The Theatres of Inigo Jones and John Webb*, pp. 85–8, must now be changed in the light of evidence produced by John Peacock, 'The French Element in Inigo Jones's Masque Designs', pp. 160 and 167 n. 52.
10. (1635), p. 1.
11. *The Characters of Two Royall Masques. The One of Blacknesse* . . . (1608), sig. A4ᵇ.
12. *Tethys Festival: or, The Qveenes Wake* (1610), sig. E3ᵃ.
13. *Tempe Restored. A Masque* (1632), p. 11.
14. (1634), sig. C2ᵃ⁻ᵇ.

15. *Britannia Trivmphans: a Masque* (1638), p. 24.
16. (1639), sig. B2^{b}.
17. Alberti, *On Painting and On Sculpture*, translated by Cecil Grayson (1972), p. 53.
18. Ibid., p. 55.
19. Published by Richard Southern, *Changeable Scenery* (1952), plate facing p. 160.
20. At Chatsworth. They are reproduced in *The Dramatic Works of Roger Boyle, Earl of Orrery*, edited by William Smith Clark, 2 vols (Cambridge, Mass., 1937), I, frontispiece, 244, 268 and 280.
21. Printed in Orrell, *The Theatres of Inigo Jones and John Webb*, plates 29 and 30.
22. Chatsworth, Devonshire Collection B59^{a}.
23. Boswell, *The Restoration Court Stage*, p. 243, citing an 'Extraordinary account' for February 1664/5–April 1665.
24. 'ffor framing and setting upp a Stage of xl^{ty} foote one way and xxvij^{en} foote an other way and vij foo: in heigth with double stayres in the Banquetting House Inclosing the same and covering it overhead with ffirrpoles & dealebourdes xlij:$^{foo:}$ in heighte', PRO E351/3267 (1633–4, for *The Triumph of Peace*). Compare Thomas Carew, *Coelum Britanicum* (1634): 'This strange spectacle gave great cause of admiration, but especially how so huge a machine, and of that great height could come from under the Stage, which was but six foot high', *Poems* (1640), p. 252.
25. Davenant, *Salmacida Spolia*, sig. B4^{a}.
26. Davenant, *Lvminalia, or The Festivall of Light* (1637), pp. 20–1.

APPENDIX: SERLIO'S VIRTUAL FIELD OF VISION

1. *On Painting and On Sculpture*, translated by Grayson, pp. 56–7.
2. $AC = 12 \times \frac{8\cdot1}{13\cdot5} = 7.2$; $AB = 12 \times \frac{32\cdot4}{27} = 14.4$; $AB = 2AC$
   Because AC represents 12 floor units at the reduced scale of the backscene, AB represents 24 units.
3. $AC = 12 \times \frac{36}{13} \times \frac{1}{9} = \frac{48}{13}$; $AB = 12 \times \frac{432}{13} \times \frac{1}{27} = \frac{192}{13}$; $AB = 4AC$
   Because AC represents 12 floor units at the reduced scale of the backscene, AB represents 48 units.
4. If the diagram be considered as a pair of large similar triangles it will be seen that they are proportioned 3 : 2. The lower horizontal is therefore $40.5 \times \frac{2}{3} = 27$ units long. A similar calculation for the Comic Scene yields an apparent depth of 81 units, where the virtual field is 96 units wide.
5. *Tvtte l'opere d'architettvra* (1566), I, fol. 9^{b}, translated by Hersey, *Pythagorean Palaces*, p. 53. Omitted from the English version of 1611.
6. *The Book of Architecture by Sebastiano Serlio*, II, fol. 24^{a}.

Index

285